PROGRAMMING FOR POETS
A Gentle Introduction Using FORTRAN
with WATFIV

PROGRAMMING FOR POETS
A Gentle Introduction Using FORTRAN with WATFIV

Richard Conway
Cornell University

James Archer
Cornell University

contributions by
Charles Van Loan
and
Kathryn Conway

Winthrop Publishers, Inc.
Cambridge, Massachusetts

Library of Congress Cataloging in Publication Data

Conway, Richard Walter,
    Programming for poets.

    Includes index.
    1. FORTRAN (Computer program language).
I.   Archer, James Elson,   joint author.
II.   Title.
QA76.73.F25C657   001.6'424   78-6469
ISBN 0-87626-722-3

©*1978 by Winthrop Publishers, Inc.*
  17 Dunster Street, Cambridge, Massachusetts 02138

All rights reserved. No part of this book may be reproduced in any form or by any means without permission in writing from the publisher. Printed in the United States of America.

10   9   8   7   6   5   4   3   2   1

CONTENTS

PREFACE xi

PART I. Elements of Programming 1

1. What is a Program? 1
   1.1 A Different Kind of Machine 2
   1.2 The Limits of Computing 5
   1.3 Understanding the Nature of Programming 6

2. Data-Printing Programs 8
   2.1 Read and Print a Single Word 8
       2.1.1 Preparation of a Card Deck 10
       2.1.2 Execution of a Program 13
   2.2 Read and Print a Single Number 17
       2.2.1 Output Format for Numbers 19
   2.3 Variables 20
   2.4 Algorithms 22
   Summary 25
   Exercises 27

3. Statement Repetition 28
   3.1 The Loop Concept 29
       3.1.1 Loop to Print each Item Twice 32
   3.2 Control Values in the Data 33
   3.3 Nested Loops 34
       3.3.1 Nested Loops and Control Values in the Data 36
   Summary 38
   Exercises 39

4. Conditional Statements 40
   4.1 Conditions 42
       4.1.1 Relations 43
       4.1.2 String Comparisons 43
   4.2 Branching 46
   4.3 Compound Statements 47
       4.3.1 A Conditional Loop 48
   4.4 A Choice of Alternatives 49
   4.5 Definite and Indefinite Repetition 50
   4.6 Nesting of Conditional Statements 52
   Summary 53
   Exercises 55

5. Output Format and Titling   57
   5.1 Printing Values of More than One Variable   57
       5.1.1 Reading Values of More than One Variable   59
   5.2 Printing Titles   59
       5.2.1 Quotes Within a String   62
       5.2.2 Continuing a Statement on a Second Line   63
       5.2.3 Upper and Lower-case Letters   64
   Summary   65
   Exercises   66

6. Computing New Values for Variables   67
   6.1 Arithmetic Expressions   68
       6.1.1 Multiplication and Division   70
       6.1.2 The Order of Arithmetic Operations   71
       6.1.3 Built-in Functions   72
   6.2 String Expressions   74
       6.2.1 Sub-Strings   75
       6.2.2 The Length of Strings   76
       6.2.3 Assignment to Sub-Strings   78
   Summary   79
   Exercises   80

7. Variables with Multiple Values   81
   7.1 Declaration of a List   82
   7.2 Reference to an Individual Value of a List   82
       7.2.1 Expressions as Subscripts   86
   Summary   87
   Exercises   88

8. Program Testing   89
   8.1 Errors Detected by FORTRAN   90
       8.1.1 Grammatical Errors   91
       8.1.2 Detectable Execution Errors   91
   8.2 Test Data   93
   8.3 Diagnostic Output Statements   94
   Summary   96

9. Preliminary Examples   97
   9.1 Compute the Sum of a List of Numbers   98
   9.2 Assemble Letters into Words   101
   9.3 Find the Maximum Number in a List   103
   9.4 Find the Maximum and Print the Values
       of a List   104
   9.5 A Program for Vowelless Printing   107
   9.6 A Program to Detect Palindromes   109
   9.7 More Sample Programs   112
       9.7.1 Print Lines of Ordered Pairs   112
       9.7.2 Expanded Printing   113
       9.7.3 First Character Replacement   113
       9.7.4 Fibonacci Sequences   114
       9.7.5 Table of Factorials   115
       9.7.6 List Values and Cumulative Sums   115

PART II. Program Examples 117

1. Some Text-Editing Programs 121
   1.1 Composing Lines from Words 122
      1.1.1 Line-Oriented Composition 126
      1.1.2 Control of Output Format 129
   1.2 Decomposing Lines into Words 133
      1.2.1 Decomposition by Copying Words 136
   1.3 Variations on Line Composition 138
      1.3.1 Justifying the Right Margin 138
      1.3.2 Altering Line Lengths 139
      1.3.3 Formatting Control Words 140
   Exercises 142

2. A Concordance Program 144
   2.1 Construction of a Word-Frequency Table 145
   2.2 Re-ordering the Lines of the Table 149
   2.3 The Complete Concordance Program 152
      2.3.1 The Program with Input Lines Rather than Words 157
   Exercises 159

3. A Statistical System 160
   3.1 User's Guide to PS-PACK 161
   3.2 The Program for PS-PACK 163
   3.3 "Real" Statistical Systems 166
   Exercises 170

4. Translation of Natural Languages 171
   4.1 A Word-Replacement Translator 172
   4.2 Obstacles to Improved Translation 177
   Exercises 180

5. Matching and Selection 181
   5.1 The PYS Retrieval System 181
   5.2 Limitations on Types of Queries 187
   5.3 Permanent Files 189
   Exercises 190

6. Random Processes 191
   6.1 The RAND Function 193
      6.1.1 The FLOAT Built-in Function 196
   6.2 Coin-Tossing Experiments 196
      6.2.1 Run-Lengths in a Coin-Tossing Experiment 200
   6.3 A Turtle Race 203
   6.4 Poetry Composition 208
      6.4.1 Sample Results from POET 215
   6.5 Simulation of a Queuing System 221
   Exercises 225

7. Interactive Computing Systems 227
   7.1 An Interactive Retrieval System 229
   7.2 Competitive Programs 233
   7.3 A Conversational Program 239
   Exercises 241

PART III. The Nature and Limits of Programming 243

1. Users and Programmers 243
   1.1 A Programming Language for Lists 245
   1.2 A Programming Language for Poems 247
   1.3 The Real Nature of FORTRAN 248
   1.4 Other Programming Languages 250
   1.5 English as a Programming Language 252
   1.6 Future Programming Languages 254

2. Some Limits on Programming 256
   2.1 Ill-Defined Problems 257
   2.2 Impossibly-Long Programs 258
   2.3 "Undecidable" Problems 261

3. Errors in the Computing Process 265
   3.1 Types of Errors 265
   3.2 Errors in Input Data 266
   3.3 Program Errors 269

4. Abuses of the Computer, 271
   4.1 The Impersonal Touch 272
   4.2 The Invasion of Privacy 273
   4.3 An Accessory to Fraud 275
   4.4 The Second Industrial Revolution 277

5. The Intelligence of the Computer 279
   5.1 What does a Computer "Understand"? 279
   5.2 Creative Programs 282
   5.3 Programs that Write Programs 285
   5.4 Artificial Intelligence 287

6. Popular Wisdom About the Computer 289
   6.1 Myth versus Fact 289
   6.2 The Computer Age 293

APPENDICES 295

- A. Summary of the Poet's Subset of FORTRAN   295
  - Miscellaneous Rules   297
  - Program Format Rules   297
  - Punctuation Rules   298

- B. Additional Topics in FORTRAN   299
  - B.1 Program Notes   299
  - B.2 Formatted PRINT statements   300
  - B.3 Formatted Input   301
  - B.4 Doubly-Subscripted Variables   302
  - B.5 Additional Built-in Functions   303
  - B.6 User-Defined Functions   304
  - B.7 Logical Connectives   305
  - B.8 WATFIV Extended IF Statements   307
  - B.9 WATFIV Conditional Loops   307
  - B.10 An Example: Queue Simulation   308

- C. WATFIV Options   311
  - Decimal Format REAL printing
  - Extension Message Supression
  - Omit Source Listing

- D. Keypunching   313

- E. Living Without the Substring Specifier   315

REFERENCES   321

INDEX   323

PREFACE

This is a book <u>about</u> programming, for readers who don't expect to do much programming themselves, but who would still like to understand what it is all about. Our objective is to explain what programs are like, without having to require that the reader become proficient in their construction. Our technique is primarily to supervise the <u>reading</u> of selected programs, rather than the writing of programs. Programs are, of course, written in a programming language, and reading them requires a certain minimal literacy in such a language. To achieve this literacy we present a gentle introduction to the basic concepts and constructs of programming, and expect the reader to become comfortable with these ideas by writing some simple programs. Up to this point, our approach is quite conventional. It becomes radical when we abruptly switch to presenting programs that are considerably longer and more complicated than the reader could be expected to construct on his own. We discuss these programs, not to help the reader become able to write similar programs, but to help him <u>understand</u> what they are, how they work, and something about why they are that way.

After this brief course in program literature, we undertake a discussion of such topics as the difference between programmers and users, and the difference between programming languages and applications programs. We discuss the nature of "computer errors" and the responsibility for them. Finally we try to explore the limits of programming by discussing processes such as "understanding" and "creating".

To explain our intent by analogy, suppose that you wanted to help someone understand something of the nature of proofs in mathematics, without his having to become a mathematician in the process. You might introduce the basic concepts and techniques of proofs in some very simple system -- perhaps plane geometry -- and expect the reader to construct a few trivial proofs. With this background, he then could read and understand proofs at some slightly higher level (beyond what he would be capable of constructing). Finally, you might attempt to draw on this reading experience to discuss proofs more generally -- why they are useful, why they are difficult, etc. To the question "why do it this way?" The answer is, that if well done, you might be able to introduce some key ideas of mathematical proofs to students who are unwilling, or unable, to take sufficient conventional mathematics courses to reach this level.

It would seem that computing has a special obligation to explain itself to laymen. Perhaps not since the internal combustion engine has a single machine possessed the potential for such pervasive influence on our society. We are already served in many ways by computers and there is every indication that this is just the beginning. We are also already often abused by human beings using the instrumentality of the computer, and we hope that this is <u>not</u> just the beginning of more of that. It would seem highly desirable, in the "computer age", that many educated people have a substantive understanding of the capabilities of this machine, and the manner in which it is instructed and controlled.

The usual approach to this educational task is a "computer appreciation" course, or a "computers and society" course -- in either case, an entirely vicarious experience in computing. What we are proposing is to introduce a measured amount of actual programming into such courses, in the belief that this will support a type of discussion and achieve a type of understanding not otherwise possible. Moreover, at least until the problems start to get complicated, most students seem to enjoy such an introduction.

Our objective is to achieve an understanding of the programming process comparable to what a student of programming per se might achieve after two or three courses. But we attempt to do this in a single course, since this is probably all that most students are willing to allocate to this area as a culturally broadening experience. The only possible way to achieve this acceleration is to carefully avoid trying to make programmers out of these students.

Deciding how to present our programs involved some difficult choices. While it would be desirable to present programs in a realistic form, in proper contemporary style, we felt obligated to explain every programming feature used, in order to exorcise any suggestion of thaumaturgy from the process. But we also believe that the amount of preparatory material the reader will tolerate is severely limited. Hence we sought a ruthlessly minimal subset of a programming language. The subset must just support our program examples, without requiring them to be written in an intolerably offensive manner. (As a compromise, as we converged on this minimal subset, the final excisions were restored in Appendix B, but not used in the examples.) The other device used to minimize the length of the introductory material is to present as fixed constructions things which are, in fact, highly variable. For example, we show every program ending with the lines:

```
STOP
END
```

and give no explanation. In our subset, every output statement is of the form:

PRINT, ...

In the same spirit, all variables are explicitly declared, all strings are CHARACTER*100, statement numbers are always in sequence, and so forth. No instructor is going to be fond of this subset -- each will wish we had included at least one or two additional features. The difficulty is that there would be little agreement as to just what the next feature to be included should be. For example, four different reviewers for the publisher wanted a total of six additional features -- but no two reviewers mentioned the same feature. If the subset were expanded to a comfortable level -- say by including the various features listed in Appendix B -- as a rough estimate, the introductory material would be half again as long, and for our limited objectives, it is just not worth it.

In the introductory material of Part I we have taken the somewhat unorthodox approach of trying to explain all of the control structures of the subset with only the input and output statements as objects to control. This permitted a substantial delay in the introduction of expressions and assignment statements. This is very much an experiment, and we may have to retreat to a more conventional order in future editions.

As far as possible, given the constraints of the langauge used and the subset chosen, we have tried to approximate the contemporary view of proper programming practice. Our basic control construct is the loop, and this is implemented with a "DO" statement rather than an "IF-GO TO". However, since neither the "WHILE-DO" nor the "IF-THEN-ELSE" constructs is generally available in FORTRAN we often had to resort to the "IF-GO TO". We did so in a carefully disciplined way, and while the number of "GO TOs" is not high (for FORTRAN programs) it is nevertheless more than we would have preferred.

The question of choice of programming language and presentation of "good" programming practice are less important here than if our objective were to train programmers. The basic ideas about computers and programming are largely independent of the details of the particular programming language used. In fact, this book was derived from an earlier version that used the PL/I language. The examples had to be converted but much of the text is essentially unchanged.

Many of our examples process character strings rather than numbers, since these are inherently easier to motivate and explain without assuming a technical background on the part of the reader. FORTRAN would not be the language of choice for such tasks and, indeed, only the use of the WATFIV dialect makes it possible at all. FORTRAN is also a venerable language that does not reflect contemporary ideas about programming languages, but the differences largely affect issues beyond the scope of this book. Whatever its comparative disadvantages, FORTRAN is the closest thing to a "universal programming language" that currently exists. Since the purpose of this book is to explain programming to a wide audience, this makes FORTRAN a reasonable vehicle.

The approach of the book is entirely non-mathematical. However, it is not really especially oriented to poets -- unless you accept Norman Cousin's notion that poets are "all those who have respect for and speak to the human spirit". The title arises in the practice, at Cornell and elsewhere, of dedicating the least technical introductory version of a subject "to poets". There is a "physics for poets", and the least technical introduction to computing inevitably became "computing for poets". Probably "Programming for Non-Programmers" would be a more descriptive title for this book, but "Programming for Poets" is more fun.

We would like to express our appreciation to our co-authors, Charles Van Loan and Kathryn Conway. Professor Van Loan suggested this approach in the first place, and his enthusiasm was infectious. He subjected his students to early drafts of this material, and contributed many improvements to both programs and explanations.

We are also indebted to our colleagues Charles Moore, Gerard Salton and Tim Teitelbaum for their helpful suggestions, and to Andy Soyring for his help in the preparation of the manuscript.

The book was produced by an editing program (FORMAT) run on the IBM 370/168 computer of Cornell's Office of Computer Services. A printer-simulator generated page images on a CRT display, from which photo plates were made.

Ithaca, N.Y.   Richard Conway
                                                          James Archer

PROGRAMMING FOR POETS
A Gentle Introduction Using FORTRAN
with WATFIV

PART I   ELEMENTS OF PROGRAMMING

Section 1   What is a Program?

A computer program is a sequence of instructions that cause a particular kind of machine called a computer to perform some specified task. The following is an example of a computer program, albeit a trivial and unrealistic one:

```
INTEGER FIRST, SECOND
READ, FIRST, SECOND
SUM = FIRST + SECOND
PRINT, FIRST, SECOND
PRINT, SUM
STOP
END
```

Each step in this sequence is a command to perform some elemental operation: "integer", "add", "print". A certain repertoire of such operations is built into the computer; each command selects one from among this list of possible operations. The program specifies one operation after another in such a way that the performance of the complete sequence accomplishes some useful task. In the example above the "task" is to read two numbers from punched cards, compute their sum, and write out this answer on the computer's printer.

The process of "programming" a computer is the process of preparing a program -- that is, the job of determining what sequence of elemental operations will accomplish the desired task. To do this, one must be familiar with the repertoire of operations the machine is capable of performing, and must have some understanding of the ways in which certain sequences of operations can be usefully employed.

One who prepares programs for a computer is called a "programmer". This is a relatively new occupation -- since computers themselves are a very recent development. It is a rapidly growing occupation -- since the use of computers is increasing at a fantastic rate. There are already several hundred thousand full-time practicing professionals in the field of programming, and each year a million or so new students are given some exposure to programming.

This growth rate is absolutely without precedent. The modern computer is less than thirty-five years old; computers have been commercially available for less than twenty-five. No other device in the entire history of mankind has come close to matching the rapidity of this development from an invention in a research laboratory to a device that is widely used, and is already indispensable in many organizations. Moreover, every informed forecast suggests that this growth rate will not soon diminish. Indeed, there are significant technological and economic arguments that suggest it is accelerating.

There are several reasons to study this phenomenon. For some, there is the prospect of employment, so the study becomes preparation for a professional career in programming. For many others, there is the prospect of acquiring a useful facility -- a tool that can be at least occasionally employed to advantage in one's job, or even in the home or avocation. But the most important reason to study computing is less practical -- it is just to obtain some insight into an inherently interesting and overwhelmingly significant development. If historians of the future call this the beginning of the computer age, it would be a sad and curious thing to have lived in this time without any appreciation of what was taking place.

1.1 A Different Kind of Machine

The key point is to understand _why_ the computer is so important. The answer is basically concerned with its flexibility -- the capability of one machine to perform so many very different kinds of tasks. So then the real question is how come this one type of machine is so nearly universally useful?

A computer is a type of machine. In general, each different type of machine has a distinctive repertoire of elemental operations. For example, an automobile is a type of machine for which a partial list of elemental operations is the following:

1. Accelerate
2. Deccelerate
3. Turn right
4. Turn left
5. Issue a loud warning noise
6. Flash a light signifying a right turn
7. Receive a quantity of fuel
8. Embark a passenger
9. Disembark a passenger
10.   etc.

In order to use such a machine, one "programs" it by specifying a sequence of operations from this list, one at a line, in a carefully prescribed order. The result of executing such a sequence is to accomplish some useful task -- presumably to transport something or somebody from one location to another.

The analogous operation list for a computer includes such things as the following:

1. Copy information from a punched card and record it within the machine.
2. Print out some information that is recorded within the machine.
3. Add two numbers and record the result.
4. Compare two numbers and decide which is larger.
5. Compare two sequences of letters and decide which is longer.
6. etc.

The particular list of computer operations varies somewhat depending upon the make and model of computer, just as the lists would vary in some details for a Chevrolet and a Porsche, or for a compact automobile and an eighteen-wheel semi-trailer truck. But the general nature of the operations is similar for all computers; the differences between various models in this regard are less important than the similarities.

The purpose of a sequence of automobile operations is a general class of task called "transport"; the purpose of a sequence of computer operations is a task called "information processing". Information processing tasks are incredibly varied. They include, for example, customer billing for an electric power utility, air traffic control at a metropolitan airport, and poetry composition. So the question remains: why is this one type of machine so tremendously flexible?

The source of a computer's flexibility lies in several characteristics. Basically, it depends upon the nature of the individual operations that the machine can perform. There is also simply the matter of speed of execution -- each individual operation on a computer is performed so rapidly that a sequence of a million separate operations can be accomplished in a second. While in principal this is just an acceleration of what other types of machines do, in practice the result becomes something substantially different. What is apparently just an <u>enormous difference in degree</u>, becomes in fact, a distinct <u>difference in kind</u>.

There is another distinguishing characteristic of a computer that is even more important. This is the fact that the computer is capable of accepting an <u>entire program in advance</u>, storing it within itself, and then obtaining its sequence of instructions from this stored copy, rather than from the programmer directly. No other kind of machine possesses this capability to anywhere close to the same degree. For example, consider the manner in which one "programs" an automobile. The programmer (the driver) selects an operation from the list of those available, specifies his choice to the machine (by means of some lever, switch, steering wheel, etc.), and observes the machine's response. From time to time the driver decides that another operation is required, and so he repeats this process. One could not conceive of specifying the entire sequence of driving operations, in precise detail, in advance, before ever going near the automobile. Yet this is <u>exactly what a computer programmer does</u>. He prepares a program, loads it into a computer -- and then can leave while the computer executes the sequence of instructions he has specified. The programmer has specified everything in advance, and does not participate in the process while the program is being executed. It may seem surprising that this is possible, let alone useful. If one were required to program an automobile in this manner, it would severely restrict the utility of the device, yet programming a computer in this way is essentially the key to the computer's power and flexibility.

One reason why this is so is simply that storing the program within the computer frees the computer to run at its own speed. If computer instructions had to be delivered to the computer one at a time, as they are executed, it would hardly matter that the computer could perform each operation in a millionth of a second. The overall process would be limited by the speed with which the programmer could specify the instructions. On the other hand, if the instructions are already stored in the machine, it can "find the next instruction" in a millionth of a second, as well as execute instructions at that speed.

For example, the contemporary hand-held electronic calculator is a machine that has certain similarities to a computer, but most current calculators <u>lack the ability to store a program</u> internally. The calculator's repertoire of instructions is similar to that of a computer but its program is supplied, one instruction at a time, by the programmer, as the program is being executed. Each instruction is executed very rapidly, but the overall process is limited by the speed with which instructions are specified by the programmer. This device is unquestionably useful -- but essentially as a convenient and economical alternative to the conventional electric desk calculator (or to the slide rule). The hand calculator is significant, but hardly revolutionary.

However, note that the more expensive current models of hand calculator are already offering some limited internal storage, and the capability of storing at least portions of a program. It is confidently predicted that by 1980 one will be able to purchase for a few hundred dollars a personal computer with computing power comparable to that offered by a university computing center machine in the mid-sixties. The implications of the widespread availability of such machines are really quite beyond reasonable prediction.

So essentially the point is that, because of this stored program concept, there exists a machine capable of performing a pre-specified sequence of elemental operations at a rate of something like a million operations per second. (The rate varies from several hundred thousand to several million, depending on the particular type of computer.) What is very difficult to appreciate is the great variety of things that can be accomplished by the execution of a few million such operations.

Some things are obvious -- certain engineering design calculations, for example. Many other things are not at all obvious -- for example, it is remarkable that a sequence of such operations can effectively play very good chess, and another sequence can compose modestly interesting poetry. These are not tasks that one ordinarily thinks of as being performed by "calculation" at all. One would have assumed that they involved some higher-level type of intellectual process. But regardless of what they involve when performed by a human, some programmer has devised a way to <u>substitute for that process</u> a very large number of simple, clerical operations. Probably the most remarkable aspect of the whole computer development has been the ingenuity with which people have found different ways of using these long sequences of simple operations.

In fact, most of the things that computers do today were not considered likely prospects for computer use when the machine first appeared. The brief history of computing has been marked by spectacular underestimates of the breadth of applicability and the rate of growth of this machine. (There is a lovely apocryphal story that at one point in the early fifties, IBM forecast the <u>total</u> market for electronic computers to be at most <u>twenty-eight machines.</u>) Even today it is difficult to guess where the next explosion of computer application will take place. Professional programmers who thoroughly understand the machine, and are actively exploiting it in one particular field, are still often surprised at the emergence of some new application in another field.

1.2 The Limits of Computing

For all practical purposes the limits on computing are the limits on programming. Not everything that can be programmed can be computed (a subject discussed in Part III), but of more practical importance, <u>nothing that cannot be programmed can be computed</u>. That is to say, if a human being cannot write a program for a particular task, then no computer can accomplish that task. Science fiction provides entertaining accounts of computers that are essentially "self-programming" -- for example, HAL in "2001" -- but this is not an accurate description of the current state of the art, or for that matter even a realistic forecast.

In order to assess the feasibility of obtaining computer assistance for a certain problem, one must assess the practicality of writing a program for the process. Such assessment is a very difficult task. So many remarkable programs have already been written in the few years that computers have been available, that it is easy to fall into the trap of believing that given enough time and effort, virtually any "information processing" task can be programmed. This is not true, and it is surprisingly difficult to forecast what can and cannot be programmed, or even how long it will take to program things that are programmable.

For example, two problems that have enjoyed considerable attention in the brief history of computing are <u>playing chess</u> and <u>translating natural languages</u>. In both cases, there were early successes, and based on these preliminary achievements there were optimistic forecasts, by experts, of complete success. A layman might guess that translation is the easier of the two tasks -- at least there are many small children who can translate between two languages quite easily, but there are few small children who play very good chess. There is also considerably more economic incentive to achieve "automatic translation" than there is to have a robot that plays chess. Yet today, after some fifteen years of work on programs to perform these two tasks, the results are just the opposite of what might have been expected. There are programs that play very good chess, although not play of world championship caliber. But translation programs have made very limited progress, and there is a growing conviction that this process is just not programmable.

Even in less sophisticated areas of programming such as business accounting applications, it is relatively difficult to estimate the magnitude of a programming task. In fact, the field has become notorious for chronic underestimates of the cost and elapsed time required to achieve working programs. Cost overruns in programming projects may be exceeded only by the overruns in military procurement projects -- and even then it is likely that programming costs are a major contributor to military project overruns.

1.3 Understanding the Nature of Programming

In every sense, the central aspect of the computing phenomenon is the programming process. If one wishes to understand computing, one must <u>learn about programming</u>. Instead of learning about the topics in solid-state physics and electronic circuits that underlie the physical hardware of the computer, it is more important to understand the nature of "variables", "loops", "algorithms" and "programming languages" -- things that underlie the process by which computers are instructed.

Unfortunately, there seems to be a limit to how deep and substantive an understanding of programming can be achieved vicariously. Programming is not a very good "spectator sport", and a certain amount of active participation seems prerequisite to understanding.

It also appears that programming is <u>not inherently a natural human process</u>. Programming textbooks may draw analogies with other familiar human processes -- for example, compare computer programming to writing instructions in a cookbook -- but there are such orders of magnitude of difference in size and complexity that the analogy is of limited value. The programming process is really quite unique. We can't think of any other human activity that is a very good model for computer programming.

For example, we used to regard Goren's books on the card game called "bridge" as "programs" to play bridge. We thought our inadequacies in actual practice were largely a consequence of inability to remember the complete program. This illusion persisted until the first time we tried to write a computer program to illustrate some trivial aspect of bridge. Then it became apparent that Goren's books consist of aphorisms and anecdotes, and not programs.

There seems to be no adequate substitute for first-hand experience in programming. If one seeks to really understand what programming involves, why it is difficult, and why the results are less than perfectly reliable, then it seems to be necessary to experience some actual programs. On the other hand, perhaps it is not really necessary to approach the process as if one were going to become a professional programmer. This present book is something of an experiment in this regard. We are attempting to maximize and accelerate the task of acquiring a general <u>understanding</u> of the programming process, by ignoring some of the aspects of the process that are necessary only if one intends to write serious programs. Rather than describe as much as possible about how to write programs, we will describe as little as is necessary to understand what programs are really like.

What you have read in these pages so far may seem plausible, but it cannot really have conveyed much of a useful impression of what a computer program is like. Essentially, the plan of this book is to <u>repeat this discussion</u> -- with more care, detail and depth -- <u>in Part III</u>, after you have achieved a certain minimal literacy in programming. Essentially you must endure Parts I and II in order to really understand the discussion of Part III.

The basic technique employed in Parts I and II is the <u>reading</u> of programs, rather than writing them. However, some actual experience in writing simple programs is highly desirable (and might even be enjoyable), and you should try your hand at it if a computer system is available to you.

Section 2 Data Printing Programs

2.1 <u>A Program to Read and Print a Single Word</u>

We will start with a trivial computing task -- just <u>read a single word</u> given as data, and <u>print that word</u> as output. This is much too simple a task to really consider using a computer -- in fact, it will soon be apparent that it is much more complicated to write the program for this task than it would be to perform the task by hand. Nevertheless, it will serve to illustrate some important points about the nature of a program, and we will rapidly build upon this trivial task until we have more interesting and realistic jobs for which computer assistance would actually be useful.

We develop a computer program in two distinct stages. The first is to <u>figure out a strategy that can be used by a computer</u> to solve the problem. This strategy must be expressed in terms of operations that the computer can perform, but the <u>strategy is described in English</u>. The second stage is to "<u>translate</u>" this English description into an <u>equivalent description in a programming language</u>. In our case the particular programming language used will be FORTRAN.

A description, in English, of a computing strategy for this trivial task would be the following:

>Set aside a segment of memory to hold a string of characters.
>Read an item from the data list, and store this value in the reserved memory segment.
>Retrieve the value from the memory segment, and print it out.
>Terminate the program.

This is obviously a complicated way to describe the performance of a very simple task -- but have faith and patience. The key point here is to note the use of the <u>computer memory</u>. This is what we meant earlier in saying the "strategy must be expressed in terms of operations that the computer can perform". The computer cannot read an item and print its value directly. It can only do this in two separate steps, using memory to save the value between steps. If memory is to be used, it must be prepared -- and that is the purpose of the "set aside" step.

   Now that we have a feasible strategy, we can translate the description, line by line, into FORTRAN. The result is:

         CHARACTER*100 STRING
         READ, STRING
         PRINT, STRING
         STOP
         END

The meaning of this FORTRAN description is exactly the same, step for step, as the previous English description, but it is now in a form that can be presented to a computer and executed. For example:

         CHARACTER*100 STRING

specifies that a memory segment should be set aside to hold a string of up to 100 characters, and that this particular segment will be referred to by the name "STRING". (We will arbitrarily use a maximum length of 100 characters in most of our examples and assume that all of our strings will actually be comfortably less than that. This is a little wasteful, but we can afford to ignore efficiency for our small problems, and this avoids having to worry much about how long the strings actually may be.) The name "STRING" was chosen arbitrarily. Some name is required, so we chose one that would help suggest what that memory segment is used for. The statement:

         READ, STRING

means: "read the next item from the data list, and store the value in the memory segment named STRING. The statement:

         PRINT, STRING

means: "retrieve the value from the memory segment named STRING (actually, just copy the value from STRING) and print this on the output page, starting on a new line on the page". The statements:

         STOP
         END

signal the end of the program. Both statements, in this order, are necessary to end the program gracefully.

   To a limited extent the meanings of the FORTRAN statements are suggested by the English meaning of the key words in the statement. For example, "READ" suggests the action of "read a value from the data list". But don't rely too heavily on such apparent meanings -- the FORTRAN meaning is very strictly defined, regardless of what you think might be implied by the English words used. You should approach the task of learning

FORTRAN almost as you would learning any other "foreign" language. You must learn a new vocabulary. Some of the new words have cognates in English and this will help you remember them, but you must learn the exact meaning in the new language.

Programming languages are unusual languages in that their vocabulary is not completely specified -- each author arbitrarily <u>invents nouns</u> to be used in a particular program. For example, in the program above, "STRING" is not a word of the FORTRAN language -- at least not in the same sense as "CHARACTER" and "READ". In effect, it is like a proper name in English -- you can invent any name you like. For example, the program could have been written in the following way:

```
CHARACTER*100 STR
READ, STR
PRINT, STR
STOP
END
```

This has exactly the same meaning as the previous version. The name "STRING" or "STR" is only used so that several different statements in the program can unambiguously refer to the same segment of memory. (We will soon have programs that use more than one memory segment.)

2.1.1 <u>Preparation of a Card Deck</u>

Now we are faced with task of communicating both the <u>program</u> and the <u>data list</u> to the computer. We will assume this is going to be done by means of punched cards. (The alternative is a typewriter-like terminal connected directly to the computer. In this case each line on the terminal corresponds to a card.) The cards are prepared (punched) on a machine called a "keypunch" and then processed by a machine called a "card reader" that is attached to the computer. People often speak of "loading cards into the computer", but this is actually a poor description of the process. A deck of cards is passed through the card reader, and as each card passes through the reader, the <u>information it contains is copied into the computer</u>. The cards may be "loaded" into the hopper that feeds the reading mechanism, but only the information from the cards is loaded (copied) into the computer.

The keypunch machine punches holes in a blank card, from the left to the right side of the card. (The punching is done in a fixed position, so the card moves under this "punch station" from right to left as you face the machine.) Each <u>column</u> of the card <u>represents one character</u> -- and is generated by one stroke on the keyboard. The keypunch also prints the character at the top of the card, over the column in which the corresponding coded holes are punched. (One hole is sufficient for an integer; for other characters two or more holes are punched in the same column.) However, this printing is solely for the human reader's benefit in verifying the correctness of what has been punched -- the card reading machine senses the holes in the card and not the printing along the top. This means that even if the keypunch is printing poorly (or not at all) the card reader can still read the information from the card.

For our purposes, a good practice is to <u>punch one card for each line</u> of program or data. This is the easiest for you to read, and the easiest way to make changes in the event you discover that mistakes have been made (which is dismayingly often).

A number of restrictions are imposed on where to enter characters on a card (which columns):

1. <u>Don't use the rightmost 8 columns</u> (numbered 73 through 80) for anything. (For some purposes, information in these columns is ignored by the computer -- the simplest thing to do is to avoid using them for anything.)

2. Use the leftmost column (numbered column 1) <u>only for "control cards" and comments</u>. Control cards are explained in some detail below. Comments are explained in Appendix B.1.

3. <u>Use columns 7-72</u> for program statements.

4. <u>Use columns 2-5</u> for statement numbers, where needed.

5. <u>Place a "$" in column 6</u> to indicate that the current card is a continuation of the previous one (columns 1-5 will be blank).

We will use a careful and consistent system of indenting lines of a program -- but only because we feel this makes it easier for a human to read. This is not required by FORTRAN and makes no difference to the computer. We will indent on the card in a corresponding way. For now, statements will simply start in column 7; later, as programs become more complicated, we will further indent some lines. The keypunch has a facility to skip to certain columns (corresponding to the "tab stops" of a typewriter) but it is easier for you to have someone demonstrate this to you than for us to try to explain it here. (See Appendix D.)

Following the above rules, punch a deck of cards for your program, and another deck for your data. For the specific example of section 2.1 the program deck will consist of five cards (since there are five lines in the program) and the data deck will consist of a single card (since there is only one item of data).

Now we need certain "control cards" to indicate the beginning and end of these sections. We will use the control cards for WATFIV as examples of what will be required. If you are not using WATFIV (and maybe even if you are), you will need to get local instructions. In the examples we will assume the use of a version called WATFIV, which is the most widely used for instruction. (WATFIV stands for WATerloo Fortran IV; WATFIV was developed at the University of Waterloo.) The program deck is preceded by a "$JOB card" to indicate the beginning of a new program in the in the FORTRAN language. The data deck is preceded by an "$ENTRY card" to indicate the beginning of the data. In both cases, the "$" must be punched in column 1 of the card.

Now the program deck and the data deck are combined (program first, data last) to form a "job deck" -- a complete job for the computer. Additional control cards are required to indicate the beginning and end of a job deck -- but the form of these cards varies so much from one computer installation to another that you will have to depend upon local instructions for details. However, there is usually some form of "job card" that identifies the beginning of a job and also the name of the user. There is also usually some form of "end-of-job card" to follow the last card of data. Sometimes there are other cards required at the beginning or end of the job, but we will just use the term "job card" to represent everything that must come before the FORTRAN program, and "end-of-job card" to represent everything that must come after the last data card. This sounds complicated at this point, but since it is exactly the same for every job, once you get used to it there is no problem. (You can reuse these control cards from one job to the next.) The job card(s) and end-of-job card(s) are control cards and (like the "$ cards") must begin in column 1 of the card.

The complete deck for the program of Section 2.1 would be the following:

```
                   ┌─column 1
                   v
first card ->  Job card(s) - get local instructions
               $JOB
                       CHARACTER*100 STRING
                       READ, STRING
                       PRINT, STRING
                       STOP
                       END
               $ENTRY
                    'FINISTERRE'
last card ->   End-of-job card(s) - get local instructions
```

There are eight cards, plus your local job card and end-of-job card -- probably ten cards in all.

Note that the data item "FINISTERRE" is enclosed in quotes (single quotes on the data card; not double quotes as used in normal text). These quotes are used to mark the beginning and end of the string on the card; they are not part of the string itself. They are not stored in memory with the string, and will not appear when the string value is printed by the program. That is, this program will print the value without the quotes as:

    FINISTERRE

2.1.2 Execution of a Program

To execute a program, the information in the program deck and the data deck must be copied into the computer. This is done by processing the job deck (consisting of program deck, data deck and various control cards as shown in Section 2.1.1) through a card reader. The job deck is loaded into the hopper of the card reader so that the job card is the first card presented to the reading mechanism.

The time required to process the small examples we will consider is negligible -- a fraction of a second -- but the time required for you to actually get the results may be considerably longer, depending upon when the computer gets around to working on your job. Generally, even when your deck has been processed by the card reader this does not mean the computer is "working on it". Usually one section of the computer serves as a queue of jobs waiting for another section that executes the program. Your program may also have to wait for access to the printer after it has been executed. But sooner or later your job will be executed and the results will be printed, and you will receive several pages of continuous-form paper. Your problem then is to learn to read this output in order to find out what happened.

There are two possible outcomes to the execution of your program:

1. Either everything went just as you intended and you have the results you wanted, or

2. Something went wrong and you don't have the required results.

It is not always easy to distinguish between these two outcomes, and in fact, sometimes it is exceedingly difficult (but more about that later).

The exact form of the output depends somewhat upon what version of the FORTRAN language your computer center is using. The output for the WATFIV version consists of three main sections:

1. source listing
2. execution output
3. run statistics

I 2.1 Program to Read and Print a Word

The source listing is a <u>copy of your program</u> deck (program only -- not the data list). The source listing for our example is shown on the next page. There is a column of numbers at the left of the page. These are the <u>statement numbers</u>, assigned consecutively by WATFIV and used in various messages used to refer to individual statements.

The next section of output is that produced by the execution of the PRINT statements in the program. In this case there is only one PRINT statement in the program and only one line of execution output:

    FINISTERRE

The end of the execution output is marked by four lines of WATFIV diagnostic information, beginning with:

    CORE USAGE   OBJECT CODE=   ...

The output from a different version of FORTRAN would be quite similar to that produced by WATFIV. If you are using a different version, you should run the example and see if you can find the corresponding information on your listing.

A photo-copy of the actual computer output for the program is shown below:

I 2.1 Program to Read and Print a Word

```
      $JOB  NOEXT,LIST,DEC
   1        CHARACTER*100 STRING
   2        READ, STRING
   3        PRINT, STRING
   4        STOP
   5        END
      $ENTRY
FINISTERRE

STATEMENTS EXECUTED=      2

CORE USAGE      OBJECT CODE=    328 BYTES,ARRAY AREA=          0 BYTES,TOTAL AREA AVAILABLE=  338720 BYTES

DIAGNOSTICS     NUMBER OF ERRORS=     0, NUMBER OF WARNINGS=     0, NUMBER OF EXTENSIONS=     0

COMPILE TIME=   0.02 SEC,EXECUTION TIME=    0.01 SEC,    13.12.39   SUNDAY   5 FEB 78     WATFIV - JUN 1977 V1L6
```

If you did not keypunch your program deck perfectly, there will probably be error messages included in your source listing. For example, if you omitted the comma in the READ statement, the source listing would be as shown below. In this case FORTRAN is able to detect the error, and provide you with an error message. Admittedly, the message probably doesn't mean much to you (or to many experienced FORTRAN programmers), but it does indicate a problem. When an error occurs, your goal is to fix it. The first step is to try to check the statement yourself to see if you can find the error(s) (with or without the messages' help). It is important to remember that there is no error too small to cause trouble; look what happened just because of a missing comma. If, after you have checked carefully, you cannot figure out the error (or the error message) you should consider asking someone who might be able to help. Notice that WATFIV attempted to run the program until it encountered an error and provided the message:

PROGRAM WAS EXECUTING LINE   2

to indicate where the problem occurred. Checking back to the source listing, line 4 is the erroneous READ statement, the expected reason for the program not working.

```
              $JOB NOEXT,LIST,DEC
       1          CHARACTER*100 STRING
       2          READ STRING
***ERROR***   VARIABLE FORMAT MUST BE AN ARRAY NAME. STRING IS INVALID
       3          PRINT, STRING
       4          STOP
       5          END

          $ENTRY
***ERROR***   SOURCE ERROR ENCOUNTERED WHILE EXECUTING WITH RUN=FREE

          PROGRAM WAS EXECUTING LINE     2 IN ROUTINE M/PROG WHEN TERMINATION OCCURRED
```

2.2 A Program to Read and Print a Single Number

The program developed in section 2.1 will read and print a string of any kind of characters -- including digits, as well as letters. For example, if the data list consisted of the following:

```
$ENTRY
'2468'
```

the execution output of the program in 2.1 would be:

```
2468
```

However, if you know in advance that the data item will be a number, then it is worthwhile writing the program slightly differently. There are two advantages to treating numbers specially. The most important is that we can perform arithmetic operations (addition, subtraction, multplication and division) on numbers, whereas this is not permitted with character strings. (This will be discussed in Section 6.) The second advantage is that numbers can be given as data in a slightly simpler form -- numbers are not enclosed in quotes.

The only change required in our problem strategy is in the specification of the memory segment to be used. The English description now becomes:

> Set aside a segment of memory to hold a number.
> Read an item from the data list, and store this value in the reserved memory segment.
> Retrieve the value from the memory segment, and print it out.
> Terminate the program.

Translating this description into FORTRAN, we have:

```
INTEGER NUMBER
READ, NUMBER
PRINT, NUMBER
STOP
END
```

This differs from the previous program only in the declaration of the memory segment, where we specify that the segment is to hold a number (rather than a string of characters). The words that describe the type of value that segment is to hold are called its "type attributes". The only types of values we will use are strings and numbers, hence the only type attributes we will be concerned with are:

I 2.2 Program to Read and Print a Number

    CHARACTER*100   for a string of up to
                                      100 characters.

    INTEGER   for an integer.

    REAL   for a number which can have a
                                      decimal point.

    In the program above we have named the memory segment "NUMBER", instead of the name "STRING" in the previous version, but recall that the name is an arbitrary choice on our part and not a special word of the programming language. It would be confusing to have a segment named "STRING" that couldn't be used for anything but a number, so we chose the name "NUMBER" simply to remind us what type of value it can hold. But there are many other names that might be equally appropriate, depending upon the particular problem. For example, NBR, QTY, HEIGHT, WIDTH, AGE, etc.

    The only restriction is that FORTRAN limits the length of names to <u>at most six characters</u>.

    For our purposes, we would like to be able to treat all numbers identically, using only REAL variables. Our programs would be somewhat less efficient, but this is not a basic concern. A more serious problem is that FORTRAN <u>insists</u> that INTEGER variables be used in many of the statements we will be using extensively. Since INTEGER values are a special case of REAL values we can not use INTEGER variables exclusively. However, INTEGER variables are ideally suited for <u>most</u> of our needs, and we will use them whenever possible, reserving REAL numbers solely for calculations where integers would be inadequate.

    REAL numbers can have decimal points, and digits to the right of the decimal point, but all numbers do not have to be written with a decimal point. For example, all of the following are valid REAL numbers:

    3.14   65   .52   0.0120   0   32768   .1

Negative numbers are written in the usual manner:

    -13   -.0602   -0.146   -32.67

    It will simplify our task if we do not try to use numbers that are "too big" or "too small". We will limit our examples to numbers that have <u>six or fewer digits</u>. That is, we will only use numbers less than one million. Or if we are using numbers with three decimal places (three digits to the right of the decimal point), they will be less than one thousand -- so the total number of digits is six or fewer. Like the assumption of 100-character strings, this 6-digit limit is just to simplify matters for our present purposes. These limits are more than adequate for the examples we will use, and they allow us to

I 2.2 Program to Read and Print a Number

avoid various complications and explanations. But don't misunderstand -- these limits are self-imposed for our convenience, and are not inherent limits of computers or the FORTRAN language.

2.2.1 Output Format for Numbers

Let us execute our program to read and print a number. For example, for the number 975 the complete jobdeck would be:

```
        Job card
    $JOB
        INTEGER NUMBER
        READ, NUMBER
        PRINT, NUMBER
        STOP
        END
    $ENTRY
     975
    End-of-job card
```

The printed output from the execution of this program will be the single line:

    975

If we had used the statement: REAL NUMBER, the printed output would have been:

    0.9750000E 03

For REAL numbers, FORTRAN normally prints values in "exponential notation", also called "scientific notation". That is, the number is printed with a zero to the left of the decimal point, and an exponent of ten is given to show where the decimal point really is. (The technical name used in computing for this type of number is "floating point number".) In this case:

    0.9750000E 03 means 0.9750000 multiplied by 10^3

Other examples are:

        9   would print as   0.9000000E 01

        97.5   would print as   0.9750000E 02

        -9   would print as   -0.9000000E 01

There is one peculiarity with REAL numbers that will occasionally be disconcerting. Because numbers are actually stored inside the computer in binary rather than decimal form, it turns out that <u>certain fractional numbers are not quite exact</u> -- they are "off" by 1 in the rightmost digit. For example, .2 is stored as .1999999; .7 is stored as .6999999. This does not apply to all fractional numbers -- for example, .5 is exact. Some examples of fractions in display form are:

      .3   would print as   0.2999999E 00

      .1   would print as   0.9999999E-01

      .01   would print as   0.9999999E-02

These approximations are "close enough" for arithmetic purposes -- they will give reasonable results when used in calculations. But they are unquestionably confusing when they appear on output.

    WATFIV provides an option (see Appendix C) which causes REAL numbers to be printed in normal decimal notation. For some purposes, but not ours, this feature produces undesirable results because it is not able to properly handle very large or very small numbers. The optional format produces much more readable output and has been used in running all of the examples in the rest of this book.

2.3 <u>Variables</u>

    In this section and the next we introduce several new terms, and describe a convention to be used in presenting examples.

    What we have been calling a "memory segment" is generally called a "variable". It is, literally, a segment of computer memory, but it is easier to have a single word for it, and we might as well introduce the word that is universally used for "a particular segment of computer memory used to store a single value". The word "variable" is borrowed from algebra, since its role is similar in many respects, but that need not really concern you. Just think of "variable" as a synonym for a "particular small portion of computer memory".

I 2.3 Variables

A variable has three significant aspects: a <u>name</u>, a <u>value</u>, and a <u>type</u>. Consider the following examples:

<u>name</u>	<u>value</u>	<u>type</u> (of value)
NBR	14	integer number
WORD	KEDGE	character string
COUNT	0	integer number
STRING	LWL 9	character string
FRACTN	0.5	real number

These examples illustrate the only real number types of values we are concerned with -- character strings and integer and real numbers.

In previous examples we have referred to "setting aside a memory segment". The technical phrase for this is "creating a variable", but nothing is actually created -- the memory already exists. A particular portion of memory is designated to have a certain name, used to refer to that variable for the duration of this one program. The meaning of the FORTRAN declaration:

    INTEGER NEWNBR

is to create a variable named NEWNBR to store values of type "integer number". The particular <u>type statement</u> specifies the <u>type</u> of <u>value</u> the <u>variable</u> is to hold:

    INTEGER   specifies the type "integer number"

    REAL   specifies the type "real number"

    CHARACTER   specifies the type "string"

The <u>name of a variable is permanent</u> -- at least it lasts for the entire program. On the other hand, the value of a variable will often be changed (which, in fact, is why it is called a "variable"). For example, the result of executing the statement:

    READ, NEWNBR

is to read the next data item and store that value in the variable named NEWNBR -- that is, changing the value of the variable NEWNBR. However, the <u>type of a variable is also permanent</u> (at least for the life of the program). A variable is declared to be either INTEGER, REAL or CHARACTER*100. If it is INTEGER it can only contain a number as a value. It may contain different numbers at different times, but it will never contain a character string, and it will never retain any value to the right of the decimal point. Conversely, a CHARACTER*100 variable may contain different strings, from time to time, but will never contain a number. (Its character string may consist of digits, and look like a number, but it will never be considered a number by FORTRAN.)

It is also important to realize that <u>creating a variable does not give that variable a value</u>. It gives it a name, and establishes the type of value it can have, but the variable is <u>empty</u> until some value is explicitly stored there. The technical term for this kind of emptiness is "uninitialized". (If you accidentally try to retrieve a value from a variable to which you have never given a value -- an error message will say the "variable is uninitialized".)

2.4 <u>Algorithms</u>

"Algorithm" is the technical term for a detailed, step-by-step plan for a computing process -- such as the descriptions of strategy that we have given in Sections 2.1 and 2.2. An algorithm is usually expressed in a natural (human) language, such as English. A "program" is an algorithm that has been translated into some particular programming language (such as FORTRAN). There is a little confusion because the verb "to program" is generally taken to include both stages of the process -- the development of the algorithm and the translation of the algorithm into a program.

It may surprise you at this point, but <u>the hard part</u> of the programming process <u>is the development of the algorithm</u>. Once you have learned the vocabulary and the grammatical rules of FORTRAN (an easy task compared to learning a real foreign language) the translation of the algorithm is quite straightforward. But the creation of the algorithm requires a complete understanding of the problem requirements, insight into how a computer operates, and considerable ingenuity. It is very important that you <u>separate the two stages</u> of the process, and not try to translate into FORTRAN terms until you know exactly what it is that has to be done. A common mistake for beginners, that makes programming more difficult than it need be, is to try to do both things at once.

An algorithm is equally useful in <u>reading</u> a program. It enables you to understand the overall organization of the program, by reading a description in a more familiar language, and in a form that is not obscured with details. You can read an algorithm to learn <u>what</u> is to be accomplished, and <u>generally how</u> the program goes about doing so. Then you can read the actual program to see, <u>in detail</u>, <u>how</u> the task is performed. Except when the program is very short and obvious, we will present an algorithm first.

In general, we will not discuss the process of <u>creating</u> algorithms. If we were principally concerned with developing your competence as a programmer we would concentrate on the development of algorithms -- since this is crucial to programming competence. But for our present purposes you need only understand what an algorithm is, and appreciate that if no algorithm can be found for a given problem, then that problem cannot be solved on a computer.

We will use a stylized, technical language for algorithms which is less verbose and more precise than normal English. For example, in Section 2.1 we described a step in detail:

> Set aside a segment of memory to hold a string of characters.

From now on we will say:

> Create a string variable STR.

or just:

> Create string STR.

As shown in this example, we will often use variable names in algorithms. This helps make algorithms clear and unambiguous, particularly when there are several variables involved. We will just anticipate the names that will be chosen when we translate the algorithm to a program, and use these names in the algorithm as well.

Whenever a programming element, such as a variable name, appears in an algorithm it will be given in uppercase (capital) letters. All other terms in the algorithm will be in normal lowercase letters.

Similarly, we will abbreviate the algorithm steps that specify input and output. For example, in Section 2.1 we wrote:

> Read an item from the data list, and store this value in the reserved memory segment.

From now on we will abbreviate such a step as:

> Read into NUMBER.

or just:

> Read NUMBER.

"Read" in an algorithm will always mean "read the next item from the data list". Similarly, we will write:

> Print NUMBER

which will always mean "retrieve the current value from the variable named NUMBER, and print it out".

Even with these abbreviations, algorithms should still be understandable without any knowledge of FORTRAN. They could in fact be translated into some other programming language, as well as into FORTRAN.

Section 2 Summary

1. An <u>algorithm</u> is a detailed plan for a program -- a sequence of steps that will solve some specific problem. An algorithm is described in an informal, abbreviated natural language, and should be understandable without having to know the details of a programming language.

2. A <u>program</u> is an algorithm that has been translated into some particular programming language -- the FORTRAN language in our case.

3. A <u>variable</u> is a location in computer memory used to store a value of a certain type. It has a <u>name</u> so it can be referred to by statements in the program.

4. We will use three different types of values: <u>real numbers</u>, <u>characters</u>, and ordinary <u>integer numbers</u>. These types of values in FORTRAN are called:

    CHARACTER*100   for strings of characters

    INTEGER   for integer numbers

    REAL   for real numbers

5. Variables are created by a <u>type declaration</u>. The FORTRAN forms for strings and numbers are the following:

    CHARACTER*100 list of names

    INTEGER list of names

    REAL list of names

    The declaration <u>creates</u> a variable, assigns it a name, and determines the type of value it will have -- but it does not give the variable any specific value.

6. The end of our programs will always be indicated by the lines:

    STOP
    END

7. The READ statement in FORTRAN reads the next item on the data list and stores its value in a specified variable. The form is:

    READ, name of variable

    The types of the data item and the variable <u>must agree</u>. If the variable is a string variable, then the next item read must also be a string. If the variable is numeric, then the next item must be a number.

8. The form in which values are given in a data list is different for strings and numbers. Numbers are given in normal form -- with or without decimal points, as required, and with a minus prefix for a negative number. String values are enclosed in single quotes.

   Each value in the data list is given on a separate card.

9. The PRINT statement in FORTRAN begins a new line of output and prints the value of the variable specified. The form is:

   PRINT, name of variable

   The value of a string is printed exactly as stored in the variable (which does not include the quotes from the data card). The value of an integer number is printed as an integer; the value of a real number is printed either in exponential or decimal form (depending on the compiler and options used) -- that is, 91.4 is printed as either 0.914000E 02 or 91.4000000, respectively.

10. A **job deck** consists of cards containing a program, followed by cards containing a data list. It also requires certain control cards.

12. The execution of a program produces three kinds of printed output:

    a. The source listing -- a copy of the program
    b. The execution output -- the result of the PRINT statements
    c. The run statistics -- how long your program ran, etc.

Section 2 **Exercises**

1. Rewrite the following numbers from exponential form into normal decimal notation:

    a. 0.1234560E 00
    b. 0.4321000E 03
    c. 0.1000000E-06
    d. 0.1040500E 02
    e. -0.5200000E 01
    f. -0.6421000E-02

2. Rewrite the following numbers into exponential form as it would appear in program output:

    a. 16
    b. 16.0
    c. -16.00
    d. 0.0004
    e. -.05

3. Write, punch and run a program to read one of the numbers in Exercise 2 as data and verify the form given on output.

4. Write a program to perform each of the following tasks (a separate program for each):

    a. Read a number from data, and print the value twice -- on two consecutive lines.
    b. Read a number from data, and do nothing with it -- don't print it.
    c. Given a data list consisting of two numbers (one on each of two cards), read and print the first number; ignore the second.
    d. Given a data list consisting of two numbers, read both numbers but print only the first.
    e. Given a data list consisting of two numbers, read and print the second number.
    f. Given a data list consisting of two numbers, read and print both numbers.

5. Write a program to perform each of the tasks listed in exercise 4, but for a string value rather than a number.

Section 3 Statement Repetition

Suppose that our task is to read and print a list of three words (rather than one, as in Section 2.1). Using only the techniques described in Section 2 we can easily develop a program for this task. In fact, there are two different algorithms we could use.

The <u>first strategy</u> would read all three items from the data list first, and then print them. This requires the use of three different variables, since at one point it is necessary to store three different values at the same time:

>Create 3 string variables: ST1, ST2, ST3.
>Read into ST1.
>Read into ST2.
>Read into ST3.
>Print ST1.
>Print ST2.
>Print ST3.
>Terminate the program.

The program that would be produced from this algorithm would be:

```
CHARACTER*100 ST1, ST2, ST3
READ, ST1
READ, ST2
READ, ST3
PRINT, ST1
PRINT, ST2
PRINT, ST3
STOP
END
```

The <u>second strategy</u> for this problem is based on the observation that by slightly changing the order of different actions one would only need a single variable:

            Create a string variable ST.
            Read into ST.
            Print ST.
            Read into ST.
            Print ST.
            Read into ST.
            Print ST.
            Terminate the program.

This single-variable strategy is possible because we never really need to have more than one value available at any one time. When we read the second item from the data list and store it in ST, we destroy the first value which was already in ST. But we have already printed out the first value, and hence have no further need of it, so its destruction by the arrival of the second value is harmless. Similarly, we read the third value only after the second value is no longer needed.

3.1 The Loop Concept

At this point, there is very little reason to prefer one of these strategies over the other. There is no real point in trying to minimize the number of variables used, or the length of the program -- although both of these will be reasonable criteria later on when we have more substantial problems.

However, note that the body of the second algorithm consists of <u>three repetitions of the same pair of steps</u>:

            Read into ST.
            Print ST.

We could make use of this repetition to rewrite the second algorithm in a different form:

            Create a string variable ST.
            Repeat the following section 3 times:
              Read into ST.
              Print ST.
            Terminate the program.

This form of the algorithm is preferable to its predecessors for several reasons. It is a little shorter, and probably easier to understand what is really taking place. But most important, in this form it is <u>very easy to change the length of the data list</u> to be processed -- just by changing the number in the "Repeat" line. This algorithm could be used for the single-word task of Section 2.1 just by performing the central section only once instead of three times. It could also be used to read and print a list of one thousand words, just by writing 1000 in place of 3. (Printing a list of one thousand words is a task that could justify computer assistance, so we have already reached the point where the problem is no longer trivial.)

I 3.1 The Loop Concept

A sequence of steps to be repeated, such as "Read...Print" in this algorithm, is called a "loop". This idea is central to computer programming, and is probably the single most important concept involved in understanding programs. <u>Every non-trivial computer program involves the use of loops</u>.

We will translate this loop algorithm into FORTRAN in several stages in order to carefully explain the FORTRAN form for a loop. To start with, we will translate only the familiar part of the algorithm, and show this part in upper-case letters. In effect, this is <u>translating everything but the loop</u>:

```
        CHARACTER*100 ST
        Repeat the following section 3 times:
            Read into ST.
            Print ST.
        STOP
        END
```

The "body" of the loop (that is, the sequence of statements to be repeated) is also familiar. This will be the FORTRAN statements:

```
        READ, ST
        PRINT, ST
```

All that remains is to specify the statements that <u>control the repetition</u>.

This control is accomplished with a "DO statement" and a "counter variable". The counter variable is an additional variable, used just to count the number of times the loop has been repeated. Say we choose the name "LOOP" for this variable. Then the DO statement would be:

```
        DO 20 LOOP = 1, 3, 1
```

This is just the FORTRAN form for the following action:

Repeat the following section of program 3 times, using variable LOOP to count the repetitions.

That is, LOOP is set equal to 1 and the body of the loop is executed. Then LOOP is set equal to 2 and the body of the loop is executed again. Finally, LOOP is set equal to 3 and the body of the loop is executed a third time. More generally, the DO statement is of the form:

```
        DO ### counter = first, last, increment
```

The "counter" is a variable (e.g. LOOP) which will be set to the value "first" before the first execution of the loop. Then the "counter" is incremented by "increment"; the body of the loop will be executed after each incrementation of "counter", as

I 3.1 The Loop Concept

long as the value of "counter" does not exceed "last". When "counter" is greater than "last", execution passes to the first statement after the loop.

To make precise just what is meant by "the following section", we denote the end of the repeated section with the keyword "CONTINUE" and give the loop a number, "###" in the model shown above. Whatever number replaces "###" in the DO statement will also appear as the statement number in the CONTINUE statement which ends the loop. FORTRAN will allow us to choose any integer which strikes our fancy as long as it is not already in use as the statement number of another statement. We will use the following guidlines in our selection of statement numbers:

1. Statement numbers appear in order, i.e. statement 10 appears before 100.

2. Statement number sequences leave room for additional statements to be inserted. Typically, this means that we will use 10, 20, 30, etc.

3. Smaller numbers are easier to punch and remember. We will use 10, 20, etc. rather than 100110, 21320, etc.

In our example, we arbitrarily choose 20. The complete loop would be written:

```
        DO 20 LOOP = 1,3,1
            READ, ST
            PRINT, ST
20          CONTINUE
```

Incorporating this loop into the program, and remembering to declare the counter variable, the complete program is:

```
        CHARACTER*100 ST
        INTEGER LOOP
        DO 20 LOOP = 1, 3, 1
            READ, ST
            PRINT, ST
20          CONTINUE
        STOP
        END
```

The first repetition of the body of the loop reads the first item of data and prints the first line of output; the second repetition of the body reads the second item and prints the second line; the third and final repetition reads the third item and prints the third line. (If there happened to be more than three items of data, the remaining data would not be read, since the body of the loop is executed only three times.)

For example, suppose this program were run with the following data list:

```
$ENTRY
 'HENRY'
 'HATTERAS'
 'FEAR'
```

The result of executing the program with this data would be to print the following three lines:

```
HENRY
HATTERAS
FEAR
```

Note again that the quotes that are required for strings in the data list are not considered part of the value and do not appear when the value is printed.

Now if we wanted to read and print a list of, say, five values instead of three, all we would have to do would be change the 3 in the DO statement to a 5, as shown below:

```
DO 20 LOOP = 1, 5, 1
```

or if we wanted to read and print a list of 1000 values the appropriate statement would be:

```
DO 20 LOOP = 1, 1000, 1
```

The amount of data provided in each case would have to agree with the number specified in the DO statement.

3.1.1 Loop to Print each Item Twice

Now suppose that our assigned task had been to read a list of three strings and to print each string twice. The program to do this differs from the previous one only in that the body of the loop, which is repeated for each data item, is now:

```
READ, ST
PRINT, ST
PRINT, ST
```

Including this loop body the complete program is:

```
          CHARACTER*100 ST
          INTEGER LOOP
          DO 20 LOOP = 1, 3, 1
              READ, ST
              PRINT, ST
              PRINT, ST
   20     CONTINUE
          STOP
          END
```

The point in presenting this slight variation is to emphasize that the mechanism for controlling the repetition of the loop is independent of the action performed on each repetition of the loop. That is, the control statements:

```
          DO 20 LOOP = 1, 3, 1

              ...

   20     CONTINUE
```

will repeat anything three times. In Part II we present programs where the body of loops is quite long and complicated -- but the idea is essentially as simple as it appears here: there is some sequence of statements to be repeated, and a mechanism, independent of the body, to control the number of times the body is repeated.

3.2 Control Values in the Data

The loop program of Section 3.1 can be slightly modified to give it even more flexibility. Suppose the DO statement in that program had been written:

```
          DO 20 LOOP = 1, DATA, 1
```

instead of:

```
          DO 20 LOOP = 1, 3, 1
```

The difference is simply that the number of repetitions for the loop is given by specifying a variable instead of a constant. The value of this variable, when the DO statement is encountered, serves in exactly the same way as the constant we used previously. That is, if the value of DATA is 3, then the loop will be repeated three times, just as previously.

The purpose of specifying the number of repetitions with a variable rather than a constant is that this makes it easier to change the number of repetitions. The value of a variable can be changed by executing a READ statement; the value of a constant can only be changed by replacing the entire DO statement.

To use this technique, the data list would begin with a number that specified how many data items follow. For example:

```
$ENTRY
3
'MONHEGAN'
'MATINICUS'
'MOUNT DESERT'
```

The program would be modified to read this control value into DATA before executing the loop (and also to declare the additional variable):

```
        CHARACTER*100 ST
        INTEGER LOOP, DATA
        READ, DATA
        DO 20 LOOP = 1, DATA, 1
            READ, ST
            PRINT, ST
20      CONTINUE
        STOP
        END
```

With this program, if we wanted to read and print a list of five words, we would only have to begin that list with the number 5. For example:

```
$ENTRY
5
'GRAVES'
'MINOTS LEDGE'
'HALFWAY ROCK'
'CLEVELAND LEDGE'
'BRENTON REEF'
```

The point is that no change whatever is required in the program to change the length of the data list it will read. The data list itself provides all the information required; exactly the same program will work for a list of any length.

3.3 Nested Loops

In Section 3.1.1 the program printed each data item twice. Now suppose that each item is to be printed ten times. Clearly, we could use the same strategy as before -- write a sequence of ten PRINT statements -- but there is obviously a better way. Now that you understand loops, you know that if you have to repeat some statement ten times you would use a loop. For example, something like the following:

I 3.3 Nested Loops

```
          DO 15 LINE = 1, 10, 1
             PRINT, ST
   15     CONTINUE
```

This loop is equivalent to a sequence of ten PRINT statements and can be written wherever those PRINT statements could be written. In particular, this loop can be <u>within the body of another loop</u>. For example:

```
          DO 20 LOOP = 1, DATA, 1
             READ, ST
             DO 15 LINE = 1, 10, 1
                PRINT, ST
   15        CONTINUE
   20     CONTINUE
```

When one loop is placed inside another loop in this manner, the loops are said to be "nested". It is a very common construction and you will see it frequently in the programs in Part II.

The trick to understanding nested loops is to consider them <u>one at a time</u>. When worrying about the inner loop, consider it independent of its context -- don't worry about whether or not it happens to be part of the body of some outer loop. When studying the outer loop, consider all inner loops as if they were single statements. They are complicated statements, running over several lines, but they perform some identifiable task, just as if there were a single FORTRAN statement to perform this task.

For example, at the algorithmic level the problem we have been discussing would be described as follows:

```
       Repeat the following section for each data item:
          Read into ST.
          Print ST 10 times.
```

At this level the algorithm has a single loop which includes a step "Print 10 times" in its body. Since there is no "PRINT 10 TIMES" statement in FORTRAN, this step is itself implemented by a loop, but that is just a detail, and doesn't affect the way in which we view the outer loop.

The algorithm could subsequently be rewritten in more detail to show both loops:

```
       Repeat the following section for each data item:
          Read into ST.
          Repeat the following 10 times
             Print ST.
```

This form is closer to what will actually appear in the program, but obviously the two forms are equivalent.

It should also be clear that this nesting could take place with more than two levels. The body of the inner loop in the example above could itself contain a loop, which could contain another loop, etc. The examples in Section 10.5 and 10.6 use nested loops, and all of the examples in Part II have two or more levels of loops. In every case the trick is still to approach them one level at a time, and understand what each level accomplishes on its own, without worrying about whether it may contain another loop or itself be contained within another loop.

In general, anything may appear in the body of a loop <u>except a declaration</u>. The creation of variables takes place at the very beginning of a program -- actually as part of the preparation for execution of the program, rather than part of the execution itself. Consequently, a <u>declaration is never repeated</u>, and never appears in the body of a loop.

3.3.1 <u>Nested Loops and Control Values in the Data</u>

Just for practice, we will give an example combining the ideas of Sections 3.2 and 3.3. That is, it will have nested loops, and the number of repetitions at each level will be controlled by values supplied in the data.

Suppose you are to read and print a list of words, where each word can be printed a different number of times. The length of the list, and the number of repetitions for each word on the list is included in the data. For example:

```
$ENTRY
4
2
'CONSTELLATION'
1
'PHILADELPHIA'
3
'ENTERPRISE'
2
'CONSTITUTION'
```

These data mean that there is a list of 4 items, the first of which is to be printed 2 times, the second 1 time, etc. The program to do this is the following:

I 3.3 Nested Loops

```
      CHARACTER*100 ST
      INTEGER LOOP, DATA
      INTEGER LINE, REPEAT
      READ, DATA
      DO 20 LOOP = 1, DATA, 1
          READ, REPEAT
          READ, ST
          DO 10 LINE = 1, REPEAT, 1
              PRINT, ST
10        CONTINUE
20    CONTINUE
      STOP
      END
```

The results produced by executing this program on the data shown above would be:

```
CONSTELLATION
CONSTELLATION
PHILADELPHIA
ENTERPRISE
ENTERPRISE
ENTERPRISE
CONSTITUTION
CONSTITUTION
```

Section 3 <u>Summary</u>

1. It is often convenient to repeat the execution of a certain group of consecutive statements in a program. Such a repeated group is called a <u>loop</u>. The control of a loop in FORTRAN is by means of the "DO statement". The form we will use is the following:

           DO ### counter = first, last, increment
              statements of the body of the loop
       ###   CONTINUE

   The "###" indicates the loop number. The counter variable will always be an integer variable (one declared INTEGER).

2. The "first", "last", and/or "increment" in the DO statement may be given as a constant, or it may be given as an integer variable -- so that its value may be supplied by the data. This latter practice allows the program to be more flexible, and accomodate different problem sizes without requiring any change in the program itself.

3. Any statement (except a declaration) may appear in the body of a loop. In particular, a loop itself can be regarded as a single statement and appear in the body of another loop. The loops are then said to be <u>nested</u>.

4. In understanding loops it is important to recognize the difference between the <u>statements that are to be repeated</u> and the <u>statements that control the number of times</u> the repetition is to take place.

Section 3 **Exercises**

1. Write a program that will read a data list of 20 numbers, and print those numbers, one per line, in the order they appear on the data list.

2. Write a program that will read a data list of numbers, the first of which specifies how many numbers follow. All of the numbers (except the first) should be printed, one per line.

3. Write a program that will read a data list of 30 numbers. The first 10 numbers are to be printed, one per line, in the order they appear on the data list. The second 10 numbers are <u>not</u> to be printed, but the third 10 are to be printed, one per line, in the order they appear on the data list. That is, the eleventh line of the output list will have the value of the 21st number on the data list.

4. Write a program that will read a data list of 20 strings, and print only the even-numbered strings -- that is, the second, fourth, sixth, etc.

5. Write a program that will read a data list of numbers, the first of which specifies how many numbers follow. Each of the numbers (except the first) should be printed twenty times.

Section 4   Conditional Statements

   Suppose that our list printing task was revised such that we are to print every word on the data list <u>unless the word happens to be "OMIT"</u>, in which case we are to skip the word and continue. Assume that a number is given at the beginning of the list, specifying how many words follow, as suggested in Section 3.2. The program to do this is obviously similar to the one shown in Section 3.2 -- except that sometimes it must skip over the PRINT statement. Alternatively, we could say that sometimes we <u>will</u> execute the PRINT statement, and sometimes not. An algorithm for this process is the following:

```
            Create a string variable ST.
            Create a numeric variable COUNTR.
            Create a numeric variable REPEAT.
            Read the first data item into REPEAT.
            Repeat the following section a number of times
                    equal to the value of REPEAT:
                Read into ST.
                If the value of ST is not "OMIT"
                    then print ST.
            Terminate the program.
```

The translation of this algorithm to FORTRAN involves a new type of statement called the "IF statement":

```
            CHARACTER*100 ST
            INTEGER COUNTR, REPEAT
            READ, COUNTR
            DO 20 COUNTR = 1, REPEAT, 1
                READ, ST
                IF (ST .NE. 'OMIT') PRINT, ST
     20     CONTINUE
            STOP
            END
```

The symbol ".NE." in the IF statement means "not equal".

Suppose this program were executed with the following data list:

```
$ENTRY
6
'STEWART'
'HULL'
'OMIT'
'DACRES'
'OMIT'
'BAINBRIDGE'
```

The execution output would be the following:

```
STEWART
HULL
DACRES
BAINBRIDGE
```

On four of the repetitions of the loop the value of ST is <u>not</u> "OMIT", so the PRINT statement is executed. On the other two executions, the value of ST is equal to "OMIT", so the PRINT statement is not executed, hence the value "OMIT" does not appear in the output.

The general form of the IF statement is the following:

IF(condition) statement

The meaning of the IF statement is essentially what is suggested by the keyword "IF". That is:

if the condition is <u>true</u>, then execute the statement,
otherwise skip the statement.

Alternatively:

if the condition is true, execute the statement,
if the condition is false, skip the statement.

The meaning of the "condition" is described in the next section. The "statement" may be any simple FORTRAN statement -- for example, READ or PRINT, but <u>not</u> DO, CONTINUE or another IF. A declaration is not a statement, strictly speaking, and cannot be made subject to a condition.

Notice that the "IF(condition)" is treated as a prefix to the statement whose execution is conditional, and both the "IF" and the conditional statement appear on the same line.

4.1 Conditions

"Conditions" are phrases in a program which are evaluated with a result that is either _true_ or _false_. The simplest kind of condition _compares the value of a variable_ to a _value given as a constant_. For example:

```
ST .EQ. 'HOOD'
COUNTR .EQ. 4
COUNTR .NE. 3
```

The first of these examples means the following:

Retrieve the current value of the variable named ST. If that value is "HOOD" then the condition is _true_. If the value is anything else, then the condition is _false_.

Similarly, the meaning of the last example is:

Retrieve the current value of the variable named COUNTR. If that value is not equal to three then the condition is _true_. If it is equal to three, then the condition is _false_.

A condition can _compare the values of two variables_ rather than compare a variable to a constant. For example:

```
ST .EQ. STRING
STRING .NE. WORD
COUNTR .EQ. REPEAT
```

The exact meaning of the condition "ST .EQ. STRING" is the following:

Compare the current value of the variable ST to the current value of the variable STRING. If these variables have the same value, whatever the value might happen to be, the condition is _true_. If these variables have different values at that instant, the condition is _false_.

A condition always involves a comparison of two values _of the same type_. That is, a character string can be compared to another character string, and a number can be compared to a number, but a _character string cannot be compared to a number_. If the condition involves two variables, they must have the same type of value. If the condition involves a variable and a constant, then the constant must be in the appropriate form for that type of variable -- that is, a quoted string if the variable is a string variable, and an (unquoted) number if the variable is a numeric variable.

4.1.1 Relations

The symbols ".EQ." and ".NE." in the examples above are called "relations". A relation specifies the kind of comparison to be performed in a condition. There are six different relations that will be used in our examples:

symbol	meaning
.EQ.	is equal to
.NE.	is not equal to
.LT.	is less than
.LE.	is less than or equal to
.GT.	is greater than
.GE.	is greater than or equal to

4.1.2 String Comparisons

The meaning of these relations is obvious when the values being compared are numbers -- it is less obvious when the values are strings. The problems have to do with the length of strings and with the ordering of characters -- what does it mean to say one character is "greater than" another.

The length question is handled by the following rule:

> Whenever two strings of unequal length are compared by a relation, the shorter string is (temporarily) increased in length by adding blanks to the right end, until it has the same length as the longer string.

For example, in the program above, we used the condition:

    ST .EQ. 'OMIT'

If the value of the variable ST is "OMIT", then the condition is obviously true. If the value is "XXX", then the condition is obviously false. However, suppose the value of ST is "OMIT " -- that is, with a blank after the "T". In this case, the condition is still true, because the value on the right is automatically extended with a blank to match the length of the left value -- and then the values are identical. On the other hand, if the value of ST is " OMIT" -- that is, with a blank before the "O", the condition is false. The right value is again extended with a blank to match the length of the longer left value -- but " OMIT" is not identical to "OMIT ". The results are quite reasonable -- they agree with commonsense, so that basically you don't have to worry about different lengths when testing for equality (or non-equality) between strings.

However, the "less than" and "greater than" relations are a little more complicated. Essentially, these relations involve "alphabetical ordering". A value is said to be "less than" another value if it comes <u>before</u> it in alphabetical ordering; it is "greater than" if it comes <u>after</u>. For example, the following are both true conditions:

    'D' .LT. 'F'   and   'M' .GT. 'K'

The alphabetical ordering applies to strings of more than one character in the obvious way:

    'BB' .LT. 'BC'
    'LWL' .GT. 'LVL'
    'AXX' .LT. 'BAA'

These three examples are all true conditions.

When the strings to be compared are of <u>unequal length</u>, the shorter string is extended on the right with blanks. For example, consider the condition:

    'A' .LT. 'AA'

Since the string on the left is shorter than the string on the right, the left string is automatically extended by adding a blank. Hence the condition is actually evaluated as if it had been written:

    'A ' .LT. 'AA'

This condition is true, since the two strings are identical in their first character and blank is less than "A" in the second character. (Blank is less than <u>any</u> other character.) Consider the following condition:

'L OA' .LT. 'LOA'

In this case the right string is shorter and is extended with two blanks to match the length of the left string. The effect is the same as if the condition had been written:

'L OA' .LT. 'LOA '

This condition is true. As another example:

'MORISON' .GT. 'MORIS'

is also a true condition. Note that this use of blanks to equalize lengths causes the results to agree with the usual convention in hand alphabetizing.

You should realize that the examples above, in which one constant is compared to another, are just for explanation. A condition comparing two constants would not ordinarily be used in a program. The reason is simply that the value of such a condition never changes -- it remains forever true or false. A condition is useful in a program only if its value can change -- be either true or false depending upon the value of some variable.

Consider the string length question when a variable is given in a condition. For example:

```
DESIGN = 'MULL'
IF(DESIGN .EQ. 'PERRY') ...
```

This means that the variable DESIGN contains "MULL" as its first four characters followed by ninety-six blanks. The comparison treats "PERRY" as if it were extended with blanks to 100 characters also.

Characters can be digits or punctuation marks as well as letters, so we must extend the concept of "alphabetical ordering" to cover all possible characters. This ordering, called the "collating sequence" of the language, is the following for WATFIV: (using "ƀ" for the blank)

ƀ.<(+|&$*);¬-/,%_>?:#=ABCDEFGHIJKLMNOPQRSTUVWXYZ0123456789

For the most part, this produces reasonable orderings -- ones consistent with common usage. For example, the following are true conditions:

'MORISON' .LT. 'MORISON, SAMUEL'

'MORISON, S.' .LT. 'MORISON, SAMUEL'

The first of these is true because a comma is greater than a blank; the second because "A" is greater than a period.

Note that blanks are highly significant in determining ordering. A human alphabetizer may well ignore leading blanks (those on the left end of the word) but FORTRAN takes them seriously. For example, a blank before the "M" causes the following to be a true condition, upsetting what might be considered normal alphabetic ordering:

```
' MORISON' .LT. 'KNOX-JOHNSON'
```

4.2 Branching

The IF statement shown in the beginning of Section 4 permits <u>only a single statement</u> to be made conditional. However, it is often necessary to have a sequence of two or more statements subject to the same condition. For this purpose (and others), we will introduce the "GO TO statement".

The GO TO statement causes execution to jump to an entirely different location in the program and continue execution from that point. We will most frequently use the GO TO in conjunction with the IF statement:

```
IF(condition) GO TO ...
```

It will either jump to a different point in the program, or continue with the next statement, depending upon the truth of the condition. Hence, it represents a <u>branch</u> point from which the course of execution depends upon some specific condition.

To identify the point in the program to which the jump is to take place, we use statement numbers just like those used to identify the end of a loop in Section 3.1. The statement number is simply punched in columns 2-5 of the statement to be executed following the GO TO. The only requirement is that the statement number is unique (only appears in columns 2-5 of one statement). The statement to be branched to is called the <u>target</u> statement; a GO TO and its target could be the following:

```
      IF(condition) GO TO 10
         ...
         ...
   10 statement
```

If the condition is true, the GO TO is executed, so the program jumps to the target and continues from there. If the condition is false, the GO TO is skipped, so execution continues in the normal way with the next statement. This means that the statements between the GO TO and the target may or may not be

I 4.3 Compound Statements   47

executed depending upon the condition controlling the GO TO. We
will always use a GO TO so that the target is positioned after
the GO TO -- that is, we will always jump forward, and never
backward in the program.

4.3 Compound Statements

   Consider again the problem of making more than one statement
depend on the truth of a single condition. For example, suppose
we want to read and print words from a data list, but with two
new restrictions:

   1. only words in the second half of the alphabet (N to Z)
      will be printed, and

   2. each word that is printed must be preceded and followed
      by special "marker lines". The form of these marker
      lines will be given at the head of the data list.

For example, suppose the data list is the following:

        $ENTRY
        '********'
        '*--**--*'
        4
        'SHEER'
        'CHINE'
        'RAKE'
        'TUMBLEHOME'

The required output for these data would be:

            ****
            SHEER
            *--**--*
            ****
            RAKE
            *--**--*
            ****
            TUMBLEHOME
            *--**--*

(This example doesn't really make any sense, but it is hard to
find a good, simple example using only the topics introduced up
to this point.) This peculiar printing requirement involves   a
three statement sequence:

        PRINT, TOP
        PRINT, WORD
        PRINT, BOTTOM

This entire printing sequence is to be executed <u>if</u> the following condition is true:

>   WORD .GE. 'N'

To do this, the printing sequence is viewed as a "compound statement" to be skipped using a conditional GO TO. The compound statement is then viewed <u>as if it were a single statement</u> to be executed if the <u>condition is false</u>. It would be written as follows:

```
          IF(WORD .LE. 'N') GO TO 20
              PRINT, TOP
              PRINT, WORD
              PRINT, BOTTOM
       20     statement
```

Now this complete unit could be written in place of the PRINT statement in a listing program such as the one given in Section 3.2. The complete program would be the following:

```
          CHARACTER*100  WORD, TOP, BOTTOM
          INTEGER   LOOP, COUNT
          READ, TOP
          READ, BOTTOM
          READ, COUNT
          DO 20 LOOP = 1, COUNT, 1
              READ, WORD
          IF(WORD .LE. 'N') GO TO 20
              PRINT, TOP
              PRINT, WORD
              PRINT, BOTTOM
       20     CONTINUE
          STOP
          END
```

4.3.1 <u>A Conditional Loop</u>

Suppose the strange listing program of Section 4.3 were changed to require printing a topmarker (but no bottommarker), and to require the repetition of the word on five lines if the word is in the last half of the alphabet. A loop should be used to repeat the line that prints the value of WORD. The program would be the following:

```
      CHARACTER*100  WORD, TOP
      INTEGER  LOOP, COUNT, LCNT
      READ, TOP
      READ, COUNT
      DO 20 LOOP = 1, COUNT, 1
         READ, WORD
         IF(WORD .LE. 'N') GO TO 20
            PRINT, TOP
            DO 10 LCNT = 1, 5, 1
               PRINT, WORD
10          CONTINUE
20    CONTINUE
      STOP
      END
```

Note that the entire loop, DO 10 ..., simply serves as a single statement within the compound statement. It just replaces the PRINT statement in the previous version.

4.4 A Choice of Alternatives

Another frequent use of the GO TO statement in our examples is to permit the selection of one of several parallel sections of program. For example, suppose that for each number on the data list, <u>exactly one</u> of the following three statements is to be executed:

         PRINT, 'VALUE TOO LARGE'

         PRINT, 'VALUE TOO SMALL'

         PRINT, 'VALUE WITHIN LIMITS'

The core of the program to do this could be something like the following:

```
      READ, COUNT
      READ, HIGH
      READ, LOW
      DO 30 LOOP = 1, COUNT, 1
          READ, NUMBER
          PRINT, NUMBER
          IF(NUMBER .LE. HIGH) GO TO 10
              PRINT, 'VALUE TOO LARGE'
              GO TO 30
   10     IF(NUMBER .GE. LOW) GO TO 20
              PRINT, 'VALUE TOO SMALL'
              GO TO 30
   20     PRINT, 'VALUE WITHIN LIMITS'
   30 CONTINUE
```

4.5 Definite and Indefinite Repetition

We can use the GO TO as an exit from a loop. For example, suppose for our data listing program, we needed the option of terminating the action if some particular string value was encountered in the list -- say the word "LAST". The program could be written as follows:

```
      CHARACTER*100 STRING
      INTEGER LOOP, COUNT
      READ, COUNT
      DO 10 LOOP = 1, COUNT, 1
          READ, STRING
          IF(STRING .EQ. 'LAST') GO TO 20
          PRINT, STRING
   10 CONTINUE
   20 STOP
      END
```

Note that in this program there are two ways out of the loop section -- either by completing the specified number of repetitions (as given by the number at the beginning of the data list), or by encountering the string "LAST". Whichever of these events occurs first will terminate the loop.

In general, we will use one of two different strategies for controlling loops. Sometimes the programs can determine in advance how many times the loop is to be executed. For example:

```
      ...
      READ, COUNT
      DO 10 LOOP = 1, COUNT, 1
          ...
```

Since it is known upon beginning the loop how many executions are to be performed, this is called definite repetition.

I 4.5 Definite and Indefinite Repetition

On the other hand, sometimes it is convenient to enter a loop without knowing in advance how many repetitions are to be performed. In this case the DO statement is written so that execution will continue <u>indefinitely</u>, and the loop is terminated by having a conditional GO TO in the body. During some execution of the body, this condition will become true and the GO TO will cause the program to <u>escape from the loop</u>. For example:

```
          CHARACTER*100 WORD
          INTEGER LOOP
          DO 10 LOOP = 1, 10000, 1
             READ, WORD
             IF(WORD .EQ. 'TERMINATE') GO TO 20
             PRINT, WORD
   10        CONTINUE
   20     STOP
          END
```

We will assume that loops in our examples will never have to be repeated as many as ten thousand times. Hence, specifying the loop control as:

            1, 10000, 1

is equivalent to saying "repeat forever". Whenever you see this particular control phrase in one of our examples, this indicates <u>indefinite repetition</u> and the loop will be terminated by a <u>GO TO escape</u> from somewhere in the body. (If 10000 is not enough, a larger number could of course be used.)

In general, this strategy of using a recognizable stopping value at the end of the data list is probably preferable to the strategy in which a control count is given at the head of the list (as in Section 3.2). The latter requires the user of the program to make an <u>accurate count</u> of the number of values on the list. With the former the user need only prepare the list, of whatever length, and then add a card with the "stopping value" to the end of the list. Of course, it does require that the word specified as a stopping signal cannot also appear as a legitimate item on the list. But in general, it should be possible to select a sufficiently unusual stopping signal that would be very unlikely to occur naturally.

4.6 Nesting of Conditional Statements

Suppose there are <u>two tests</u> that must <u>both be satisfied</u> before a statement is to be executed. This can be done by making one IF statement subject to another IF statement.

For example, suppose a word is to be printed only if it falls in the middle of the alphabet -- say between "f" and "r", inclusive. The following program would accomplish this:

```
      CHARACTER*100 WORD
      INTEGER LOOP, COUNT
      READ, COUNT
      DO 30 LOOP = 1, COUNT, 1
         READ, WORD
         IF(WORD .LE. 'F') GO TO 30
            IF(WORD .GT. 'R') GO TO 30
               PRINT, WORD
30    CONTINUE
      STOP
      END
```

Nesting like this can be carried to any required number of levels. Appendix B.7 describes additional language features which can be used to provide an alternate solution to this problem.

Section 4 **Summary**

1. The execution of a statement can be made to depend upon the truth of a certain condition by the IF statement:

    IF(condition) statement

    If the condition is <u>true</u> the statement is executed; if the condition is <u>false</u> the statement is skipped.

2. A <u>condition</u> is a comparison between two different values. The kind of comparison is specified by a <u>relation</u>:

    .EQ.   for equals
    .NE.   for not equals
    .GT.   for greater than
    .GE.   for greater than or equals
    .LT.   for less than
    .LE.   for less than or equals

    The two values being compared by the relation must be of the <u>same type</u> -- either both strings, or both numbers.

    A condition is evaluated, and the result is either <u>true</u> or <u>false</u>.

3. In comparing strings of different length, the shorter string is automatically extended with blanks on the right until the two strings have the same length.

4. The comparison of strings is based on an extension of alphabetical ordering that determines when one string is less than another.

5. Any statement can be made conditional, except DO, IF, CONTINUE and declarations.

6. **The** conditional statement appears on the same line as the IF.

7. The form of the branching statement is:

    GO TO ###
    ...
    ### statement

    The "###" stands for any legal statement number (e.g. 10, 250). This means continue execution with the statement marked by the target number (rather than the statement following the GO TO).

8. The target statement is always placed <u>after</u> the GO TO -- always branch forward and never backward.

9. The execution of a group of consecutive statements -- can be made to depend upon a condition:

```
          IF(condition) GO TO ###
             group of statements to be skipped
          ### first statement not conditional on IF
```

10. A primary use of the GO TO is as an exit from a loop. The GO TO is one of the statements in the body of a loop; the target is a statement after the CONTINUE of the loop.

    A GO TO exit will frequently be used with a DO statement that specifies <u>indefinite repetition</u>.

11. Another frequent use of the GO TO is to permit the selection of one of several parallel alternatives.

Section 4 **Exercises**

1. Which of the following conditions are true, which are false, and which are neither because they are not properly formed?

    a. 3 .EQ. 2
    b. 2.00 .EQ. "2.00"
    c. -4.3 .LT. -4.29
    d. 7 .GE. 6.41
    e. 'A B' .GE. 'AB'
    f. ' A' .GE. ' A'
    g. '-4' .GT. '-3'
    h. 'HOOD, FREDERICK, JR.' .GT. 'HOOD, FREDERICK'
    i. 2.2 .LT. 2.20

2. Write a statement that will print the value of the string variable S4 only if that value is not equal to "OMIT".

3. Write a statement that will print the value of the string variable STR only if that value is not equal to "STR".

4. Write a program segment that will print two lines, with each line consisting of six decimal points, only if value of the numeric variable COUNT is 13.

2. Write a program segment that will print fifty lines, with each line consisting of six decimal points, if the value of numeric variable COUNT is greater than 1.

6. Write a program segment such that, if the value of numeric variable COUNT is greater than 1, the program will print COUNT lines, each line consisting of six decimal points.

7. Write a statement that will read the next data item into NBR only if the previous value of NBR is zero.

8. Write a program segment that will print the value of numeric variable COUNT only if that value is between 17 and 35.

9. Write a program that will print the values of a list of numbers (given as data) until either a negative value, a zero value, or a value greater than 20 is encountered (whichever occurs first). Do not print the "stopping signal value".

10. Write a program that will print the values of a list of strings (given as data) until two consecutive values are the same. Do not print the second of these values.

11. Fill in the following program so that it will print just one value -- the value of A, B or C, whichever is greatest. (Assume the values are all different.)

        REAL A, B, C
        READ, A
        READ, B
        READ, C
        ...
        STOP
        END

Section 5   Output Format and Titling

Up to this point we have only used the PRINT statement to retrieve and display the value of a <u>single variable</u>. The form of the statement has been:

      PRINT, name of variable

The result of this statement is to <u>begin a new line</u> of output, and to <u>print the current value</u> of the variable whose name is specified. Now we will introduce two minor extensions of the use of the PRINT statement -- to accomodate more than one variable, and to print titles.

5.1 <u>Printing Values of More than One Variable</u>

Suppose there are three variables in a program, with values as shown below:

      <u>variable</u>   <u>value</u>

      START   1
      STOP   10
      INCR   2

To print out the values of these variables, we would use three PRINT statements:

      PRINT, START
      PRINT, STOP
      PRINT, INCR

The resulting output would appear in the format shown below:

      1
      10
      2

But suppose we wanted <u>all three values to appear on the same line</u>:

I 5.1 Printing Several Variables

```
        1       10      2
```

To achieve this we would simply <u>list all three variables in the same PRINT statement</u>.

```
    PRINT, START, STOP, INCR
```

The rule is that <u>each separate PRINT statement begins a new line</u> of output. But one statement can include a list of several variables, whose values will be printed, one after another, on the same line. If there are too many values to fit on a single line, they will automatically be continued onto the next line.

It is not necessary that the variables in the list have the same type of value. That is, both numeric and string variables can be printed by the same PRINT statement. For example, if ST is a string variable and NBR is a numeric variable, you could write:

```
    PRINT, NBR, ST
```

As an example of the use of a PRINT statement with more than one variable, suppose you wanted to read and print <u>values in pairs</u>, with the output in two columns instead of one. This program to print value pairs is just a variation of the listing program of Section 4:

```
        INTEGER NBR1, NBR2
        INTEGER COUNTR, DATA
        READ, DATA
        DO 10 COUNTR = 2, DATA, 2
            READ, NBR1
            READ, NBR2
            PRINT, NB1, NB2
    10      CONTINUE
        STOP
        END
```

Note that each repetition of the loop in this case reads and prints <u>two values</u>, so the loop should be executed only <u>half as many times</u> as the earlier version. To accomplish this, notice that the variable COUNTR that controls the loop starts with value 2, and then is increased by 2 on each repetition.

5.1.1 Reading Values of More than One Variable

Now that we have described the effect of giving a list of variables in a PRINT statement, you might wonder whether the same thing can be done in a READ statement. It can, but the result is not quite comparable to what happens in a PRINT. A READ statement with a list of variables is <u>exactly equivalent</u> to a sequence of READ statements specifying the same variables in the same order. For example, each of the following four alternatives has exactly the same effect in execution:

```
READ, V1
READ, V2
READ, V3

READ, V1, V2
READ, V3

READ, V1
READ, V2, V3

READ, V1, V2, V3
```

Note that in each of these alternatives the <u>same variables</u> appear in exactly the <u>same order</u>. This is critical since it determines which data values are assigned to which variables. But the number of READ statements used is immaterial. Consequently we will normally use a single statement with a list as long as necessary, at each point in the program where data is to be read. For example, from now on in a program such as the one given in Section 5.1 a single statement:

```
READ, STR1, STR2
```

would be given instead of the pair:

```
READ, STR1
READ, STR2
```

5.2 Printing Titles

Titles can be printed by a PRINT statement just by placing actual <u>values</u> rather than <u>variable names</u> on the list. For example:

```
PRINT, 'FEB. 20 RACE RESULTS:'
```

Execution of this statement will begin a new line of output and print the value:

```
FEB. 20 RACE RESULTS:
```

Note that the quotes are crucial in order for the PRINT statement to know whether it is being given a _value_ or a _variable_ from which a value is to be retrieved. For example, suppose there is a variable named PART that at one point during execution of a program has the value "GUDGEON". If the following PRINT statement is executed at that point:

```
PRINT, PART
```

the _value_ of the _variable_ PART will be printed. That is, the following line will be printed:

```
GUDGEON
```

However, if the PRINT statement were written:

```
PRINT, 'PART'
```

then the line printed would be:

```
PART
```

That is, the quotes in the second case make "PART" _just a value_, even though it happens to be the name of a variable. When the quotes are not present, it is interpreted as the name of a variable, and the value of that variable is printed.

Two common reasons for putting such constants in a PRINT statement are to provide _titles_ on output, and to print _messages_ to explain the meaning of the output. For example, our previous program could include such statements:

```
      INTEGER NBR1, NBR2
      INTEGER COUNTR, DATA
      READ, DATA
      PRINT, 'LIST PAIRS OF VALUES'
      PRINT, ' '
      DO 10 COUNTR = 2, DATA, 2
          READ, NBR1, NBR2
          PRINT, NBR1, NBR2
   10     CONTINUE
      PRINT, ' '
      PRINT, 'END OF LIST'
      STOP
      END
```

Notice that in addition to the titles that mark the beginning and end of the value list, there are additional PRINT statements that print a string consisting of a _single blank character_. Since this value won't show on the printed page, these statements serve to skip a line on the output.

Variables and values can both be given the same PRINT statement. For example, the program above could be written as follows (only the first part is shown):

I 5.2 Printing Titles

```
      INTEGER NBR1, NBR2
      INTEGER COUNTR, DATA
      READ, DATA
      PRINT, 'LIST OF', DATA, 'DATA VALUES'
      PRINT, ' '
      ...
```

If the first item of data for this program was the number 14, the line printed by the first PRINT statement would be:

```
   LIST OF         14 DATA VALUES
```

The format of the line that results from a PRINT statement is determined by the length of the items to be printed plus the spacing between the items provided by WATFIV. For example, our standard 100-character strings can only be printed one to a line. Shorter strings may be printed more than one to a line. It is important to remember that the length of the string is the number of characters specified in the CHARACTER declaration, not the number of characters that you can see, or the number of characters that appeared between the quotes on the data list. The length of a quoted literal string is the number of characters between the quotes. The length of the printed representation of a number is determined by the type (INTEGER or REAL) of the number.

You can achieve a little control over horizontal spacing by printing blank strings. For example, suppose you wanted to print pairs of values, two on each line, but wanted them spaced over farther than they would otherwise be in order to more aesthetically place them on the page. The PRINT statement could be written as follows:

```
         ...
         DO 10 COUNTR = 2, DATA, 2
            READ, NBR1, NBR2
            PRINT, '        ', NBR1, '          ', NBR2
   10    CONTINUE
```

This PRINT statement actually has four values for each line, but since the first and third values are blank they will not show on the page.

This is a very crude and limited type of formatting, but it will suffice for our immediate purpose. FORTRAN has very elaborate and flexible facilities for formatting output -- enough to specify any kind of format you might want. But the techniques to do this take some time to describe, and it is just not worth it for our purposes. However, some additional format capability is given in Appendix B.2. (Some versions of FORTRAN do not provide the simple formatting that we use, requiring the use of the capabilities given in Appendix B.3.)

5.2.1 Quotes Within a String

Eventually you will encounter a title that <u>includes</u> a quote -- that is, an apostrophe. For example, suppose you want to head a data list with the title:

TODAY'S RACE RESULTS:

If you write the PRINT statement as shown below, you will get an interesting surprise:

PRINT, 'TODAY'S RACE RESULTS:'

FORTRAN would consider the quote after "Y" to terminate the title. Since the "S" is then unquoted, it is assumed to be a variable, (even though it was not declared as such). Since S is a variable, there must be a missing comma preceeding it. Things get even more confused when FORTRAN tries to figure out what to do with the rest of the line -- all because of the apostrophe in "TODAY'S".

The solution is curious -- if you want to put a single quote (apostrophe) in the value, you must put <u>two consecutive quotes</u> in the input. (This means two consecutive single quotes -- not the double quote, which is a different character altogether.) The PRINT statement would be written:

PRINT, 'TODAY''S RACE RESULTS:'

To illustrate the point, the following statement mixes quotes and commas in a deliberately confusing way. Some of the commas separate items and some are in the content of strings; some of the quotes mark the ends of strings and some are in the content of strings:

PRINT, ',',''',''',',',',''','

If you study this carefully you will discover that the list consists of three quoted strings, and the value that would be printed is the following:

, ',', ,'

5.2.2 Continuing a Statement on a Second Line

The PRINT statement with long titles will probably be the first time you need to know how to split a statement between two lines. The rules are simple, and apply to any kind of statement:

1. Split a statement between any two elements, but don't divide a single element between two lines.
2. Place a $ in column six of the continuation card(s).

An "element", for this purpose is a keyword -- like PRINT, READ, IF, etc., a variable name, a number, or a string constant. That means you cannot divide a PRINT statement in the middle of a title. The following is <u>not proper</u>:

```
       PRINT, 'THE RESULTS OF', QUANTITY, 'VALUES
     $              ARE LISTED BELOW'
```

The easiest way to divide the statement is after one of the commas of the list. The following would be proper:

```
       PRINT, 'THE RESULTS OF', QUANTITY,
     $              'VALUES ARE LISTED BELOW'
```

Note that these three items (two titles and one variable) will all be <u>printed on one line</u> of the execution output. The fact that the PRINT statement itself won't fit on one line in the program does not affect the action of the PRINT statement. All of the following variations of the same statement are proper, and all produce exactly the same output when executed:

```
       PRINT, 'THE RESULTS OF',
     $              QUANTITY, 'VALUES ARE LISTED BELOW'

       PRINT, 'THE RESULTS OF',
     $              QUANTITY,
     $              'VALUES ARE LISTED BELOW'

       PRINT,
     $              'THE RESULTS OF',
     $              QUANTITY,
     $              'VALUES ARE LISTED BELOW'
```

If a single title is too long to fit on a single line, it is necessary to break it up into two (or more) titles so that these can be separated onto different lines. For example:

```
       PRINT, 'THIS IS AN EXAMPLE OF A',
     $     'VERY LONG TITLE BEING',
     $     'DIVIDED OVER SEVERAL LINES'
```

This long title will still print on a single line when the program is executed.

5.2.3 Upper and Lower-case Letters

We should also comment on upper and lower-case letters. Some printers used with computers can print both upper and lower-case -- this book was produced on such a printer. But printers that are limited to upper-case letters are generally either faster or cheaper, so these are used for most general-purpose work. We will make no distinction -- and all output will be shown in upper-case letters, but when you reach the point where more attractive output is important, it is possible to process and display data so as to distinguish between upper and lower-case letters.

Section 5 **Summary**

1. The form of the PRINT statement is:

    PRINT, list of variables and values

    This begins a new line, and prints the values from left to right.

2. Values in the list must be quoted if they are strings.

3. Blank strings can be given in the list to skip value positions on the line.

4. The value list can consist of a single blank string to leave a blank line in the output.

5. To include a single quote in the value of a string, give two consecutive quotes in the input.

6. Divide a statement (over two lines) between any two elements -- but do not split any single element. In particular, do not split a string value. Place a $ in column six of each continuation card.

Section 5 **Exercises**

1. Write a statement that will repeat the value of numeric variable X three times across a line.

2. Write a statement that will repeat the value of numeric variable X in the first, fourth and fifth value positions on a line.

3. How will the results of the following statements differ?

    a. PRINT, ' '
    b. PRINT, ' ', ' '
    c. PRINT, ' '
    d. PRINT, ',',' '

4. What would be printed by the following statement?

    PRINT, 'PRINT, LINE'

5. Write a sequence of statements that will print the following output (in exactly this form):

    "SEA FEVER"
        -A POEM
            BY JOHN MASEFIELD

6. Write a sequence of statements that will print the title output as required in Exercise 5, enclosed in a box of asterisks.

7. Write a program that will print a 10 by 10 array of asterisks -- 10 rows of 10 asterisks each. (Use a loop -- don't write out 10 PRINT statements.)

Section 6   Computing New Values for Variables

Up to this point the only method we have used to assign a new value to a variable is by supplying that value on the data list and reading it by executing a READ statement. Now we will introduce the "assignment statement" which will compute a value from values already in memory and assign this new value to some specified variable. The form of the assignment statement in FORTRAN is:

```
        name of variable              formula
        to recieve value        =     to compute new value
```

An example of an assignment statement with a very simple formula for obtaining a new value, is the following:

```
        WORD = STRING
```

The meaning of this statement is the following:

1. Retrieve the current value of the variable named STRING.

2. Store this value in the variable named WORD.

In effect, the action is to copy the value of the right-side variable (STRING) into the left-side variable (WORD). This action destroys the previous value of the left-side variable (WORD), just as it would if we had read a new value into WORD from the data list. It does not change the value of the right-side variable (STRING) -- its value is only copied.

Another very simple form of assignment statement gives a value directly, rather than specifying the name of a variable for the right-side. For example:

```
        WORD = 'STRAKE'
```

The meaning is similar -- the right-side is a formula to produce a value (very simply in this case, since the value is given directly), and the left-side specifies where to store that value. Another example is a statement that will "clear" a specified variable to a value that consists of a blank:

```
        WORD = ' '
```

Comparable examples for numeric variables are the following:

```
        COUNT = NBR

        NBRLIN = 14

        COUNTR = 0
```

Note that in each assignment statement the <u>value types of the left and right sides are the same</u>. That is, if the variable on the left is a string variable, then the formula on the right must produce a string value. If the variable on the left is a numeric variable, then the formula on the right must produce a number. These two cases are examined separately in the next two sections.

6.1 Arithmetic Expressions

A <u>formula to produce a value</u> is called an "expression". If the value produced is a number, the formula is called an "arithmetic expression". In the examples above we considered two very special cases of expressions -- just the name of a variable or a constant. Now we examine more complicated expressions that involve the performance of some arithmetic operations. For example, consider the following assignment statement, involving numeric variables X, Y and Z:

```
        X = Y + Z
```

The meaning is the following:

1. Obtain a new value (a number) by adding the current value of the variable Y to the current value of the variable Z.

2. Store this sum as the new value of the variable X.

As before, neither the value of Y or Z is changed by this operation -- their values are merely copied. The previous value of X, whatever it might have been, is destroyed when the new value is stored there. Another example is:

```
        X = Y - Z + 4.3
```

The meaning is the following:

1. Obtain a new value by subtracting the current value of variable Z from the current value of variable Y; add the constant 4.3 to the result.

2. Store the final result as the new value of variable X.

I 6.1 Arithmetic Expressions

It is permissible, and in fact very common, for the same variable to appear on both sides of an assignment statement. For example:

        COUNT = COUNT + 2

In spite of the multiple occurrence of variable COUNT, the statement is interpreted just as before:

1. Obtain a new value by adding 2 to the current value of variable COUNT.

2. Store this new value in variable COUNT.

The value of COUNT is not changed by its role on the right-side of the statement, but the value is changed by its appearance on the left-side. This illustrates how important it is to understand that the assignment process takes place in two distinct steps:

1. A new value is obtained by evaluating the expression on the right-side. This step only copies values and does not change any.

2. The new value is stored in the variable specified on the left-side, destroying whatever previous value this variable had.

Since these steps are separate, and take place in the order indicated, it is quite reasonable for the variable named on the left to also appear on the right and contribute its earlier value to the computation of the new value. In fact, it happens very often.

  An example of a problem that would use this type of assignment statement would be to compute the sum of a list of numbers. Suppose that it is known that none of the numbers is zero -- then a zero can be appended to the end of the list as a stopping signal. Although it might not seem so at first, the program to do this is very similar to the data listing program we have been using as an example. The algorithm for the summing program could be the following:

    Create a numeric variable NBR to receive numbers from data.
    Create a numeric variable SUM to act as a running sum.
    Prepare SUM by initially setting it equal to 0.
    For each number on the data list until zero is encountered:
      Read into NBR.
      Add NBR to SUM.
    Print results.
    Terminate the program.

The key step in the algorithm is "Add NBR to SUM" This is

implemented by the FORTRAN statement:

        SUM = SUM + NBR

The complete program is the following:

        INTEGER NBR, SUM, LOOP
        SUM = 0
        DO 20 LOOP = 1, 10000, 1
            READ, NBR
            IF (NBR .EQ. 0) GO TO 30
            SUM = SUM + NBR
     20   CONTINUE
     30 PRINT, 'SUM IS:', SUM
        STOP
        END

6.1.1 Multiplication and Division

The operations of multiplication and division can be specified in an arithmetic expression, much as addition and subtraction have been used in our examples -- but the notation is a little peculiar. Multiplication is designated by an asterisk:

        X = Y * Z

This means:

   1. Obtain a new value by multiplying the current value of the variable Y by the current value of the variable Z.

   2. Store this new value in the variable X.

Multiplication can only be indicated with the asterisk -- there is no other form. In particular, you <u>cannot</u> use an "x", or a dot, or just write two variables next to each other -- XY is not the product of X and Y; it is just a different variable named XY.

The symbol for division is the slash:

        X = Y / Z

This means divide the value of Y by the value of Z and assign the quotient to X. The notation for division is a little different when the denominator and/or the numerator consists of more than a single term, since everything must be written on a single line. For example, where you might ordinarily write

$$\frac{A + B}{C - D}$$

in a FORTRAN expression you would have to write:

$$(A + B)/(C - D)$$

Parentheses must be used to show exactly what constitutes the numerator and the denominator of the operation. If the parentheses were omitted from this expression -- that is, if it were written as

$$A + B / C - D$$

It would be interpreted to mean:

$$A + \frac{B}{C} - D$$

which is quite different from the original.

6.1.2 The Order of Arithmetic Operations

The previous section used parentheses to specify the extent of the numerator and denominator for division when the numerator or denominator are not a single term. Actually, what the parentheses indicate is the <u>order in which the different arithmetic operations are to be performed</u>. The expression:

$$(A + B)/(C - D)$$

means to perform the addition of A and B, and the subtraction of D from C <u>before</u> the division. In general the rule is to <u>perform operations in parentheses first</u>.

The value obtained from an expression will often depend upon the order in which operations are performed. For example, consider the expression:

$$4 * 3 + 2$$

If the multiplication is performed first the resulting value is 14, but if the addition is performed first the resulting value is 20. So you should write this expression either as :

$$(4 * 3) + 2$$

or

$$4 * (3 + 2)$$

to make clear exactly what order you intend.

As expressions become more complicated it sometimes becomes necessary to <u>nest parentheses</u> -- that is, to include one pair of parentheses within another pair. For example:

            (Z * (X + Y))/(X - 3)

This means the expression is to be evaluated in three stages:

1. Obtain the sum of X and Y, and the difference of X minus 3.

2. Multiply the sum of X and Y by Z.

3. Perform the division.

In general, when parentheses are nested -- work from the <u>inside out</u>. That is, <u>perform the operations in the innermost parentheses first</u>.

6.1.3 Built-in functions

In addition to the basic arithmetic operations (add, subtract, multiply and divide) there are various other operations that are generally useful in programs. In FORTRAN these are provided by a mechanism called a "built-in function". A built-in function is a mechanism that <u>receives a value</u>, <u>performs some specified operation</u> on that value, and <u>produces a new value as a result</u>.

For example, there is a built-in function to "obtain the absolute value". (Recall that the "absolute value" of a number is the number without it's sign. That is, the absolute value of -4 is 4; the absolute value of +4 is also 4.) The name of the built-in function depends on the type of number. ABS is used for real variables and IABS is used for integer variables and constants. They are written in the following form:

        ABS(real argument)
        IABS(integer argument)

"Real argument" and "integer argument" specify those numbers whose absolute values are sought. For example, you could write:

        IABS(-4)

The resulting value of IABS(-4) is 4. The resulting value of IABS(10) is 10, etc. These functions are generally used with variables (rather than constants) as their arguments. For example, to obtain the value of the real variable X, but without the sign of that value, you could write ABS(X). This says:

1. Retrieve the value of the variable X, and pass this as argument to the built-in function ABS.

2. ABS removes the sign of this value.

I 6.1 Arithmetic Expressions

Since a built-in function <u>produces a value</u> it can be used in an expression. For example, you could write:

    ABS(X) + Z

This says to retrieve the value of X and use ABS to remove its sign; retrieve the value of Z; and add these two values together. Another example might be:

    ABS(X) + ABS(Y) + ABS(Z)

This says to retrieve the values of X, Y and Z, remove their signs, and add the resulting values together.

Another built-in function called SQRT is used to obtain the <u>square root</u> of a real value. For example, to obtain the square root of the value of variable X you would write:

    SQRT(X)

Expressions including built-in functions can be used on the right side of assignment statements. For example, the statement:

    Y = SQRT(X)

says to retrieve the value of X, take its square root, and assign this square root of X as the new value to the variable Y. Other examples are the following:

    VAL = IABS(VAL)

    SUMSQRT = SQRT(X) + SQRT(Y)

    TERM = SQRT(LEVEL) + ABS(TEMP) - 14.7

    NEXT = SQRT(LAST) * (CHANCE - 14.73)

An <u>expression</u> can be given as the <u>argument</u> of these built-in functions. For example:

    SQRT(X + Y)

    IABS(NEXT * -3)

    SQRT(X * (A + B))

Since a built-in function can be <u>part of an expression</u>, and an <u>expression can be given as argument</u> to a built-in function, it follows that <u>one built-in function can be given in the argument</u> of another. For example:

ABS(Y + SQRT(X))

SQRT(ABS(X) * ABS(Y))

SQRT(SQRT(Y - X) + ABS(Z) - 73.2)

To illustrate the use of a built-in function, suppose you wanted to read a list of numbers, and for each number tabulate the value, the value squared, and the square root of the value. Assume that all of the numbers are positive, and a 0 is added at the end of the list as a stopping signal. This is accomplished by the following program:

```
      REAL  NBR, NSQD, NSQRT
      INTEGER  COUNT
      PRINT, '    NUMBER          ', 'SQUARED    ',
     $       '       SQUARE ROOT'
      PRINT, '    ------          ', '-------    ',
     $       '       ------ ----'
      DO 10 COUNT = 1, 10000, 1
         READ, NBR
         IF(NBR .EQ. 0) GO TO 30
         NSQD = NBR * NBR
         NSQRT = SQRT(NBR)
         PRINT, NBR, NSQD, NSQRT
   10 CONTINUE
   30 STOP
      END
```

There are many other built-in functions in FORTRAN. We will use a few others, and explain them when we use them. Some other examples are given in Appendix B.5, but this is far from a full list.

6.2 <u>String Expressions</u>

Now we will consider assignment statements where the left-side variable is a string variable, hence the formula on the right must produce a string value. A formula to produce a string value is called a "string expression". At the beginning of Section 6 we illustrated the simplest kinds of string expressions:

WORD = STRING

STR = 'STEM'

These expressions consisted of a string variable or a string constant. Now we consider more complicated expressions with more than one term -- comparable to the arithmetic expressions of Section 6.1. The key difference is in the operations that

I 6.2 String Expressions

are performed. You <u>cannot perform arithmetic operations upon strings</u> -- not even if the characters in the string happen to be integers. Once you quote an integer, it becomes a string and is no longer eligible for arithmetic. That is, the following is <u>not proper</u>:

    '2' + '4.3'

The only operations we can perform upon strings are to take them apart, and put them together. These operations are discussed in the following sections.

6.2.1 Sub-strings

 Strings are taken apart using the "sub-string specifier". This <u>selects certain consecutive characters from the string</u> variable that it qualifies. For example:

  WORD(4:5)

retrieves a sub-string of two characters from the string variable named WORD, starting with the fourth character (from the left) of WORD, through the fifth character of WORD. If WORD happens to be "ABCDEF", then the value of WORD(4:5) is "DE".

 For further examples of string expressions, suppose the value of string variable W is "ABCDEFGH". Then the values of the following expressions are as shown below:

expression	value
W(1:4)	ABCD
W(5:8)	EFGH
W(4:8)	DEFGH
W(1:8)	ABCDEFGH
W(2:2)	B
W(20:20)	
W(150:150)	error

The next to the last example shows that (assuming W is CHARACTER*100) a string variable that has been assigned a short value will be filled out with blanks. The last example would be an error, since W has a maximum of 100 characters.

 Sub-string specifiers can be used in <u>conditions</u>. For example:

```
              IF (W(1:1) .EQ. 'B') ...
```

This means "if the value of string variable W begins with the character "B", then ...".

6.2.2 The Length of Strings

Unfortunately, most strings have two "lengths": the length of the string variable and the length of the current value of the string variable. The former is fixed by the string declaration (e.g. 100); the latter will vary, depending upon the length of the most recent value stored in that variable. FORTRAN only deals with the declared lengths. As poets, however, we are going to want to deal with words and lines of poetry in a manner which requires that the word "and" be three characters long (instead of 100).

For English words, we can straightforwardly find the length of a word by searching for the first blank:

```
              LENGTH = 0
              DO 10 POS = 1, 100, 1
                  IF (WORD(POS:POS) .EQ. ' ') GO TO 20
                  LENGTH = LENGTH + 1
       10     CONTINUE
       20     ...
```

Note that an all-blank variable causes LENGTH to be zero. Our program segment has a problem, however. It would decide that the string "TWO WORDS" has a length of three, when we would like it to be nine. This problem is solved by searching from the end of the string for the first non-blank character:

```
              LENGTH = 100
              DO 10 POS = 1, 100, 1
                  IF (WORD(LENGTH:LENGTH) .NE. ' ') GO TO 20
                  LENGTH = LENGTH - 1
       10     CONTINUE
       20     ...
```

We will adopt this as our LENGTH function. For convenience, we will define LENGTH as a function, which when applied to a CHARACTER*100 variable will give the number of characters preceding the final string of blanks, the "length" of the current value of the variable. For example:

```
              ...
              STR = 'ABC'
              PRINT, LENGTH(STR)
```

will cause the value "3" to be printed. This function is not a part of FORTRAN (or WATFIV), but it is something we will find

I 6.2 String Expressions

very useful. The following should be placed following the END statement of any program referring to the LENGTH function:

```
          INTEGER FUNCTION LENGTH(STRING)
          CHARACTER*100 STRING
          INTEGER POS
          LENGTH = 100
          DO 10 POS = 1, 100, 1
              IF (STRING(LENGTH:LENGTH) .NE. ' ') GO TO 20
              LENGTH = LENGTH - 1
   10         CONTINUE
   20     RETURN
          END
```

A brief discussion of how functions can be created is included in Appendix B.6, but for now, all that is necessary is that you be able to use the function. LENGTH(...) can be used anywhere FORTRAN expects a number.

For example, suppose you want to extract the last character (the rightmost character) of the value of string variable S. The substring specifier will obviously extract the character -- but it must be told which position it is. This can be done by using the LENGTH function to give the values of the substring specifier. That is, the last character of S is:

```
          S(LENGTH(S): LENGTH(S))
```

Since the function requires time to determine the length of a string, the following would be more efficient:

```
          LEN = LENGTH(S)
          ... S(LEN:LEN) ...
```

Consider the task of printing each individual character of a variable named WORD. The substring specifier is used to extract the characters, one at a time, from left to right, but the LENGTH function is required to determine how long to continue the process. The program segment is the following:

```
          LEN = LENGTH(WORD)
          DO 10 POSN = 1, LEN, 1
              PRINT, WORD(POSN:POSN)
   10         CONTINUE
```

6.2.3 Assignment to Sub-Strings

The sub-string specifier has a property that will often be useful -- it can be used on the left side of an assignment statement. A sub-string specifier is used on the left side when you want to change part of the value of a string variable, but not all of it. For example:

        ST(2:2) = 'G'

will replace the second character (from the left) of string variable ST by the character "G". The other characters of ST are unchanged. Consider the following string assignment statements, assuming the value of string variable ST is "ABCDEFGH":

statement	resulting value in ST
ST(4:5) = ' '	ABC FGH
ST(1:3) = ST(4:6)	ABCABCGH
ST(9:3) = 'IJK'	ABCDEFGHIJK

Section 6 <u>Summary</u>

1. The form of the assignment statement is one of the following:

    numeric variable = arithmetic expression

    string variable = string expression

2. The assignment takes place in two steps:

   a. evaluate the expression to produce a value

   b. assign that value to the left-side variable.

3. The operations that can be performed in an arithmetic expression are addition, subtraction, multiplication and division. The symbols are +, -, *, and /.

4. The order of operations can be specified by use of parentheses. Operations are performed from the innermost parentheses to the outer.

5. Certain additional operations can be performed by functions built-into the FORTRAN language. Examples of such functions are IABS and ABS for absolute value and SQRT for square root. In both ABS and SQRT, the arguement is a real expression and the result is a real number; in IABS, the arguement is an integer expression and the result is an integer number.

6. A portion of a string can be extracted by using a substring specifier of the form:

    str(nbr1:nbr2)

   The result is a string value.

7. A portion of the value of a string variable can be altered by using the substring specifier on the left-side of an assignment statement:

    str(nbr1:nbr2) = string expression

8. The current length of a string value can be obtained from the LENGTH function developed in this section. The argument of LENGTH is a string variable; the result is a number:

    LENGTH(str)

Section 6 **Exercises**

1. There are three numeric variables X, Y and Z. Write a program segment that will assign to Z the greater of the values of X and Y.

2. There are three string variables R, S and T. Write a program segment that will assign to T:

    a. the greater (according to the collating sequence) of the values of R and S,

    b. the longer of the values of R and S.

3. There are three numeric variables SIDE1, SIDE2 and HYPOT. If SIDE1 and SIDE2 represent the lengths of the sides of a right triangle, write a single assignment statement that assigns to HYPOT the value of the length of the hypotenuse of that triangle.

4. WORD is a string variable with an even number of characters. Write an assignment statement that will:

    a. delete the second half of the original value of WORD,

    b. delete the first half of the original value of WORD.

5. CHR is a string variable whose value is a single character. NBR is a numeric variable whose value is a positive integer. REPEAT is a string variable. Write a program segment that will assign a value to REPEAT equal to the value of CHR repeated NBR times.

6. Write a complete program that will read a list of numeric values from data (value 0 denotes the end of the list) and print a single value -- the maximum that occurs on the list.

7. The speed potential of a heavy displacement hull is proportional to the square root of its waterline length. Write a program that will tabulate, for each length from 15 to 40 feet, in increments of one foot, the length, the square root of the length, and 1.4 times the square root of the length. 1.4 times the square root of the length is called the "hull speed" (measured in knots). Title the columns appropriately.

8. In 1890 the New York Yacht Club promulgated a Rule for calculating the handicap Rating for racing yachts. The NY-Rating of a yacht is equal to one-half the product of its length and the square root of its sail area. Write a program that will tabulate Rating values for all combinations of length and sail area, for lengths from 25 to 40 (in increments of 1 foot), and sail areas from 600 to 1200 square feet (in increments of 50 square feet).

Section 7   Variables with Multiple Values

We have only one more significant concept to describe before discussing more interesting program examples. This idea is deceptively simple -- <u>permit certain variables to have several values at the same time</u> -- but it is very powerful. It will be essential in most of our examples.

To motivate this idea, we return to a variation of our data listing problem: suppose you wish to list the items appearing on the data list -- but in <u>reverse order</u>. That is, the last item of the data list is to be the first item of the printed list; the second-last item of the data list, the second on the printed list, etc. The algorithm for this form of the problem is completely different from the algorithm for printing in the same order. The algorithm for the normal-order printing version is essentially the repetition of the pair of steps:

        Read the next value.
        Print the value just read.

This won't work for the reverse-order printing version, since the printing cannot begin until the last data item has been read. All of the data items must be read in order to get to the last item, and they must all be saved for later printing. (You are only allowed to read the data list <u>once.</u>) So while the normal-order version can use a single variable, and reuse it for each data item, the reverse-order version requires <u>all of the data items to be stored at once</u>. In effect, the algorithm is basically:

        Read and store all of the data items.
        Retrieve and print the data items, in reversed
           order.

With simple variables -- the kind we have been using up to this point -- we would have to have as many different variables as there are data items, since each variable can store only a single value (at any one time). For example, if the list consisted of only three values, the program could be written as follows:

```
      CHARACTER*100 ST1, ST2, ST3
      READ, ST1, ST2, ST3
      PRINT, ST3
      PRINT, ST2
      PRINT, ST1
      STOP
      END
```

However, this program would only work for a list of three values. For a list of any other length the program would have to be substantially changed. Ever since Section 3, our programs have enjoyed the convenient property that they would work without change for lists of any length. Now, just because the problem says "in reverse order" this useful property has been lost. We recover it by using a special type of variable that can have more than one value at a time.

7.1 Declaration of a List

A variable with more than one value can be called a "list variable" or just a "list". It is also called an "array" or a "vector" in programming literature, but we will call it a list. The declaration is similar to what we used before, in that it specifies the type of value and a name, but now it also specifies the number of values that the list is to accommodate. For example:

```
      CHARACTER*100 STR(50)
```

specifies the creation of a list variable named STR with fifty values, each of which is a string such as the ones we have been using all along. Similarly:

```
      INTEGER NBR(40), X(10)
```

specifies the creation of two lists -- NBR with forty values and X with ten -- both of whose values are "integer numbers".

7.2 Reference to an Individual Value of a List

Suppose we declare a list as follows:

```
      CHARACTER*100 ST(5)
```

The name ST refers to a list of five different string values. We need a way to refer to one particular value out of these five. We do this by appending a "subscript" to the variable name. The name "subscript" comes from algebra, where it is usually a character depressed below the normal printing line, but since in programming everything must be written on the same line, subscripts are written after the variable name and

I 7.2 Reference to an Individual Value of a List

enclosed in parentheses. For example, ST(2) refers to the second of the five different values of the list named ST; ST(3) refers to the third of the five values, ST(5) to the fifth of the values. This <u>subscripted name can be used in exactly the same way as the name of a simple variable</u> has been used in our previous examples:

```
READ, ST(1)

ST(4) = ST(1)(1:5)

PRINT, ST(4)
```

So far, we haven't really gained anything. We have a list of five values, with individual names ST(1), ST(2), ST(3), ST(4), and ST(5). We could just as well have called them ST1, ST2, ST3, ST4, and ST5 and declared them as ordinary single-valued variables. The difference comes when we write their names with a <u>variable rather than a constant</u> as the subscript. Consider the following program:

```
CHARACTER*100 ST(5)
INTEGER ITEM
ITEM = 2
READ, ST(ITEM)
PRINT, ST(ITEM)
STOP
END
```

This program doesn't need a list of variables -- in fact, it only uses one of the five values of its list, but it illustrates the vital idea of using one variable as a subscript for another variable. Consider its execution in detail. The declarations create a list named ST having five string values, and a numeric variable named ITEM. The next statement assigns the value 2 to the variable ITEM. The next statement reads the first string from the data list and assigns it as value to some variable in storage. The question is "which variable?" The name ST is obvious -- but which of the five different elements of the list ST? The specification of one particular value of ST is given by a subscript -- but in this case the subscript is not given as an integer, it is given as another variable ITEM. So the value of the variable ITEM is retrieved from memory, and this value is used as the subscript of ST. Since the value of ITEM is 2, the statement

```
READ, ST(ITEM)
```

is executed exactly as if it had been written

```
READ, ST(2)
```

The same thing happens in the execution of the PRINT statement. The statement

        PRINT, ST(ITEM)

is executed exactly as if it had been written

        PRINT, ST(2)

There was no point in using a variable as a subscript in this particular program -- except to illustrate how it works. The purpose of using a variable as a subscript becomes apparent when the program changes the value of that variable. For example:

```
        CHARACTER*100 ST(5)
        INTEGER ITEM
        ITEM = 1
        READ, ST(ITEM)
        PRINT, ST(ITEM)
        ITEM = ITEM + 1
        READ, ST(ITEM)
        PRINT, ST(ITEM)
        STOP
        END
```

At the time the first READ and PRINT statements are executed the value of ITEM is 1, so these statements are executed as if they had been written:

        READ, ST(1)
        PRINT, ST(1)

When the second READ and PRINT statements are executed the value of ITEM is 2, so they are executed as if they had been written:

        READ, ST(2)
        PRINT, ST(2)

Although the two pairs of READ and PRINT statements are _written exactly the same way_ in the program, their effect when executed is different, just because the value of ITEM has been changed. This idea can be used to write our normal-order data listing program in a different form:

```
        CHARACTER*100 WORD(50)
        INTEGER ITEM, COUNT
        READ, COUNT
        DO 10 ITEM = 1, COUNT, 1
            READ, WORD(ITEM)
            PRINT, WORD(ITEM)
   10       CONTINUE
        STOP
        END
```

This program works for any data list of length 50 or less. The list has a number added at the beginning to specify how many strings follow -- the technique introduced in Section 3.2. We create a list of 50 values -- some of which may not be used,

I 7.2 Reference to an Individual Value of a List   85

depending upon the length of the particular data list used with this program. Now the variable used to control the repeated section of the program is also used as a subscript for the list WORD. The effect is to read the first data item into WORD(1) and then retrieve it and print it. The second data item is read into WORD(2), retrieved and printed; the third into WORD(3), etc. The program obviously doesn't <u>need</u> the list, since we have accomplished the same task since Section 3 using only a single simple variable. But it does work. Now let us change the order of reading and writing:

```
      CHARACTER*100 WORD(50)
      INTEGER ITEM, COUNT
      READ, COUNT
      DO 10 ITEM = 1, COUNT, 1
          READ, WORD(ITEM)
10        CONTINUE
      DO 20 ITEM = 1, COUNT, 1
          PRINT, WORD(ITEM)
20        CONTINUE
      STOP
      END
```

This version <u>reads all</u> of the data, and <u>then prints all</u> of the values, rather than alternately reading and printing.

From this form it requires only a simple modification to get the program to print the values in <u>reversed order</u>:

```
      CHARACTER*100 WORD(50)
      INTEGER ITEM, COUNT, REVERS
      READ, COUNT
      DO 10 ITEM = 1, COUNT, 1
          READ, WORD(ITEM)
10        CONTINUE
      DO 20 ITEM = 1, COUNT, 1
          REVERS = (COUNT + 1) - ITEM
          PRINT, WORD(REVERS)
20        CONTINUE
      STOP
      END
```

All that was required was to count backwards from COUNT. This is accomplished by subtracting the control variable, ITEM, from COUNT + 1 thus when ITEM is 1, REVERS is COUNT; when ITEM is 2, REVERS is COUNT - 1 and so on until each of the values of WORD has been printed in reverse order.

7.2.1 Expressions as Subscripts

Alternatively, we could achieve the same reverse-order printing using a slightly different technique. This involves the use of a more complicated subscript -- one which is an arithmetic expression. The constants and variables we have shown as subscripts up to this point are just special cases of expressions. In fact, more general expressions involving arithmetic operations can be used as subscripts. That is, we can write such things as:

```
      WORD(ITEM + 1)
```

The following program uses this technique:

```
         CHARACTER*100 WORD(50)
         INTEGER ITEM, COUNT
         READ, COUNT
         DO 10 ITEM = 1, COUNT, 1
            READ, WORD(ITEM)
   10    CONTINUE
         DO 20 ITEM = 1, COUNT, 1
            PRINT, WORD(COUNT - ITEM + 1)
   20    CONTINUE
         STOP
         END
```

In this version of the program, the variable REVERS has been replaced by an expression which is used to calculate the values of REVERS in the previous version.

Section 7 **Summary**

1. A variable with a list of different values can be declared in one of the following ways:

    CHARACTER*100 name(number of values)

    INTEGER name(number of values)

    REAL name(number of values)

   All of the values of a given variable are of the same type -- either all string, all integer, or all real.

2. An individual value of a variable with multiple values is referenced by giving a subscript in parentheses after the name:

    name(arithmetic expression)

   The value of the subscript expression must be an integer.

3. The substring of an individual value of a string variable with multiple values is specified by giving the name of the value followed by the substring specifier:

    name(subscript)(first character:last character)

4. The utility of subscripted variables arises in the fact that the subscript can involve a variable whose value is changed during execution of the program. In this way, different values can be referenced by the same statement.

Section 7 **Exercises**

1. X is a numeric variable with 20 values. SUM is a simple numeric variable. Write a program segment to assign to SUM the value of the total of the 20 values of X.

2. ST is a string variable with 12 values. LONGST is a simple string variable. Write a program segment to assign to LONGST the <u>longest</u> of the 12 values of ST.

3. WORDS is a string variable with 15 values. COUNTA is a simple numeric variable. Write a program segment to assign to COUNTA a value giving the number of values of WORDS that begin with the character "A".

4. PHR is a string variable with 20 values. LENPHR is a numeric variable with 20 values. Write a program segment that will assign to each value of LENPHR a number giving the length of the corresponding value of PHR. That is, if the value of PHR(5) is "ABCD", your program should assign the value 4 to LENPHR(5).

Section 8   Program Testing

In Section 2.1.2 we showed the result of a program that contained an error -- by now you probably have some experience of your own in this regard. Unfortunately it is rare for a program to be entirely correct on the first try. It is just too complicated a process, with too many opportunities to make errors, to expect to be able to design, write and punch a program that is perfect. Hence the process of detecting the imperfections, and correcting them, is an essential part of the overall programming task.

This is not only true of neophyte programmers; it is equally true of professionals, who are skilled and experienced. To be sure, they don't often make mistakes of misunderstanding the meaning of a particular FORTRAN statement, but nevertheless oversights and keypunch mistakes are still a painful part of their life. A good, careful programmer can learn to make relatively few errors -- but he will still make some, so he must learn to find hidden errors in his program.

There is much that can be said about this search for errors. There are special tools and techniques that must be learned. We will give a brief introduction to the topic -- commensurate with the limited type of programming we are considering. To the extent that we are concerned with <u>reading</u> programs, rather than constructing them, this topic can be slighted. But we assume you are also writing short programs, to help learn the language, so you need some facility in finding errors. Moreover, some knowledge of what types of errors exist, and how they can be exorcised, is essential to understanding the issues of reliability and responsibility -- topics discussed in Section III.3.

8.1 Errors Detected by FORTRAN

Whenever you make an error and violate some rule of the FORTRAN language you are rewarded with an "error message". The system automatically announces that some error has been detected, and prints a message intended to give some hint as to the nature of the error. You shouldn't take these hints too seriously -- they often describe some symptom of the problem, rather than its cause. But at least they are unmistakable evidence that <u>something</u> is wrong. As long as error messages are present, your programming job isn't finished.

An interesting change in attitude often takes place as you learn to program. At first FORTRAN seems to be an adversary, and you consider these messages an affront to your programming competence. However, eventually you realize that testing is a very difficult process, and that you need all the help you can get. The easy part of the process is finding the errors that FORTRAN calls to your attention; the hard part is finding errors of kinds that <u>cannot be detected by FORTRAN</u>.

For example, suppose you intended to write the following assignment statement in a program:

    SUM = SUM + NUMBER

Suppose your finger slipped and what actually was punched was:

    SUM = SUN + NUMBER

You did not intend there to be a variable named SUN, and never declared one. But FORTRAN has an unfortunate characteristic (which we have not mentioned before, but you probably have discovered on your own). That is, if you <u>use</u> a variable that was never declared it is assumed that you forgot the declaration -- so an "implicit declaration" is supplied. The variable is created, arbitrarily assigned certain "default" type attributes, and <u>no mention is made</u> of this misguided charity. But since the implicit declaration only <u>creates</u> the variable, and <u>does not give it an initial value</u>, when the statement is executed SUN has no value and the expression on the right side cannot be evaluated. At this point the WATFIV version of FORTRAN indicates that an error has been made. (Incredibly, standard FORTRAN does not detect this error -- it just finds some random value for SUN in memory, and proceeds, with no warning whatever that anything untoward has happened.) The point is that the error message in this case is a real benefit -- it calls your attention to an error that would otherwise be very hard to find.

By contrast, suppose that what happened to get punched was:

    SUN = SUM + NUMBER

Again there is an implicit declaration of the variable SUN, but in this case the statement assigns a value to SUN rather than attempts to retrieve a value from SUN. As a consequence there is no problem of a missing value and, in fact, <u>no violation of the rules of the language</u>, so not even WATFIV can give any indication that an error exists. The new value is quietly stored away in variable SUN, and since you are unaware of SUN's existence you will never use this value. But the variable SUM, which was to receive this value, contains an incorrect value from that point onward. There is no error message of any sort, but the program is flawed and its results are wrong. This type of insidious error must be detected and eliminated if the program is to be correct, but this must be done without any help from the automatic detection features built-into the programming language.

8.1.1 Grammatical Errors

The first (and easiest) type of error to be eliminated in testing a program consists of errors in the <u>construction of statements</u>. These grammatical or "syntactic" errors can be detected by the language, and messages are produced in the source listing.

Typical sources of grammatical errors are:

1. mispelling of keywords and names

2. mistakes of punctuation

3. misunderstanding of the required form of a statement.

While mistakes of misunderstanding will diminish as your experience increases, mistakes in keypunching will inevitably continue, so elimination of this type of error is always the first phase of the testing process.

8.1.2 Detectable Execution Errors

Some violations of language rules are not detected as the program is loaded into memory, but only when it is being executed. The mispunched assignment statement, described in Section 8.1:

SUM = SUN + NUMBER

is an example of such an error. This statement is in <u>legal form</u>, but it cannot be legally executed. During execution it is discovered that SUN has no initial value, so the expression on the right side of the statement cannot be evaluated. However, the error message is deceptive:

VALUE OF SUN IS UNDEFINED

The problem, of course, is not that the value of SUN has not been defined, but that there is not supposed to be a variable SUN in the first place.

As another example, consider the following section of a program:

```
      INTEGER N
      REAL NBR(10), SUM
      ...
      SUM = 0
      DO 10 N = 1, 15, 1
         SUM = SUM + NBR(N)
10    CONTINUE
```

On the eleventh repetition of the loop the value of the variable SUM will be 11, so NBR(N) will reference a value that does not exist. WATFIV will detect an error when this happens (standard FORTRAN will not). But the WATFIV error message will point to the <u>assignment statement</u>:

```
      SUM = SUM + NBR(N)
```

since that is the statement that could not be executed when N became too large. But the problem is not really in the assignment statement; the difficulty is that the size of NBR in the REAL type declaration, and the maximum value of N in the DO statement do not agree. All the error message really tells you is that <u>something is wrong</u> somewhere, and the result is that the assignment statement indicated is not executable. There is nothing (reasonable) you can do to the assignment statement to make the message go away. But with this slim clue you must find the flaw somewhere else in the program, and fix it.

In general, the execution errors that you are most likely to have reported to you by WATFIV are the following:

1. An attempt to retrieve a value from a variable that has never been assigned a value.

2. An incorrect value of a subscript -- a value that is too small or too large.

3. An attempt to execute a READ statement after the data list has already been read.

4. An attempt to execute a READ statement where the type of variable in the does not match the type of the next value on the data list.

Unfortunately, <u>these errors are almost always symptoms</u> and <u>not causes</u>, as illustrated by the examples above. Nevertheless, they serve to warn you that something is wrong and you must find and fix it.

8.2 Test Data

Once the obvious errors have been eliminated from your program you are ready to <u>begin</u> serious testing. That is, when there are no more "helpful" messages from FORTRAN in either the source listing or the execution output, you are ready to see whether or not the program "works". At this point, the program is in some sense "valid" -- at least FORTRAN no longer finds any objection to it, but this does not yet mean that it is useful, or that the output has any resemblance to what the problem requires.

Now you are faced with an interesting paradox. On the one hand, how do you know the program is working correctly, unless you know what the correct answer is supposed to be? But on the other hand, if you know what the answer is, why bother to write and run the program anyway?

The answer is that you test the program by running it on several problems for which you <u>already know the answer</u>. If the program behaves properly on all of these test problems, then you <u>infer</u> from that success that it will run correctly on <u>all similar problems</u> -- even those for which you don't know the answer. If the program performs satisfactorily on test problems which are <u>deliberately designed to be difficult</u>, and to reveal flaws, then you begin to have confidence that the program is really correct, and will work properly for normal, reasonable data.

Unfortunately, this course is terribly risky -- fraught with peril, as the saying goes. More often than not, testing stops too soon -- that is, while one or more errors still lurk in the dark recesses of the program. With natural optimism (or sheer desperation, as the case may be) we stop testing when there is the least encouragement that the program is beginning to work, rather than persevering until there is massive evidence that it does not fail.

The problem is that the "last error" in a program does not have any special distinguishing marks, so you never know when you have found it. When you find an error you know the program (including this error) was wrong; when you fail to find an error -- either the program is correct, or you aren't testing it vigorously enough. All too often, the latter is the case. We will discuss this dilemma further in Section III.3; at this point we just observe that you must run the program on several different test problems for which you know the answer, and the program must <u>behave perfectly on every</u> one of these test problems. The slightest hint of trouble on any of these tests means that you aren't done yet.

"Test data" are the data lists for these carefully contrived test problems. It is very much an art to be able to contrive good test data. These tests should exercise the program vigorously, making sure that every branch and every option is executed at least once.

The author of a program has certain advantages in testing -- he knows the program, and should know where to probe for weaknesses. On the other hand, having written it he is either:

a. proud of it, and doesn't want it to fail, or

b. tired of it, and doesn't want it to fail -- since that will require more work.

In either case, it is easy to understand a certain lack of enthusiasm in designing maliciously difficult test data. But realistically, it is much less embarassing to bring on a failure yourself, while you can still effect repairs privately, than to pronounce the program "correct", and then have it fail when it is being used (or being graded).

An effective strategy in designing test data is the following:

1. Construct a _first test_ that is as _gentle as possible_ -- give the newborn program every chance to do something successfully. (The program may have no emotions, but its author will be greatly encouraged by some sign of success.)

2. Then, once the program has passed this preliminary test, pretend it was written by someone else, and show how much smarter you are by discovering all of the flaws in "his" program.

8.3 Diagnostic Output Statements

The basic difficulty in diagnosing a sick program is that you never have enough information about just what went on during execution. The solution is quite simple (at least in principle) -- _run the program again, after modifying it so you get more information_. "Modifying" means inserting some extra PRINT statements just to tell you what is going on in more detail than is revealed by the display of final results. Of course, after you have found the trouble and repaired it, these extra PRINT statements must be removed so that only the required output will be printed.

Where to put the extra PRINTs is the question. The idea is to gradually localize the difficulty -- to segregate the sections where you know everything is correct from sections where you aren't sure yet. This means _inserting PRINT statements between sections_ to display the actual state of affairs as execution moves from one section to the next.

Another generally useful type of information is to confirm the data values actually read, by following each READ statement

I 8.3 Diagnostic Output Statements

with an immediate PRINT. For example:

```
READ, X, Y
PRINT, 'IN READ LOOP, X AND Y ARE:', X, Y
```

Note that the extra PRINT statement <u>identifies itself</u> when it is executed, and also <u>identifies the variables</u> whose values are displayed. Without this identification, the information provided by these statements is much more difficult to use.

Once you accept the fact that programs rarely are entirely correct on the first try, you realize it is foolish to waste the first try just to discover that the program is not correct. A prudent and efficient programmer plans his testing while he is writing the program. Extra PRINT statements are included in the very first run, so that even this run yields as much diagnostic information as possible.

It is hard to exaggerate the value of this technique. Too often a great amount of time is wasted staring at a faulty program waiting for the error to suddenly reveal itself (which rarely happens). Then more time is spent paging through textbooks and manuals, or waiting in line to see a "programming consultant". Usually the best kind of consulting advice is simply what you could have done in the first place -- <u>run it again, with some extra PRINT statements inserted</u> to see what is really going on.

The disparity in skill exhibited by different programmers in testing is at least as great as that involved in constructing the programs in the first place. If you spend much time in the company of neophyte programmers you will discover that there are two kinds. One kind seems to find testing a challenging form of contest, and develops a systematic technique for the tracking and killing of "bugs". The second kind, usually more numerous, find testing unspeakably frustrating, and become ex-programmers as soon as possible.

Section 8 **Summary**

1. Programs are rarely correct on the first try. Systematic testing is an essential part of the programming process.

2. The first step in testing is the elimination of <u>grammatical errors</u>, (syntactic errors) as noted by FORTRAN in the source listing.

3. The second step is the elimination of errors detected by FORTRAN during <u>execution</u> of the program.

4. Test data must be devised so the program can be executed on problems for which the <u>correct answer is known</u>. In general, a simple first test should be followed with multiple tests that are very demanding, and that test every segment of the program. Confidence in the correctness of a program is only achieved by satisfactorily performing an exhaustive set of test cases.

5. In general, diagnostic information should be obtained by inserting <u>extra PRINT statements</u> at significant points in the program to display the values of key variables. These statements should identify themselves, and identify the particular variables whose value is displayed. When you are satisfied as to the program's correctness, these statements must be removed.

Section 9   Preliminary Examples

   The examples in the previous sections have been very
artificial, and intended just to illustrate the meaning and use
of some particular feature of the FORTRAN programming language.
They have been short, and quite unrepresentative of "real"
programs. On the other hand, the examples in Part II take a
particular problem and use whatever programming techniques are
necessary for its solution. They are also intended to be more
realistic, so there is a considerable jump in both size and
complexity -- the shortest program in Part II is longer than the
longest program presented up to this point.

   Section 9 is intended to help bridge this gap, by presenting
a group of programs that are somewhat longer and more
complicated than the previous ones, but still not overwhelming.
These examples are oriented to a problem statement, similar to
those in Part II, rather than a particular programming concept.
Furthermore, several of these problems are actually simplified
forms of tasks that will appear again as parts of the problems
in Part II.

   You might well regard this section as optional. Try going
directly to Part II; if the programs there are too formidable
then come back and warm up on the easier examples in this
section.

9.1 Compute the Sum of a List of Numbers

Our first example is a program to compute the sum of a list of numbers. Suppose that we are only concerned with non-negative numbers -- that is, numbers greater than, or equal to, zero. The program is to be a <u>general summing program</u>, that will work for <u>any list</u> of non-negative numbers, rather than for just one particular list. It should not be necessary to make any change in the program itself to adapt it to a particular data list.

The program establishes a variable to be used as a "running sum". Each new number is read from the data list and added to this running sum. When the last number has been read and added, the running sum is the sum of the entire list -- which is the required answer. The algorithm for the program is the following:

```
         Repeat for each number on list:
         Read number.
         Add number to sum so far.
Print sum.
```

We need to specify how the program can recognize the last number on the list. Two techniques for this have been illustrated in previous sections -- either append a special, recognizable value to the end, or specify initially how many values follow. In this case, since negative values are not allowed, we chose the former strategy and specified a particular negative value (-999) to denote the end of the list. Also note that the program must initially set the summing variable to zero, so that the step "Add number to sum so far" will work properly on its first execution.

A minimal version of the program is given below:

```
           REAL SUM, NEWNBR
           INTEGER LOOP
           SUM = 0
           DO 20 LOOP = 1, 10000, 1
               READ, NEWNBR
               IF (NEWNBR .EQ. -999) GO TO 30
               IF (NEWNBR .GE. 0) SUM = SUM + NEWNBR
     20        CONTINUE
     30    PRINT, SUM
           STOP
           END
```

This is a "bare bones" version of the program. It might be adequate for a situation where it would be used briefly and then discarded, but if it were intended to be used by anyone other than its author, and/or used for any length of time, then it should be made more elaborate. In particular, the <u>output should be suitably labeled</u>, and there should be some <u>protection against improper data</u>. It might also be useful to report how many data

I 9.1 Compute the Sum

items contributed to the final answer, even though the problem statement does not explicitly require this. An expanded version of the program, providing these additional features, is shown below:

```
       REAL   SUM, NEWNBR
       INTEGER  LOOP, NUMBER, ERRORS
       PRINT, 'SUMMING PROGRAM FOR NON-NEGATIVE NUMBERS'
       PRINT, ' '
       SUM = 0
       NUMBER = 0
       ERRORS = 0
       DO 20 LOOP = 1, 10000, 1
          READ, NEWNBR
          IF(NEWNBR .EQ. -999) GO TO 30
          IF(NEWNBR .GE. 0) GO TO 10
             PRINT, 'NEGATIVE NUMBER:', NEWNBR, 'IGNORED'
             ERRORS = ERRORS + 1
10        SUM = SUM + NEWNBR
          NUMBER = NUMBER + 1
20     CONTINUE
30     PRINT, ' '
       IF(ERRORS .GT. 0) PRINT, ERRORS,
     $        'NEGATIVE NUMBERS DISCARDED'
       PRINT, NUMBER, 'NON-NEGATIVE NUMBERS IN SUM'
       PRINT, 'SUM IS:', SUM
       STOP
       END
```

As an example of the execution of this program, suppose it were used to process the following data list:

```
     $ENTRY
      120
      -17
       .3
      -1
       0
      45
      -999
```

The resulting execution output would be:

```
SUMMING PROGRAM FOR NON-NEGATIVE NUMBERS

NEGATIVE NUMBER:         -17.00000000 IGNORED
NEGATIVE NUMBER:          -1.00000000 IGNORED

            2 NEGATIVE NUMBERS DISCARDED
            6 NON-NEGATIVE NUMBERS IN SUM
SUM IS:        147.29990000
```

It is interesting to note that the expanded version of this program requires twenty-three FORTRAN statements, while the minimal version requires only eleven. Since they both perform the same basic task this must seem like a high price to pay for the additional features of the expanded program. But for anything except trivial use, this additional effort on the part of the programmer is worthwhile. The titling will help each subsequent user of the program to properly interpret the output. But most important, the expanded program is much less likely to be misused by accident. It would be easy to forget that these programs work <u>only for non-negative values</u>. If the minimal program were accidentally used for data that included negative values, it would <u>give an incorrect answer</u> with no warning that anything was wrong. Under the same circumstances the expanded program would remind the user of the restriction that was built into the program.

It is even more striking to realize that in either program there are only <u>three statements</u> that really perform the basic task:

```
...
READ, NEWNBR
...
SUM = SUM + NEWNBR
...
PRINT, 'SUM IS:', SUM
...
```

All of the other lines in the program prepare for these statements, control when and how often they are executed, protect them from erroneous data, label results, etc.

9.2 Assemble Letters into Words

The next example is a program to take a data list consisting of individual letters, and assemble these letters to form a "word". For example, given a data list consisting of the four letters:

```
'S'
'K'
'E'
'G'
```

the program should construct and print the word "SKEG".

This task is quite similar to the summing problem of the last section, except that the substring specifier operation (recall Section 6.2.2) replaces the operation of addition. The algorithm is the following:

```
Repeat for each letter on data list:
    Read letter.
    Add letter to right end of word.
```

As in the summing problem, we must decide how to have the program recognize the end of the data list. We will make a comparable choice and use an asterisk as a recognizable stopping value. The program must also initially clear the word to a blank string, just as the summing program initially cleared SUM to zero.

The following is a minimal form of the program:

```
      CHARACTER*100 WORD, LETTER
      INTEGER LEN, LOOP
      WORD = ' '
      LEN = 0
      DO 10 LOOP = 1, 10000, 1
         READ, LETTER
         IF(LETTER .EQ. '*') GO TO 20
         LEN = LEN + 1
         WORD(LEN:LEN) = LETTER(1:1)
10       CONTINUE
20    PRINT, WORD
      STOP
      END
```

Just as in the case of the summing program, if this word-composition program is intended for non-trivial use, it should be expanded to provide adequate labelling of results and testing of data. An expanded version is shown below:

```
      CHARACTER*100 WORD, LETTER
      INTEGER  LOOP, ERROR, LEN
      PRINT, 'WORD COMPOSITION PROGRAM'
      PRINT, ' '
      WORD = ' '
      ERROR = 0
      LEN = 0
      DO 30 LOOP = 1, 10000, 1
      READ, LETTER
         IF(LETTER .EQ. '*') GO TO 40
         IF(LENGTH(LETTER) .NE. 1) GO TO 10
         IF(LETTER .LT. 'A') GO TO 10
         IF(LETTER .GT. 'Z') GO TO 10
            IF(LEN .LE. 100) GO TO 20
               PRINT, 'TOO MANY LETTERS, PROCESSING TERMINATED'
               GO TO 40
10         PRINT, 'IGNORED DATUM IS NOT A LETTER:', LETTER
           ERROR = ERROR + 1
           GO TO 30
20      LEN = LEN + 1
        WORD(LEN:LEN) = LETTER(1:1)
30      CONTINUE
40    PRINT, ' '
      IF(ERROR .GT. 0) PRINT, ERROR, 'ITEMS DISCARDED'
      PRINT, LEN, 'LETTERS USED'
      PRINT, 'WORD IS:', WORD
      STOP
      END
      INTEGER FUNCTION LENGTH
         ...
```

   While this program is generally comparable to the expanded summing program of Section 9.1, it includes one additional test. This is a test for an excessive number of letters that would "overflow" the capacity of the variable WORD. Actually a comparable overflow <u>could</u> occur in the summing program, if it were presented with so many or such large numbers that their sum exceeded the capacity of the variable SUM. However, in that case the computer would <u>automatically detect the overflow</u> condition and issue an error message, so it was not necessary to explicitly test for arithmetic overflow in the summing program.

9.3 Find the Maximum Number in a List

The next example is a program to find the maximum value in a list of non-negative numbers. The algorithm is:

> Repeat for each number on the list:
>   Read number.
>   Compare number with maximum found so far,
>   save if new number is greater.
> Print maximum for entire list.

As in Section 9.1, -999 is used as a stopping value.

A variable MAXVAL is used to record the maximum value encountered so far during execution. Initially MAXVAL is set to an artificially small value, say -1, to ensure that the first value on the list will become the first real value of MAXVAL.

This program is quite similar in structure to both the summing program and the word composition program of the last two sections. However, in this case the key statement, instead of adding or concatenating, is the following:

> IF(NEW .GT. MAXVAL) MAXVAL = NEW

Since the program is similar in structure to the last two, the skeletal version is not given. The expanded form is shown below:

```
      REAL NEW, MAXVAL
      INTEGER LOOP, NUMBER, ERROR
      PRINT, 'FIND MAXIMUM OF NON-NEGATIVE NUMBERS'
      PRINT, ' '
      MAXVAL = -1
      NUMBER = 0
      ERROR = 0
      DO 20 LOOP = 1, 10000, 1
         READ, NEW
         IF(NEW .EQ. -999) GO TO 30
         IF(NEW .GE. 0) GO TO 10
            PRINT, 'NEGATIVE NUMBER:', NEW
            ERROR = ERROR + 1
            GO TO 20
10       IF(NEW .GT. MAXVAL) MAXVAL = NEW
         NUMBER = NUMBER + 1
20    CONTINUE
30    PRINT, ' '
      IF(ERROR .GT. 0) PRINT, ERROR, 'NEGATIVE NUMBERS'
      PRINT, NUMBER, 'NON-NEGATIVE NUMBERS'
      PRINT, 'MAXIMUM IS:', MAXVAL
      STOP
      END
```

9.4 Find the Maximum and Print the Values of a List

Now consider a program to perform a <u>compound</u> task -- say, two of our previous tasks to be performed by a single program. For example, given a list of non-negative numbers, find and report the <u>maximum value</u> (as in Section 9.3), and <u>print the values</u> on the list (as in Section 3.2). Clearly we could use the two separate programs we have already described, but it is interesting to consider a single program capable of performing both tasks.

What makes the problem interesting is that the nature of the program depends importantly upon the <u>format</u> in which the answers are to be displayed. For example, suppose the data list consisted of the following six numbers:

    5.2   13   2.01   7   9   6.94

Consider three possible alternative arrangements for the results:

```
5.2                    MAXIMUM IS: 13      5.2
13                                         13    (MAXIMUM)
2.01                   5.2                 2.01
7                      13                  7
9                      2.01                9
6.94                   7                   6.94
                       9
MAXIMUM IS: 13         6.94
```

The leftmost format lists the values first and then reports the maximum. The center format is just the opposite of that. The rightmost format lists the values and identifies the maximum as it is listed. Any of these three (or some other variation) might be <u>preferred by the user</u> of the program, and hence could be specified as part of the problem requirements. Surprisingly, this seemingly arbitrary choice turns out to be crucial to the way the program has to be constructed.

The key point is that the program cannot discover which value on the list is the maximum <u>until it has read the entire list</u>. (The maximum could be the last value.) Consequently, if either the center or right format is required, then the program <u>cannot begin to print</u> the list <u>until after it has finished reading</u> the list. On the other hand, for the left format, the program can <u>print the list as it reads</u> it, testing for the maximum value as it reads, and then report the maximum value as a final step after the reading and list printing is completed.

Any of these formats <u>can</u> be produced, but the left format is <u>more natural</u> in terms of the way the task must be performed, and consequently the program for that format is simpler. In fact, the program would be just a trivial variation of the program given in Section 9.3. It would only require the addition of a single statement:

I 9.4 Find Maximum and Print List

```
            PRINT, NEW
```
in the loop:
```
            DO 20 LOOP = 1, 10000, 1
                ...
                NUMBER = NUMBER + 1
                PRINT, NEW
       20   CONTINUE
```

You may wonder why the center and right format could not be as easily programmed just by reading the data list twice -- once to find the maximum value, and the second time to print the values. Curiously, that would be considered a very unattractive strategy. Reading cards is one of the slowest and most expensive operations the computer performs, so most systems are designed so that the program is allowed <u>only one pass through the data cards</u>. Therefore, if you want to effectively read the cards twice, you must <u>make an internal copy</u> of the data list when you read it the first time. Then you can scan that internal copy as many additional times as you find necessary.

To illustrate this process, we present a program to provide results in the center format of the three choices shown above. The algorithm is the following:

```
            Repeat for each number on the data list:
                Copy number into an internal list.
            Repeat for each number on the internal list:
                Compare to MAXVAL and save if greater.
            Print MAXVAL.
            Repeat for each number on the internal list:
                Print number.
```

The program employs a "list variable" (as described in Section 7) for the internal copy of the data list. The program shown below uses a list of fifty elements, which means that it can only accomodate a data list of up to fifty items. If a longer data list was required, a larger internal list could be declared -- within reason. (If more than several hundred items is involved, the internal list strategy becomes complicated and is beyond the scope of this book.)

```
       REAL NEW, MAXVAL, VALUE(50)
       INTEGER NBRVAL, VALNBR
       INTEGER ERROR
       PRINT, 'FIND MAXIMUM AND LIST DATA'
       PRINT, ' ', '(FOR NON-NEGATIVE VALUES)'
       PRINT, ' '
       ERROR = 0
       NBRVAL = 0
       DO 30 VALNBR = 1, 10000, 1
           READ, NEW
           IF (NEW .EQ. -999) GO TO 40
```

I 9.4 Find Maximum and Print List

```
              IF (NEW .GE. 0) GO TO 10
                  PRINT, 'NEGATIVE VALUE', NEW
                  ERROR = ERROR + 1
                  GO TO 30
      10      IF (NBRVAL .LE. 50) GO TO 20
                  PRINT, 'TOO MUCH DATA'
                  GO TO 40
      20      NBRVAL = NBRVAL + 1
              VALUE(NBRVAL) = NEW
      30      CONTINUE
      40  MAXVAL = -1
          DO 50 VALNBR = 1, NBRVAL, 1
              IF (VALUE(VALNBR) .GT. MAXVAL) MAXVAL = VALUE(VALNBR)
      50      CONTINUE
          PRINT, ' '
          IF (ERROR .GT. 0) PRINT, ERROR, 'NEGATIVE VALUES IGNORED'
          PRINT, 'NUMBER OF VALUES IS:', NBRVAL
          PRINT, 'MAXIMUM VALUE IS:', MAXVAL
          PRINT, ' '
          DO 60 VALNBR = 1, NBRVAL, 1
              PRINT, ' ', VALUE(VALNBR)
      60      CONTINUE
          PRINT, ' '
          PRINT, 'END OF LIST'
          STOP
          END
```

To illustrate the execution of this program, suppose it was run with the following data list:

```
    $ENTRY
     45
     -26
     17.2
     -.05
     101
     16
     -999
```

The execution output would be the following:

```
FIND MAXIMUM AND LIST DATA
   (FOR NON-NEGATIVE VALUES)

NEGATIVE VALUE            -26.00000000
NEGATIVE VALUE             -0.05000000

         2 NEGATIVE VALUES IGNORED
NUMBER OF VALUES IS:          4
MAXIMUM VALUE IS:        101.00000000

         45.00000000
         17.19999000
        101.00000000
         16.00000000

END OF LIST
```

9.5 A Program for Vowelless Printing

The following program is quite different from those of the last four sections. It is presented to illustrate the use of <u>nested loops</u>, a concept introduced in Section 3.3.

The problem is to read and print the words given in a data list, but the words are to have <u>all vowels deleted</u> before they are printed. For example, if

      'ASSATEAGUE'

is given on the data list, the corresponding word printed would be:
      SSTG

An algorithm for this process is the following:

      Repeat for each word on data list:
         Repeat for each letter in the word:
            Delete letter if it is a vowel.
         Print word with vowels deleted.

Two levels of loop are apparent in the algorithm, and the step "Delete letter ... " is also accomplished using a loop, so loops are nested three levels deep in the program. The "deletion" is actually accomplished by <u>copying</u> the letters which are not vowels -- and failing to copy the vowels. The program follows:

```
      CHARACTER*100 INPUT, COPY
      INTEGER WDNBR, LTNBR, VNBR, CNBR, LEN
      CHARACTER*100 VOWEL(5)
      VOWEL(1) = 'A'
      VOWEL(2) = 'E'
      VOWEL(3) = 'I'
      VOWEL(4) = 'O'
      VOWEL(5) = 'U'
      PRINT, 'WORD LIST WITHOUT VOWELS'
      PRINT, ' '
      DO 30 WDNBR = 1, 10000, 1
         READ, INPUT
         IF(INPUT .EQ. 'LAST') GO TO 40
         CNBR = 0
         COPY = ' '
         LEN = LENGTH(INPUT)
         DO 20 LTNBR = 1, LEN, 1
            DO 10 VNBR = 1, 5, 1
               IF(INPUT(LTNBR:LTNBR) .EQ. VOWEL(VNBR)) GO TO 20
10          CONTINUE
            CNBR = CNBR + 1
            COPY(CNBR:CNBR) = INPUT(LTNBR:LTNBR)
20       CONTINUE
         PRINT, ' ', COPY
30    CONTINUE
40    PRINT, ' '
      PRINT, 'END OF LIST'
      STOP
      END
```

To illustrate the execution of this program, consider the following set of data. It consists of lines, rather than individual words, but note that there is nothing in the program that detects blanks. Hence each data item is considered a single word as far as the program is concerned.

```
      $ENTRY
       'EVERY DRUNKEN SKIPPER TRUSTS TO'
       'PROVIDENCE.  BUT ONE OF THE WAYS OF'
       'PROVIDENCE WITH DRUNKEN SKIPPERS IS'
       'TO RUN THEM ON THE ROCKS.'
       'LAST'
```

The resulting execution output is:

```
WORD LIST WITHOUT VOWELS

  VRY DRNKN SKPPR TRSTS T
  PRVDNC. BT N F TH WYS F
  PRVDNC WTH DRNKN SKPPRS S
  T RN THM N TH RCKS.

END OF LIST
```

9.6 A Program to Detect Palindromes

Another example concerned with processing character data is a program to detect the presence of a "palindrome". A palindrome is a word (or sentence) that reads exactly the same backwards as it does forwards. For example, "noon", "redivider" and "edit a tide" are all palindromes. The detection program given below reads words from a data list and reports whether each one is or is not a palindrome.

The algorithm is the following:

>   Repeat for each word on data list:
>   Test for perfect reflection.
>   Print word and test result.

The reflection test involves a loop that examines letters from the left to the middle of the word, checking to see whether the corresponding rightside letter is the same.

The reflection test loop examines letters "from 1 to LENGTH(WORD)/2". This is obviously halfway through the word <u>if the word has an even number of letters</u>, but what happens if the word has an odd number of letters? For example, say the word has five letters. Then the value of LENGTH(WORD)/2 is 2.5, which is truncated to 2. In that case the loop is executed twice: once for LTR equal to 1, and again for LTR equal to 2. The next potential value of 3 is greater than the calculated value 2 (and the specified limit of 2.5), so the loop is <u>not</u> executed for LTR equal to 3. This happens to be just what the problem requires, since the odd center letter does not require

I 9.6 Detection of Palindromes

any test. A test is required to make sure that there are actually characters to be checked.

The program is given below:

```
      CHARACTER*100 WORD, RESULT
      INTEGER  WDNBR, LTR, RVRS, LEN, NBRPAL
      INTEGER  LEN2
      NBRPAL = 0
      PRINT, 'TEST WORDS FOR PALINDROMES'
      PRINT, ' '
      DO 30 WDNBR = 1, 10000, 1
         READ, WORD
         IF(WORD .EQ. 'LAST') GO TO 30
         RESULT = 'NO'
         LEN = LENGTH(WORD)
         LEN2 = LEN/2
         IF(LEN2 .EQ. 0) GO TO 15
         DO 10 LTR = 1, LEN2, 1
            RVRS = LEN - LTR + 1
            IF(WORD(LTR:LTR) .NE. WORD(RVRS:RVRS)) GO TO 20
10       CONTINUE
15       RESULT = 'YES'
         NBRPAL = NBRPAL + 1
20       IF(RESULT .EQ. 'YES') PRINT, '  IS A PALINDROME:', WORD
         IF(RESULT .EQ. 'NO') PRINT, '  NOT A PALINDROME:', WORD
30    CONTINUE
      PRINT, ' '
      PRINT, 'END OF LIST'
      PRINT, NBRPAL, 'PALINDROMES FOUND'
      STOP
      END
```

The following is a set of sample data on which to exercise this program:

```
      $ENTRY
       'REVIVER'
       'LON NOL'
       'A'
       'MADAM, I''M ADAM'
       'ABLE WAS I ERE I SAW ELBA'
       '*|*--<<|>>--*|*'
       'I '
       'LAST'
```

The resulting execution output would be:

```
TEST WORDS FOR PALINDROMES
    IS A PALINDROME: REVIVER
    IS A PALINDROME: LON NOL
    IS A PALINDROME: A
    NOT A PALINDROME: MADAM, I'M ADAM
    IS A PALINDROME: ABLE WAS I ERE I SAW ELBA
    NOT A PALINDROME: *Y*--<<¶>>--*¶*
    IS A PALINDROME: I

END OF LIST
          5 PALINDROMES FOUND
```

This program is very strict in what it considers a palindrome. <u>All characters</u> in the input string, including blanks and punctuation marks, are considered and must be balanced. Common practice usually permits blanks and punctuation marks to be ignored and only letters considered significant. This admits many more interesting possibilities, such as:

Was it a bar or a bat I saw?

'Naomi, sex at noon taxes,' I moan.

Doc, note, I dissent. A fast never prevents a fatness. I diet on cod.

Norma is as selfless as I am, Ron.

He goddamn mad dog, eh?

These examples and others -- including an incredible 450-letter palindromic poem -- are given in Espy's "Almanac of Words at Play" (Potter, New York, 1975).

9.7 More Sample Programs

This section presents a group of programs without the usual preliminary explanation and algorithm -- just so you can practice reading a program "unassisted". Previously, you have been told _what_ a program does, and have read the program to see _how_ it is done. In this section you must figure out what is done from the program itself. These examples are similar in size and complexity to those of the previous sections. They are not intentionally deceptive or tricky. The variables are given names that should help suggest what they do, and the statements that title and label output should also be helpful in figuring out what the program accomplishes.

After studying each of these programs you should be able to:

1. Write out the algorithm corresponding to the program.

2. Write a detailed program description -- precisely what the program is intended to accomplish.

3. Prepare several test sets of data for the program, ranging from easy to demanding (see Section I 8.2). These data should test all aspects of the program, including various error tests and limit tests.

4. Sketch out what the execution output will look like for your test cases.

9.7.1 Print Lines of Ordered Pairs

```
      CHARACTER*100  LEFT, RIGHT, LINE
      INTEGER  PAIRS
      PRINT, 'PRINT LINES MAKE UP WORD PAIRS'
      PRINT, 'IN ALPHABETICAL ORDER'
      PRINT, ' '
      PRINT, ' '
      DO 30 PAIRS = 1, 10000, 1
         READ, LEFT
         IF(LEFT .EQ. 'LASTWORD') GO TO 40
         READ, RIGHT
         IF(RIGHT .EQ. 'LASTWORD') GO TO 40
         IF(LEFT .GT. RIGHT) GO TO 10
            LINE = LEFT(1:25)
            LINE(26:50) = RIGHT(1:25)
            GO TO 20
10       LINE = RIGHT(1:25)
         LINE(26:50) = LEFT(1:25)
20       PRINT, LINE
         PRINT, ' '
30    CONTINUE
40    PRINT, ' '
```

```
      PRINT, 'END OF LIST'
      STOP
      END
```

9.7.2 Expanded Printing

```
      CHARACTER*100  WORD, LINE
      INTEGER  COUNT, CHR, LEN, POS
      PRINT, 'PRINT WORD LIST IN EXPANDED FORM'
      PRINT, ' '
      PRINT, ' '
      DO 10 COUNT = 1, 10000, 1
         READ, WORD
         IF(WORD .EQ. 'LASTWORD') GO TO 30
         LEN = LENGTH(WORD)
         IF(LEN .GT. 50) LEN = 50
         LINE = ' '
         POS = 1
         DO 10 CHR = 1, LEN, 1
            LINE(POS:POS) = WORD(CHR:CHR)
            POS = POS + 2
10       CONTINUE
         PRINT, ' ', LINE
         PRINT, ' '
20       CONTINUE
30    PRINT, ' '
      PRINT, 'END OF LIST'
      STOP
      END
```

9.7.3 First Character Replacement

```
      CHARACTER*100  WORD, LINE
      CHARACTER*100  FIRST, REPL
      INTEGER  COUNT, CHR, POS, LEN
      PRINT, 'PRINT WORD LIST REPLACEMENT'
      PRINT, ' '
      READ, REPL
      PRINT, 'REPLACE EACH OCCURRENCE OF FIRST CHARACTER WITH:'
     $        REPL
      PRINT, ' '
      PRINT, ' '
      DO 20 COUNT = 1, 10000, 1
        READ, WORD
        IF(WORD .EQ. 'LASTWORD') GO TO 30
```

```
          FIRST = WORD(1:1)
          LINE = ' '
          POS = 1
          LEN = LENGTH(WORD)
          DO 10 CHR = 1, LEN, 1
              IF(WORD(CHR:CHR) .EQ. FIRST) LINE(POS:POS) = REPL
              IF(WORD(CHR:CHR) .NE. FIRST)
     $            LINE(POS:POS) = WORD(CHR:CHR)
              POS = POS + 1
   10     CONTINUE
          PRINT, ' ', LINE
          PRINT, ' '
   20     CONTINUE
   30 PRINT, ' '
      PRINT, 'END OF LIST'
      STOP
      END
```

9.7.4 Fibonacci Sequence

```
      INTEGER   FIRST, SECOND, NEXT
      INTEGER   TERMS, COUNT
      PRINT, 'PRINT FIRST N TERMS OF FIBONACCI SEQUENCE'
      PRINT, ' ', '(WHERE N IS GIVEN IN DATA)'
      PRINT, ' '
      READ, TERMS
      FIRST = 0
      PRINT, 'TERM:', 1, 'IS:', FIRST
      SECOND = 1
      PRINT, 'TERM:', 2, 'IS:', SECOND
      DO 10 COUNT = 3, TERMS, 1
         NEXT = FIRST + SECOND
         PRINT, 'TERM:', COUNT, 'IS:', NEXT
         FIRST = SECOND
         SECOND = NEXT
   10    CONTINUE
      STOP
      END
```

9.7.5 Table of Factorials

```
          INTEGER   LASTN, NCOUNT
          INTEGER   FACT, MULT
          PRINT, 'TABULATE FACTORIALS UP TO N'
          PRINT, '(WHERE N IS GIVEN IN DATA)'
          PRINT, ' '
          READ, LASTN
          IF(LASTN .GE. 1) GO TO 10
             PRINT, 'IMPROPER CHOICE OF N'
             GO TO 40
  10      DO 30 NCOUNT = 1, LASTN, 1
             FACT = 1
             DO 20 MULT = 1, NCOUNT, 1
                FACT = FACT * MULT
  20         CONTINUE
             PRINT, 'FACTORIAL OF', NCOUNT, 'IS:', FACT
  30      CONTINUE
  40      STOP
          END
```

9.7.6 List Values and Cumulative Sums

```
          INTEGER   COUNT, ITEM
          REAL   VALUE(50), CUM(50)
          READ, COUNT
          IF (COUNT .LE. 50) GO TO 10
             PRINT, 'ERROR: TOO MUCH DATA'
             COUNT = 50
  10      IF(COUNT .GE.1) GO TO 20
             PRINT, 'ERROR: NOT ENOUGH DATA'
             GO TO 60
  20      PRINT, 'LIST LENGTH IS:', COUNT
          DO 30 ITEM = 1, COUNT, 1
             READ, VALUE(ITEM)
  30      CONTINUE
          PRINT, ' '
          PRINT, 'PRINT LIST IN BOTH ORDERS:'
          DO 40 ITEM = 1, COUNT, 1
          PRINT, ' ', VALUE(ITEM), VALUE(COUNT-ITEM+1)
  40         CONTINUE
          PRINT, ' '
          PRINT, 'PRINT LIST AND CUMULATIVE VALUES:'
          CUM(1) = VALUE(1)
          PRINT, ' ', VALUE(1), CUM(1)
          DO 50 ITEM = 2, COUNT, 1
             CUM(ITEM) = CUM(ITEM-1) + VALUE(ITEM)
             PRINT, ' ', VALUE(ITEM), CUM(ITEM)
  50         CONTINUE
  60      STOP
          END
```

PART II   PROGRAM EXAMPLES

Part II consists of a series of examples of programs. The short examples and segments of programs in Part I were intended only to illustrate particular aspects of the programming language. Now, these longer examples illustrate how a particular problem can be solved. These examples use only the language elements you have seen in Part I (except for two additional functions, introduced in Section 6). These programs contain more statements, but this just means more instances of the statement types you have already seen in Part I. You should be able to understand the meaning and action of each individual statement in any of these programs.

In general, the way to read these programs is to first <u>study their overall structure</u>. That is, figure out roughly what each major section of the program is intended to accomplish. For example, the general pattern for all of these programs is the following:

        Create the required variables.
        Read control values from data; test the values
           and report any difficulties.
        Print titles and headings.
        Perform the principal action.
        Print final results.

The heart of each program is the fourth section -- "Perform the principal action" -- but this section of the program can sometimes be obscured by the rest of it. As we start to make the programs more realistic, the sections involved in testing data and labelling output grow rapidly, but as long as you can identify these separate tasks, and recognize when a different task begins, a program is not really hard to read. If it is well-organized and carefully presented, a program of two hundred statements is not hard to understand. If it is not well-organized a program of twenty statements can be impossible to understand (even by its own author).

Usually the principal action of a program will be a loop. That is, the "perform" step of the algorithm will actually be something of the form:

> Repeat for each ...
> Action to be performed on each ...

It will help in understanding programs if you look for this structure. Try and discover what object is the <u>basis of the main repetition</u>. For example, it might be any of the following:

> Repeat for each input item:
>
> Repeat for each output line:
>
> Repeat a definite numbers of times:
>
> Repeat a number of times given in the data:
>
> Repeat until some particular result is achieved:

Once you understand what the basis of repetition of the main loop is, it is usually not difficult to decipher how that repetition is described in FORTRAN terms. Sometimes this is contained entirely within the DO statement that initiates the loop; sometimes the DO just keeps the loop going, and an exit test with an IF ... GO TO is included in the body of the loop.

The next thing to do is figure what has to be done <u>on each repetition</u>. This is the task performed in the body of the main loop. Of course, as the programs get more complicated the body of the main loop will itself include other loops. But each of these can be approached in essentially the same way: figure out what is the basis of repetition, and then figure out what task has to be performed on each individual repetition.

In general, we will explain the principal action of a program by giving an algorithm before presenting the program. In some cases, the algorithm is presented in several levels of elaboration. You should use the algorithm to understand <u>what</u> the program is going to do, and <u>róughly how</u> it is going to go about it, before attempting to read exactly how this is specified in FORTRAN.

While we are primarily concerned here with <u>reading</u> programs, rather than writing them, an essentially similar process is involved in writing programs. That is, a program is designed by working on the algorithm first, usually working out several levels of algorithm with increasing degrees of detail at each successive level. The examples here are longer than you might be expected to write as a class assignment, but if you worked carefully from algorithm to program, there really is no reason you could not produce programs of similar size. The principal consequence of our concern with <u>understanding</u> a given program, rather than with <u>constructing</u> a program to solve a given problem, is that we will not spend as much time discussing the process by which an algorithm is developed. We will use the algorithm as a tool to <u>explain</u>, rather than as a tool to <u>create</u> -- which is its customary role. If a book is serious about

II Program Examples

teaching programming it should spend most of its pages discussing the development of algorithms -- since this is the hard and critical part of the process. Strangely, many programming texts do not do this.

Our intent in having you read these sample programs is to help you develop some feeling for what a "real" program is. That is, you should gain some appreciation for how much of a program is required to accomplish a given task. You should also begin to understand how a program should be designed to make it useful and convenient for the eventual user -- who, in practice, is generally not the same person who wrote the program. Finally, you should begin to appreciate the type of checking that must be built into a program if it is to become a dependable servant to fallible human users.

Some discussion of these points accompanies the program examples, but this is primarily concerned with understanding what the program does, and how it might be used. More general discussion of the significance of these examples is deferred to Part III.

The different sections of Part II are relatively independent. It is not necessary to read them in order, or for that matter, to read them all. (An exception is Section 1, which presents programs used in several other sections.) You might choose to read several sections in detail -- really study the programs -- and read just the problem descriptions and algorithms in other sections. Later, when reading Part III, if the discussion refers to a program you skipped, you can come back and read whatever is required. In order to make these sections independent we have resorted to a certain amount of redundant description. That is, we draw your attention to various points in the programs in a way that would not be necessary if we were to assume that all the examples would be considered in the sequence given.

These examples are not intended to be representative samples of important computer applications -- they clearly are not. Although several are related to common and important applications (Sections 1 and 3, in particular) they have all been chosen just because they seem interesting, and because they help to illustrate some points about programming. Our intent is to use these examples to help you understand programming in general, and not because it is important that you should be familiar with these particular programs.

For example, Section 2 is concerned with a literary tool called a "concordance". This example should suggest ways in which a computer could be used for non-numerical work, but it is not intended to imply that concordances are especially important applications of a computer. Section 2 is <u>not</u> entitled "The Computer and the Humanities", and it is not intended to be read as a survey or an assessment -- it is just a single interesting program.

These programs are also not presented as examples of particularly good programming style. Their style is reasonable, given the language subset that we presented in Part I, but a serious programmer would use language features that we have omitted (see Appendix B), and consequently their programs would be different in many details -- although similar in general concept. As a token example of the differences that the subset imposes, the program written in the subset language in Section 6.5 is given in Appendix B.10 using the additional language features.

Section 1 Some Text-Editing Programs

There are many programs that process data that consists of <u>natural language text</u>. For example, this book was produced by such a program. Other programs that require this capability are discussed in Sections 2, 4 and 6. Very frequently such programs are faced with the task of <u>composing</u> a text line from individual words. The opposite task is also common -- the job of <u>decomposing</u> a text line into individual words. We treat these tasks as independent problems in Sections 1.1 and 1.2 and present programs for them. Then in later sections these programs will be used without detailed explanation, whenever line decomposition or line composition is required in other problems.

1.1 Composing Lines from Words

It is a common task in text-processing to be given a series of individual words, and to have to construct lines from these words. To be specific, consider the following form of this task:

> Given data items that consist of individual words, compose these words into lines and print the lines. The maximum line length (number of characters) should be given as the first data item (a number), and when the next word cannot be included in the current line without exceeding this length, then the current line is considered complete and a new line is begun. The end of the data list is denoted by the word "last".

There are two different ways of viewing this process. One might be called word-oriented, and the second called line-oriented. Algorithms for these two different strategies are given below:

A word-oriented algorithm:

> Repeat for each input word:
>   Read word.
>   If new word cannot be added to current line:
>   Print current line.
>   Prepare new line.
>   Add word to line.

A line-oriented algorithm:

> Repeat for each line composed:
>   Prepare new line.
>   Repeat for enough words to fill line:
>   Read word.
>   Add word to line.
>   Print line.

At this point either of these algorithms seems reasonable. However, it will develop as we examine the resulting programs that one is better than the other.

The key step in each of these algorithms is "Add word to line." This is the step that actually performs the "composition". The FORTRAN statement corresponding to this step will use the substring specifier, described in Section I.6.2.1. Assuming the variable LINE contains the partially-constructed line, and variable NEWORD contains the word to be added to this line. A statement to accomplish this is:

```
LINE(LENGTH(LINE)+2:100) = NEWORD
```

The character at position "LENGTH(LINE)" is the last character of its current contents; "LENGTH(LINE)+2" causes a single blank

II 1.1 Composing Lines

space to be left between the words. Unfortunately, it also causes a blank space at the beginning of the line. This can be circumvented by keeping a variable whose value is the next position on the line; making the line construction statement:

```
LINE(NEXT:100) = NEWORD
```

After a line is completed and printed, the variable LINE must be cleared and prepared to start a new line. This is done by assigning a "blank string" as the value of LINE and setting the next position to 1:

```
LINE = ' '
NEXT = 1
```

A complete program for the first strategy -- the word-oriented approach -- is given below:

```
      CHARACTER*100  LINE, NEWORD
      INTEGER  MAXLEN, WRDNBR, NEXT
      READ, MAXLEN
      LINE = ' '
      NEXT = 1
      DO 20 WRDNBR = 1, 10000, 1
         READ, NEWORD
         IF(NEWORD .EQ. 'LAST') GO TO 30
         IF(LENGTH(LINE)+LENGTH(NEWORD) .LE. MAXLEN) GO TO 10
            PRINT, LINE
            LINE = ' '
            NEXT = 1
10       LINE(NEXT:100) = NEWORD
         NEXT = LENGTH(LINE)+2
20    CONTINUE
30       PRINT, LINE
      STOP
      END
```

It is interesting to note in this program that there are actually <u>only three statements that do the real work</u>:

```
      ...
      READ, NEWORD
      ...
      LINE(NEXT:100) = NEWORD
      NEXT = LENGTH(LINE)+2
      PRINT, LINE
      ...
```

All the rest of the statements serve only to support these three, and to control the order in which they are executed.

This is also a good place to comment on why algorithms can be short and clear, and programs are longer and more obscure. For example, in the algorithm for this program we could simply specify the loop control as:

>   Repeat for each input word:

After translation to our subset of FORTRAN this becomes:

```
        DO 20 WRDNBR = 1, 10000, 1
            READ, NEWORD
            IF(NEWORD .EQ.'LAST') GO TO 30
               ...
    20      CONTINUE
    30  ...
```

The proliferation of lines is due to the fact that our subset of FORTRAN has no direct way of saying "for each input word". (Complete FORTRAN is not a great deal better in this regard.) Extra lines also arise in the fact that we can use indentation in the algorithm to indicate the extent of each loop, but while we also indent the lines of the program, this is just for the human reader. FORTRAN does not consider the indentation of the lines, and requires the "CONTINUE lines" to indicate the extent of each loop.

There is also the matter of various details, which can be omitted from the high-level algorithm, but must be completely specified in the program. For example, the algorithm says simply:

>   Add word to line.

The program must worry about inserting a blank between words. The program must also recognize that when the stopping signal "last" is encountered there will, in general, be a partially-constructed line. This line must also be printed, so that the last few words will not be lost.

As an example of the execution of this program, suppose the following data list is given:

```
$ENTRY
 21
 'THE'
 'SEA'
 'APPEARS'
 'TODAY'
 'JUST'
 'AS'
 'IT'
 'DID'
 'ON THE'
 'FIRST'
 'DAY'
 'OF'
 'CREATION.'
 'LAST'
```

The resulting execution output is shown below:

```
THE SEA APPEARS TODAY
JUST AS IT DID ON THE
FIRST DAY OF CREATION.
```

1.1.1 <u>Line-Oriented Composition</u>

A program for the second strategy -- the line-oriented approach -- is given below. (We warn you that this initial version of the program is <u>not quite correct</u>. We will discuss the difficulty following the program, but you might try to discover the flaw for yourself.)

```
      CHARACTER*100 LINE, NEWORD
      INTEGER  MAXLEN, WRDNBR, LINNBR, NEXT
      READ, MAXLEN
      DO 30 LINNBR = 1, 10000, 1
         LINE = ' '
         NEXT = 1
         DO 10 WRDNBR = 1, 10000, 1
            READ, NEWORD
            IF(NEWORD .EQ. 'LAST') GO TO 40
            IF(LENGTH(LINE)+LENGTH(NEWORD) .GT. MAXLEN) GO TO 20
               LINE(NEXT:100) = NEWORD
               NEXT = LENGTH(LINE)+2
10       CONTINUE
20       PRINT, LINE
30    CONTINUE
40 PRINT, LINE
   STOP
   END
```

The program as shown above doesn't quite work. The algorithm is reasonable, but some of the details were not handled right in the translation. There are <u>no violations of the rules of FORTRAN</u> -- hence there will be no warning messages. Nevertheless, the <u>results will be wrong</u>. The difficulty is in the way the algorithm step "Repeat for enough words to fill line:" has been implemented. The program always has to read an <u>extra word</u> in order to learn that a line has been completed. However, this extra word gets lost when the program begins a new line. For example, suppose the input data was the following:

```
      $ENTRY
      30
      'THE'
      'SHIP'
      'TORE'
      'ON,'
      'LEAVING'
      'SUCH'
      'A'
      'FURROW'
      'IN'
      'THE'
      'SEA'
      'AS'
      'WHEN'
      'A'
```

II 1.1 Composing Lines

```
          'CANNON'
          'BALL,'
          'MISSENT,'
          'BECOMES'
          'A'
          'PLOUGHSHARE'
          'AND'
          'TURNS'
          'UP'
          'THE'
          'LEVEL'
          'FIELD.'
          'LAST'
```

The resulting output from this (incorrect) program would be:

```
THE SHIP TORE ON, LEAVING SUCH
FURROW IN THE SEA AS WHEN A
BALL, MISSENT, BECOMES A
AND TURNS THE LEVEL FIELD.
```

   This problem can be remedied by initializing a new line with the word in NEWORD, rather than with a blank string. That is:

```
        DO 30 LINNBR = 1, 10000, 1
            LINE = NEWORD
```

However, this repair causes a problem in starting the loop. In the first execution of the loop, NEWORD does not have a value, hence the statement:

```
        LINE = NEWORD
```

would cause an error message to be printed (by WATFIV, but not by FORTRAN). If this new difficulty is repaired by reading a value for NEWORD <u>within the body of the loop</u>:

```
        DO 30 LINNBR = 1, 10000, 1
            READ, NEWORD
            LINE = NEWORD
```

then the first execution of the loop will be alright, but every subsequent execution of the loop will be incorrect (since it will discard one word per line). Hence, this initial READ must be positioned <u>outside the loop</u> where it is executed only before the first execution of the loop:

```
      READ, NEWORD
      DO 30 LINNBR = 1, 10000, 1
         LINE = NEWORD
```

Now the only problem that remains is the special case when <u>no</u> <u>list of words is given</u> -- that is, the first word of data is "last". The program will not detect "last", so it will stumble on looking for more data.

It may seem strange to worry about this, on the grounds that no reasonable user would use this program to do nothing. But in fact, this sort of extreme condition is very common and very important in computing. Very often one program obtains its input from the output of another program, without any human intervention to decide what is "reasonable". It may be quite reasonable for the first program to generate no output (except "last"), and the second program must be prepared to handle this special case with aplomb. Hence an additional test for "last" must be added. Note that the first test for "last" does not go to a print statement, since LINE does not have a value if no words have been read. The complete, corrected program is the following:

```
            CHARACTER*100  LINE, NEWORD
            INTEGER  MAXLEN, WRDNBR, LINNBR
            READ, MAXLEN
            READ, NEWORD
            IF(NEWORD .EQ. 'LAST') GO TO 50
            DO 30 LINNBR = 1, 10000, 1
               LINE = NEWORD
               DO 10 WRDNBR = 1, 10000, 1
                  READ, NEWORD
                  IF(NEWORD .EQ. 'LAST') GO TO 40
                  IF(LENGTH(LINE)+LENGTH(NEWORD) .GT. MAXLEN)GO TO 20
                  LINE(LENGTH(LINE)+2:100) = NEWORD
10             CONTINUE
20             PRINT, LINE
30          CONTINUE
40       PRINT, LINE
50       STOP
            END
```

Presented with the same data list shown above, this revised program will produce the following output:

```
THE SHIP TORE ON, LEAVING SUCH
A FURROW IN THE SEA AS WHEN A
CANNON BALL, MISSENT, BECOMES A
PLOWSHARE AND TURNS THE LEVEL
FIELD.
```

This program still has the property that it will occasionally print an extra blank line at the end -- whenever it happens that "last" would begin a new line. (The first program had the same characteristic.) Since the extra line is blank this may not be objectionable. But if it is objectionable, the final PRINT statement could be made conditional:

        IF(LINE .NE. ' ') PRINT, LINE

   The point of this discussion is primarily to illustrate that there is often more than one algorithm for a problem, each representing a different strategy. It can turn out that a strategy that is apparently reasonable at the algorithmic level, will be clumsy when translated into a program. Rather than feel committed to translating a particular algorithm, the programmer should also weigh the option of revising (or replacing) the algorithm to find one that will translate more naturally.

1.1.2 Control of Output Format

   Suppose you wanted to give the user (not the programmer) of this composition program some additional control over the format in which the output is displayed. In effect, he has already been given some control in that he can specify the maximum line length, so just enrich this control. For example, suppose the user needs the option of specifying whether the line output is to be single or double spaced, and also the option of printing the input words as well as the output lines. With these additional options, the instructions for use of the program might be the following:

   1. The first word of input to the composition program will be treated as a title, and displayed as given.

   2. The second word of input is either 'SINGLE' or 'DOUBLE' to specify whether single-spaced or double-spaced output should be printed.

3. The third word of input is either 'SHOWINPUT' or 'NOSHOWINPUT' to specify whether or not the input words should also be printed.

4. The fourth item of input is a number to specify the maximum line length. This number must be an integer less than 100.

5. The fifth item of input is the first word of text data; the sixth is the second word of text data; etc.

6. The last word of input is the special word 'LAST', which denotes the end of text data. 'LAST' is not considered part of the text and will not be printed.

A revised program to provide this additional control is shown below. "Comments", the cards with a "C" in column 1, have been added to break the program into visually recognizable sections. These comments have no effect on the execution of the program. This is based on the word-oriented program of Section 1.1:

```
      CHARACTER*100  LINE, NEWORD
      INTEGER  MAXLEN, NEXT
      CHARACTER*100  TITLE, SPACE, SHOW
      INTEGER  WRDNBR
C
      READ, TITLE
      PRINT, ' ', TITLE
      PRINT, ' '
C
      READ, SPACE, SHOW, MAXLEN
      LINE = ' '
      NEXT = 1
C
      DO 20 WRDNBR = 1, 10000, 1
         READ, NEWORD
         IF(NEWORD .EQ. 'LAST') GO TO 30
         IF(NEXT+LENGTH(NEWORD) .LE. MAXLEN) GO TO 10
            PRINT, LINE
            IF(SPACE .EQ. 'DOUBLE') PRINT, ' '
            LINE = ' '
            NEXT = 1
   10    IF(SHOW .EQ. 'SHOWINPUT') PRINT, ' ', NEWORD
         LINE(NEXT:100) = NEWORD
         NEXT = LENGTH(LINE)+2
   20 CONTINUE
C
   30 IF(LINE .NE. ',') PRINT, LINE
      PRINT, ' '
      PRINT, ' '
      PRINT, 'END OF:', TITLE
      PRINT, 'PRINTED WITH LINES UP TO:', MAXLEN
      STOP
      END
```

Note that this program has the same <u>structure</u> as the first version of the composition program in Section 1.1. The length of the program has increased, as further functions and tests are added. This is a very common phenomenon in programming. What starts out as a very simple, single-purpose program becomes the basis of further development. New features are added, and the program grows -- often at a surprising rate that seem disproportionate to the capability added. If the program was not carefully and cleanly designed in the first place, its structure will soon disappear under the layers of repairs and additions. If the program becomes obscure and hard to understand, then it becomes increasingly likely that future modifications will cause trouble. They may not only fail to correctly implement the added function; they can also damage the initial function which presumably was handled satisfactorily before the change. This is a major reason why programmers must be concerned with the <u>readability</u> and understandability of their programs. The presentation of a program (indenting, choice of names for variables, use of comments, etc.) doesn't matter at all to FORTRAN, but it matters a great deal to humans who must read and understand the program.

An example of the use of this expanded program is shown below. Suppose the data presented to the program are the following:

```
$ENTRY
 'BYRON:'
 'SINGLE'
 'SHOWINPUT'
 27
 'THOU'
 'GLORIOUS'
 'MIRROR,'
 'WHERE THE'
 'ALMIGHTY''S'
 'FORM'
 'GLASSES'
 'ITSELF'
 'IN'
 'TEMPESTS.'
 'LAST'
```

The output printed by execution of the program would be:

```
    BYRON:

    THOU
    GLORIOUS
    MIRROR,
THOU GLORIOUS MIRROR,
    WHERE THE
    ALMIGHTY'S
    FORM
WHERE THE ALMIGHTY'S FORM
    GLASSES
    ITSELF
    IN
GLASSES ITSELF IN
    TEMPESTS.
TEMPESTS.


END OF: BYRON:
PRINTED WITH LINES UP TO:         27
```

Suppose the control words at the beginning of the data were changed to the following:

```
$ENTRY
 'BYRON:'
 'DOUBLE'
 'NOSHOWINPUT'
 27
 'THOU'
 ...
```

Then the resulting output would be:

```
   BYRON:

THOU GLORIOUS MIRROR,

WHERE THE ALMIGHTY'S FORM

GLASSES ITSELF IN

TEMPESTS.


END OF: BYRON:
PRINTED WITH LINES UP TO:          27
```

1.2 Decomposing Lines into Words

The opposite of line composition is "line decomposition". This is also a common task in text-processing: given a "line", separate its contents into individual "words". The assumption is that some of the characters in the line are blanks, so a "word" is defined as a sequence of non-blank characters, preceded either by a blank or by the beginning of the line, and followed either by a blank or by the end of the line. For example, consider the lines:

```
        The fourteenth of August
                    was the day fixed
        upon for       the       sailing
              of the     brig               "Pilgrim",
```

The word list based upon these lines is the following:

II 1.2 Decomposing Lines into Words

```
The
fourteenth
of
August
was
the
day
fixed
upon
for
the
sailing
of
the
brig
"Pilgrim",
```

Note that the spacing of the words in the original lines is irrelevant -- as long as a blank is not inserted in the middle of a word. But wherever one blank can appear, there could just as well be several blanks. Our definition of a word as a sequence of non-blank characters, means the words will <u>include any punctuation</u> marks that are not separated by <u>blanks</u>. Alternatively, one could define a word to exclude punctuation, and the program could strip them off, but our program does not do this.

As in the case of line composition, there are several different approaches to decomposition. All of them obviously involve searching through the characters of a line, testing for blanks, but this can be done in several different ways. Perhaps the simplest way is to scan the line, and move each non-blank character, one at a time, from the line to another variable (say, WORD). Then whenever a blank is encountered, the contents of WORD are printed. In more detail, the algorithm is the following:

```
Begin decomposition program:
    Create variables, including LINE and WORD.
    Repeat for each line of data:
        Read LINE.
        Clear WORD.
        Repeat for each character in LINE:
            If character is non-blank
                Copy character into WORD.
            If character is blank
                Print WORD.
                Clear WORD.
        End of character repetition.
    End of line repetition.
End of decomposition program.
```

The program for this task uses the substring specifier both to test individual characters in LINE, and to copy characters from LINE into WORD. (You may need to review Section I.6.2.2.)

II 1.2 Decomposing Lines into Words

The program is given below:

```
      CHARACTER*100  LINE, WORD
      INTEGER   LINNBR
      INTEGER   CHAR, POS
C
      DO 30 LINNBR = 1, 10000, 1
         READ, LINE
         IF(LINE .EQ. ')LAST(') GO TO 40
         WORD = ' '
         CHAR = 1
         DO 20 POS = 1, 100, 1
            IF(LINE(POS:POS) .NE. ' ') GO TO 10
               IF(WORD .NE. ' ') PRINT, WORD
               WORD = ' '
               CHAR = 1
               GO TO 20
10          WORD(CHAR:CHAR) = LINE(POS:POS)
            CHAR = CHAR + 1
20       CONTINUE
30    CONTINUE
40    STOP
      END
```

As an example of the execution of this program, consider the following data:

```
      $ENTRY
      'WHEN WINDS ARE RAGING O''ER THE UPPER OCEAN'
      '     AND BILLOWS WILD CONTEND WITH ANGRY ROAR,'
      '''TIS SAID, FAR DOWN BENEATH THE WILD COMMOTION'
      '    THAT PEACEFUL STILLNESS REIGNETH EVERMORE.'
      ')LAST('
```

The resulting execution output would be:

```
WHEN
WINDS
ARE
RAGING
O'ER
THE
UPPER
OCEAN
AND
BILLOWS
WILD
CONTEND
WITH
ANGRY
ROAR
'TIS
SAID,
FAR
DOWN
BENEATH
THE
WILD
COMMOTION
THAT
PEACEFUL
STILLNESS
REIGNETH
EVERMORE.
```

1.2.1 Decomposition by Copying Words

   An alternative approach to the decomposition problem is to scan the text line looking for blanks, in order the find the first (leftmost) and last (rightmost) characters of a word. But in this case, the <u>entire word is copied</u>, in a single statement, rather than copying each character separately. The algorithm is the following:

```
        Begin new program:
           Create variables.
           Repeat for each input line:
              Repeat for each word in line:
                 Find left-most character of word.
                 Find right-most character of word.
                 Copy word from line and print it.
                 Remove word from line.
              End of word-section.
           End of line-section.
        End of program.
```

   In the program developed from this algorithm, probably the trickiest part is associated with the step "Copy word". This involves the use of the substring specifier to copy the word. Suppose the line being decomposed is in variable LINE and the word to be extracted is to be placed in WORD. The program

II 1.2 Decomposing Lines into Words

specifies the extent of this word by assigning to variable LPOSN the position of the leftmost character of the word, and assigning to RPOSN the position of the rightmost character of the word. Recall that the substring specifier requires a starting position and an ending position. Therefore, the word can be copied by the statement:

```
WORD = LINE(LPOSN:RPOSN)
```

The word is "removed" from the line by advancing FIRST past the end of the word just printed. The starting position of the rest of the line, excluding the left-end word is RPOSN+1.

The complete program is shown below:

```
      CHARACTER*100  LINE, WORD
      INTEGER   LINNBR, WRDNBR, FIRST
      INTEGER   LPOSN, RPOSN
C
      DO 60 LINNBR = 1, 10000, 1
         READ, LINE
         IF(LINE .EQ. ')LAST(') GO TO 70
         FIRST = 1
         DO 50 WRDNBR = 1, 10000, 1
C
            DO 10 LPOSN = FIRST,  100, 1
               IF(LINE(LPOSN:LPOSN) .NE. ' ') GO TO 20
   10       CONTINUE
            GO TO 60
   20       FIRST = LPOSN + 1
C
            DO 30 RPOSN = FIRST, 100, 1
               IF(LINE(RPOSN:RPOSN) .EQ. ' ') GO TO 40
   30       CONTINUE
   40       RPOSN = RPOSN - 1
            WORD = LINE(LPOSN:RPOSN)
            PRINT, WORD
            FIRST = RPOSN + 2
   50    CONTINUE
   60 CONTINUE
   70 STOP
      END
```

An example of the use of this program is shown below. If the input data are:

```
        $ENTRY
          'WE ARE ALL JOINED'
          'BY A COMMON INTEREST,'
          'A COMMON DEVOTION'
          'AND LOVE FOR THE SEA.'
          ')LAST('
```

the program will produce the following output:

```
WE
ARE
ALL
JOINED
BY
A
COMMON
INTEREST,
A
COMMON
DEVOTION
AND
LOVE
FOR
THE
SEA
```

1.3 Variations on Line Composition

In this section we will describe three interesting variations of the line composition problem, but not give programs for them.

1.3.1 Justifying the Right Margin

The first variation of line composition would be to require that all the <u>lines have exactly the same length</u>. This would result in having the right margin as well as the left margin "justified". The lines produced by the programs in Section 1.2 have varying numbers of blanks at the right end -- only occasionally does the last word of a line happen to fill out the maximum line length exactly. When one imposes the additional constraint that the last word <u>must</u> fill out the line exactly, then the problem is what to do with the extra blanks. In normal type-set printing this is answered by distributing the extra space throughout the line -- wider characters are used. (Actually only certain characters are widened, and the result is scarcely noticeable.) In simple computer-text-editing the extra blanks are distributed <u>between</u> the words. That is, in places where there would normally be only one blank, now there can be several. (The lines you are reading now were produced by such a program.) In most lines the result is fairly reasonable, but when there are many blanks to distribute and not many places to put them, the result is somewhat unattractive and hard to read.

Our composition programs could be readily modified to right-justify their lines. This would be done by inserting a blank-distributing segment immediately before the PRINT statement that prints the line. That is, after the line has been completed, and the number of excess blanks is known, this segment reformats the line to distribute these blanks between the words.

1.3.2 Altering Line Lengths

A second variation would be to combine the line decomposition program of Section 1.2 and the line composition program of Section 1.1 to give a program that would change the length of given lines. The decomposition program has text lines of any length as input, and produces individual words as output. The composition program has individual words as input, and lines of a specified length as output. Obviously, instead of printing the words produced by the decomposition, you could pass these words to the composition program, which would recombine them into lines of the desired length. You could regard the entire composition program as a replacement for the PRINT statement of the decomposition program -- or alternatively, regard the entire decomposition program as a replacement for the READ statement of the composition program.

To actually write such a combined program, the best thing to do would be to write one or the other of these sections as a "subroutine" (see Appendix B.6). Say the main program is considered to be the composition section, and the decomposition section is to be the subroutine. The decomposition section would be written at the end of the program in such a way that it would behave much like the built-in functions -- ABS, SQRT, etc. The name of the subroutine might be NXTWRD, and it could be designed so that each time it was used it would supply the next word to the user, just as if it was being read from the data list. For example, the statement:

    READ, NXTWRD

in the composition program could be replaced by the statement:

    NEWORD = NXTWRD(LINE)

The right side of this assignment statement computes a new value (this is the action of the right side of any assignment statement). It does so in this case by executing the subroutine named NXTWRD which obtains the next word from the decomposition process. This right-side value is then assigned to the variable named on the left-side (just like any assignment statement), and the result is that NEWORD has received the next word as it's value, just as if it had been read from the data list.

1.3.3 Formatting Control Words

A third variation could be to <u>include various formatting commands</u> in the input data list. The purpose of these commands would be to control the format of <u>particular</u> output lines. (This differs from the program of Section 1.1.2, where commands were given to control the entire program.) For example, if an input word is ")L", this could specify that the next word should begin a new line, regardless of how much space remains in the current line. Another command might be ")P" to mean that the next word should begin a new paragraph, by skipping a blank line, and indenting the next line a certain number of spaces. (These happen to be two of the commands used by the text-editor employed for this book.) For example, the data list might be the following:

```
$ENTRY
99
')L'
'IT''S'
'NORTH'
'YOU'
'MAY'
'RUN'
')P'
'TO'
'THE'
'RIME-RINGED'
'SUN'
')L'
' '
')L'
'OR'
'SOUTH'
'TO'
'THE'
'BLIND'
'HORN''S'
'HATE;'
'LAST'
```

The lines composed should be the following (assuming a paragraph indentation of five spaces):

```
    IT'S NORTH YOU MAY RUN

         TO THE RIME-RINGED SUN

    OR SOUTH TO THE BLIND HORN'S HATE;
```

To implement these formatting commands, the program must first <u>recognize</u> them when they occur in the data list. This would be done by inserting statements to test the value of the data item as soon as it is read in -- much as the earlier programs test for the special word "last". These testing statements would be something like the following:

```
      ...
      READ, NEWORD
      IF(NEWORD .EQ. 'LAST') GO TO 100
      IF(NEWORD .EQ. ')L') GO TO 200
      IF(NEWORD .EQ.')P') GO TO 300
      ...
```

It would be easier, more efficient, and more understandable, if the form of the commands was chosen so that all commands could be recognized by a single test. For example, suppose the special word for stopping was chosen to be ")E", instead of "last". Then all commands could be recognized by the following single test:

```
      ...
      READ, NEWORD
      IF(NEWORD(1:1) .EQ. ')') GO TO 100
      ...
```

The program segment beginning at statement number 100 would contain the tests to distinguish between the different commands, but these tests would only be performed when it had already been discovered that some command had been received. Since commands are presumably relatively rare, compared to text words, the program written in this way would execute fewer statements overall.

Obviously, the form of the commands should be designed so that the commands are not themselves words that would be likely to occur in the text being processed. In that sense, our choice of "last" as a stopping command in the previous examples was very poor practice. Our examples (carefully) avoided including this word, but sooner or later the program would be presented with a passage of text that included the word "last" within its body. When that happened the program would fail, and the user, when he realized what had caused the failure, would be entitled to criticize the programmer for making a poor design choice. Some "unnatural" word, such as ")E", would have been a much better choice.

Section 1 **Exercises**

1. In the line composition program of Section 1.1, what would happen if the first data value presented to the program is 150?

2. In the line composition program of Section 1.1, what would happen if the data words presented to the program included blanks? In particular, how would each of the following cases be treated?

          a. 'FLEMISH DOWN'
          b. 'WORM '
          c. ' PARCEL'
          d. '   '
          e. ' FLAKE '

3. In the line composition program of Section 1.1 what would happen if a single word of data happened to be longer than the specified maximum line length (MAXLEN)?

    What should be done about this?

4. In the line composition program of Section 1.1.2, show how tests could be added to check that the values of the four initial controls given in the data are "reasonable". If they are not, the program should print an appropriately informative message and then terminate processing.

5. In Exercise 4, suppose the action to be taken in the event of an unreasonable control value is to print a message, make some repair, and continue processing. Write the appropriate statements to accomplish this.

6. In the line composition program of Section 1.1, suppose the user instructions specified that the value of maximum-line-length was an integer <u>less than 101</u>. How would this cause difficulty in the program?

7. The following program is intended to generate "personalized credit letters" of varying degrees of severity. The "user instructions" that should accompany this program have been mislaid. Write a new set of user instructions, and devise a set of test data to demonstrate the use of the program.

```
      INTEGER   SEVERE
      CHARACTER*100   TIMING(3), REMIND(3), PERSON(3)
      CHARACTER*100   FNAME, LNAME, SEX, STREET, CITY
      CHARACTER*100   TITLE, LINE
      INTEGER   NOTES, I
C
      DO 10 I = 1, 3, 1
         READ, TIMING(I), REMIND(I), PERSON(I)
   10 CONTINUE
```

```
C
      READ, NOTES
      DO 20 I = 1, NOTES, 1
         READ, SEVERE
         READ, FNAME, LNAME, SEX
         TITLE = 'MR.'
         IF(SEX .EQ. 'F') TITLE = 'MS.'
         READ, STREET, CITY
C
         PRINT, '    THE POET''S LOAN COMPANY'
         PRINT, ' '
         PRINT, ' '
         LINE = TITLE
         LINE(5:100) = FNAME
         LINE(LENGTH(LINE)+ 2:100) = LNAME
         PRINT, LINE
         PRINT, STREET
         PRINT, CITY
         PRINT, ' '
         LINE = 'DEAR'
         LINE(6:8) = TITLE
         LINE(10:100) = LNAME
         LINE(LENGTH(LINE)+1:100) = ':'
         PRINT, LINE
         PRINT, ' '
         LINE = ' '
         LINE(5:100) = TIMING(SEVERE)
         LINE(LENGTH(LINE)+2:100) = 'WE LOANED A TRIFLING'
         PRINT, LINE
         PRINT, 'AMOUNT OF CASH TO YOU AT A VERY REASONABLE'
         LINE = 'RATE OF INTEREST.'
         LINE(20:100) = REMIND(SEVERE)
         PRINT, LINE
         PRINT, 'THE MEANING OF ''SIX-FOR-FIVE-ON-FRIDAY''. TO'
         LINE = 'DISCUSS YOUR PROBLEM,'
         LINE(23:25) = TITLE
         LINE(27:100) = LNAME
         LINE(LENGHT(LINE)+1:100) = ', WE ARE SEND-'
         PRINT, LINE
         LINE = 'ING OUR COLLECTION ENGINEER, '
         LINE(30:100) = PERSON(SEVERE)
         PRINT, 'TO CALL AT YOUR PLACE OF RESIDENCE.'
         PRINT, ' '
         PRINT, '           SINCERELY,'
         PRINT, ' '
         PRINT,'         C. VAN LOAN'
         PRINT, '        CHIEF OF COLLECTIONS'
         PRINT, ' '
         PRINT, ' '
         PRINT, ' '
20    CONTINUE
      STOP
      END
```

Section 2 A Concordance Program

A concordance is an analytical tool of the literary researcher. It is essentially an analysis and summary of the pattern of word usage in a passage of text -- the frequency with which particular words occur, and their position relative to other words. Presumably individual writers have highly characteristic patterns in this regard, hence a concordance can be used to establish the authorship of an apocryphal work by comparing it to works of known provenance. The technique was used long before the modern computer became available, but the computer has suddenly made it possible to perform more detailed analyses of voluminous text at very modest cost. (But there are many difficulties -- see page 118 in Van Tassel.)

We will present a program only for the simplest aspect of the production of a concordance -- the determination of the frequency of occurrence of individual words. Text is presented to this program as data, and the program <u>counts the number of times each different word is used</u>. The results are presented as a list of all of the different words that appear at least once in the text, along with a count of the number of times each appears. We will assume that this list is most useful if it is given in <u>order of decreasing frequency</u> -- that is, with the most common word first.

At the highest level of description, one possible algorithm for our limited concordance problem is the following:

     Read the text.
     Construct a word-frequency table.
     Rearrange the table entries so the frequencies
          are in decreasing order.
     Print the table.

Since "Read the text" is a separate step in this algorithm, it would require us to read the <u>entire text into memory</u> before beginning the construction of the word-frequency table. While this might be possible, it is not necessary, since the table can be constructed "on the fly" as the text is read. Doing it this way it is only necessary to store one line of text at a time. Consequently, the algorithm we will use for this problem is the following:

> Read the text and construct a word-frequency table.
> Rearrange the table entries so the frequencies are in decreasing order.
> Print the table.

We will discuss each step of this algorithm as if it were a separate problem. Section 2.1 considers the problem of reading text and constructing the table. Section 2.2 considers the problem of re-ordering the table. Then in Section 2.3 the complete program is put together, and sample runs are presented.

2.1 Construction of a Word-Frequency Table

Constructing the word-frequency table involves a process called "searching a list", or sometimes "table look-up". This occurs in many different programs, and is worth considering in some detail.

A word-frequency table for a particular passage of text might look something like the following:

frequency of occurence	word
217	THE
8	COASTAL
4	BERM
29	OF
11	EBB
...	...

There would be a line in the table for every <u>different</u> word that occurs in the text, and the line would indicate <u>how many times</u> that word appears.

Suppose, as a starting point, we assume that we are given the right half of the table. Then for each line of the table we have to count the number of times the word on that line occurs in the text, and enter that count on the left half of that line. An obvious algorithm would be:

> Repeat for each line of the table:
>   Count the number of occurrences of the word.
>   Enter the count in left-side of line.

However, this algorithm implies <u>multiple passes</u> over the text, and that is not convenient in computing. We can actually read the input data only <u>once</u>, so this would require storing the entire text in memory so it could be scanned repeatedly. As noted earlier, it is possible to store the entire text, but if you can find an algorithm that avoids doing so, it would generally be preferable.

Another way of viewing the problem would be to think of it as being "driven" by the text, rather than the table. From this approach the algorithm would be:

> Repeat for each word of input text:
>   Find the line in the table for this word.
>   Increase the count in this line by 1.

This algorithm will produce exactly the same table as the first algorithm, but it has re-ordered the action in a way that is much more convenient to program. This is an example of the point that one must generally know something of how the computing process operates in order to choose reasonable algorithms.

The heart of this algorithm is the step "find the line", so we will examine that subtask first. Suppose the table consists of fifty lines, and is implemented in the form of two lists:

```
      CHARACTER*100 WORD(50)
      INTEGER FREQ(50)
```

The pair WORD(1), FREQ(1) represent the first line of the table; WORD(2), FREQ(2) represents the second line, etc. Suppose that the variable NEWORD contains the word whose occurrence is to be recorded in the table. The simplest program segment to do this would be the following:

```
          DO 10 LINNBR = 1, 50, 1
             IF(NEWORD .EQ. WORD(LINNBR))
     $          FREQ(LINNBR) = FREQ(LINNBR) + 1
   10     CONTINUE
```

While this segment will do the job, it is unnecessarily inefficient since it always searches through the complete table -- that is, it continues its search even after it has found the proper line. It could be improved by terminating the search after the proper line has been found:

```
          DO 10 LINNBR = 1, 50, 1
             IF(NEWORD .NE. WORD(LINNBR)) GO TO 10
             FREQ(LINNBR) = FREQ(LINNBR)+1
             GO TO 30
   10     CONTINUE
   30     ...
```

Now consider the situation if we do not assume that the complete right half of the table is given. Say we are some point in the process where we have constructed part of the table, but not necessarily all of it. Now it is very possible that a particular search of the table will not be successful. In fact, this will occur each time we encounter a particular word for the first time. Now there are two ways that the loop

II 2.1 The Word-Frequency Table

segment can complete: it can branch out to 30, indicating that it has found an appropriate line, or the loop can search all the lines without success. When the latter happens we need to add a new line to the table.

If the length of the table increases in this manner we would need a variable, say LAST, to keep track of the last line that has been used. The program segment would now be:

```
        DO 10 LINNBR = 1, LAST, 1
           IF(NEWORD .NE.  WORD(LINNBR)) GO TO 10
              FREQ(LINNBR) = FREQ(LINNBR) + 1
              GO TO 30
 10     CONTINUE
        LAST = LAST + 1
        WORD(LAST) = NEWORD
        FREQ(LAST) = 1
 30     ...
```

This segment is capable of <u>building</u> the word-frequency table, adding lines when new words are encountered, and increasing the count in an existing line when a word re-occurs.

One should pay special attention to the manner in which a program such as this <u>gets started</u>, and the manner in which it handles <u>overload</u> situations. That is, is this segment capable of "self-starting" -- will it work properly when the table in empty and is presented with its first new word? In this case, presumably the initial value of LAST will be 0 and the question is, what does FORTRAN do with the statement

```
        DO 10 LINNBR = 1, LAST, 1
```

when the last value happens to be <u>less</u> than the first value? There is no point in trying to reason out what you think FORTRAN <u>should</u> do in this case -- you must find out what it <u>actually does</u>. You could find out either by looking it up in a reference manual for the FORTRAN language (if you look back to where we introduced the DO statement you will find that we never mentioned this detail), or you could write a short program just to try it out. In general, language reference manuals are notoriously hard to use, and it would be easier to try it. Either way, you would discover that WATFIV prints an error and halts execution. Most other FORTRAN's would execute the loop once, regardless. To be safe, we will check to make sure that the value of LAST is appropriate.

On the other hand, assuming the table is fifty lines long, consider what happens when the fifty-first different word is encountered. The word is not in the table so the search will continue to the end of the table and not be successful. Therefore the program will increase the value of LAST by one (to 51) and then attempt to execute the statement:

```
        WORD(LAST) = NEWORD
```

Since LAST is 51 this refers to a <u>non-existant</u> line in the table. WATFIV will recognize the inconsistency in this situation and will report an error. Surprisingly, many versions of FORTRAN do not consider this an error -- they will just store the value of NEWORD in memory right after the table (as if the table had 51 lines), but in doing so it will destroy the value of some other variable that is using that memory space. Then, at some time later in the execution, that damaged variable is going to supply an incorrect value, without giving any warning of the trouble that has occurred. This is clearly not tolerable behavior, hence a program intended for serious use must protect itself against this sort of overload situation. One way of doing this would be to insert after the line

```
        LAST = LAST + 1
```

the following program segment:

```
            IF(LAST .LE. 50) GO TO 20
               LAST = 50
               PRINT, 'TABLE OVERFLOW'
               PRINT, 'LAST LINE HAS BEEN OVERLAID'
         20 WORD(LAST) = NEWORD
```

If the condition "LAST .LE. 50" ever became false, the results of the program would be incorrect -- but at least the user of the program would be <u>warned that they were incorrect</u>. Without this explicit test, the user of this program (in FORTRAN but not WATFIV) would have incorrect results -- but <u>not know they were incorrect</u>. This is a situation that must be avoided in any program.

In a "real" program, the number of statements required to test against such exceptional situations may well exceed the number in the rest of the program. Like fire insurance, one hopes that this protection will never be used, but when the exceptional event occurs, it is very nice to have some protection. Although we believe strongly in the necessity of such tests, we have in general omitted them from our sample programs. We excuse this deliberate omission on the grounds that to provide realistic levels of protection would, in general, make our programs much harder to read and understand. Thus you should bear in mind throughout, that practical versions of these programs could well be <u>twice as long</u> as what we have shown, just because of the addition of numerous tests.

We also need some means of indicating the end of the text data. We should use some "unnatural" word, not likely to appear in the text, for this purpose -- say ")LAST(". Then the complete program to build the word-frequency table (omitting the declarations) would be:

```
          WORD(1) = ' '
          LAST = 0
C
          DO WRDNBR = 1, 10000, 1
             READ, NEWORD
             IF(NEWORD .EQ. ')LAST(') GO TO 40
             IF(LAST .EQ. 0) GO TO 15
             DO 10 LINNBR = 1, LAST, 1
                IF(NEWORD .NE. WORD(LINNBR)) GO TO 10
                   FREQ(LINNBR) = FREQ(LINNBR) + 1
                   GO TO 30
 10          CONTINUE
 15          LAST = LAST + 1
             IF(LAST .LE. 50) GO TO 20
                LAST = 50
                PRINT, 'TABLE OVERFLOW'
                PRINT, 'LAST LINE HAS BEEN OVERLAID'
 20          WORD(LAST) = NEWORD
             FREQ(LAST) = 1
 30       CONTINUE
C
 40       ...
```

2.2 Re-ordering the Lines of the Table

The table produced by the program of Section 2.1 will have its lines in the order that different words occur in the given text. The results would probably be more useful, or at least the use would be more convenient, if the lines were rearranged before the table is printed. Two possible orderings might be helpful -- either in terms of decreasing values of FREQ, or in terms of alphabetical order for the values for WORD. We will consider the task of ordering by decreasing values of FREQ. The program to order the lines alphabetically by WORD is very similar; we leave that as an exercise.

The process of re-ordering a list is called "sorting", and it is very important in computing. In fact, it is probably more widely used than any other single task. The version presented here is a very simple form of sorting procedure. Its virtue is simplicity of explanation; its vice is comparative inefficiency in execution. Since we are not concerned with efficiency for our short examples, this is an appropriate strategy, but we should note that considerably more sophisticated and efficient schemes are used in actual practice.

To simplify our explanation, initially ignore the WORD list portion of the table and assume we are only concerned with sorting the FREQ list. When we have shown how to do this, it will be very easy to sort both lists at once. We will also initially assume that FREQ has exactly 50 values. With these assumptions our task is to rearrange the 50 values of FREQ so that:

FREQ(1) .GE. FREQ(2) .GE. ... .GE. FREQ(49) .GE. FREQ(50)

Our strategy is very simple: we will find the largest value and move it into position 1, find the second-largest value and move it into position 2, etc. More precisely, we will search the list and find which value is the largest, and where it is in the list. Then we will interchange the positions of this largest value and the first value. Then ignoring the first value (which is now the largest and is already in the proper position), we will consider the remaining 49 values and repeat the process. That is, we will find the largest of the 49 values and interchange it with the value in position 2. Then we will repeat the process for the values from position 3 to 50. Finally, when we do this for the sublist consisting of only positions 49 and 50, the list will be in the required order.

To illustrate the process, consider a list of only five values. Suppose the values are initially in the following order:

6 42 12 73 19

On the first "pass" through the list we find the maximum value in position 4, and interchange it with the value in position 1. The result is:

73 42 12 6 19

The second pass ignores position 1 and finds the maximum value from positions 2 to 5 and interchanges this value with the value in position 2. It happens that the maximum already is in position 2, but this doesn't matter -- this process still works. We go through the exercise of interchanging position 2 with position 2 and achieve the following "result":

73 42 12 6 19

On the next pass, considering only positions 3 to 5, we find the maximum value in position 5 and interchange it with position 3. The result is:

73 42 19 6 12

find the maximum value in position 5, and interchange it with position 4. The final result is:

73 42 19 12 6

The algorithm for this process could be described as follows:

II 2.2 Re-ordering the Table

           Repeat for each sublist from 1-50 to 49-50:
             Find the largest value in the sublist.
             Interchange the largest value and the first value
                of the sublist.

The task of "finding the largest value in a list" is itself a repetitive process (review Section I.9.3). A reasonable algorithm is:

           Create variables to hold the "largest value so far"
                and the "position of that value". Call
                them LSOFAR and POSNFL.
           Initialize LSOFAR and POSNFL with
                first value of the list.
           Repeat for positions 2 to end of the list:
             If value greater than LSOFAR
                Replace LSOFAR with new value.
                Record position of new value in POSNFL.

The program segment for this part of the task is shown below. Assume a variable START gives the first position of the sublist:

```
           LSOFAR = FREQ(START)
           POSNFL = START
           NEXT = START + 1
           DO 500 LINNBR = NEXT, 50, 1
              IF(FREQ(LINNBR) .LE. LSOFAR) GO TO 500
                 LSOFAR = FREQ(LINNBR)
                 POSNFL = LINNBR
     500   CONTINUE
```

   The task of interchanging two values is simple -- but perhaps not quite as simple as you might at first think. For example, suppose you need to interchange the values of two variables A and B. The following program segment will not accomplish this:

```
           A = B
           B = A
```

The first statement gives A the value of B properly, but in doing so it destroys the earlier value of A. Hence the second statement does not do what is required. It assigns the value of A to B, but the value assigned is not the original value of A, which was destroyed by the previous statement. Hence, the interchange requires the use of a third variable, as a place to temporarily set aside the initial value of one of the principal variables. For example:

```
           TEMP = A
           A = B
           B = TEMP
```

   Now, using these subprograms to "find the largest" and "interchange the values", a simple sorting process is performed by the following program:

```
            DO 600 START = 1, 49, 1
                LSOFAR = FREQ(START)
                POSNFL = START
                NEXT = START + 1
                DO 500 LINNBR = NEXT, 50, 1
                    IF(FREQ(LINNBR) .GE. LSOFAR) GO TO 500
                        LSOFAR = FREQ(LINNBR)
                        POSNFL = LINNBR
        500         CONTINUE
                TEMP = FREQ(START)
                FREQ(START) = FREQ(POSNFL)
                FREQ(POSNFL) = TEMP
        600     CONTINUE
```

All that remains is to make our program sort only the portion of the list used, and to rearrange the values of WORD as well as those of FREQ. The former is done just by replacing the constant "50" by the variable LAST. The rearrangement of WORD is achieved just by expanding the "interchange" section. The rearrangement is still <u>determined by the values of FREQ</u>; the interchange of values in WORD just rides along with it. With these minor changes our final sorting program is the following:

```
            NXTLST = LAST - 1
            DO 600 START = 1, NXTLST, 1
                LSOFAR = FREQ(START)
                POSNFL = START
                NEXT = START + 1
                DO 500 LINNBR = NEXT, LAST, 1
                    IF(FREQ(LINNBR) .LE. LSOFAR) GO TO 500
                        LSOFAR = FREQ(LINNBR)
                        POSNFL = LINNBR
        500         CONTINUE
                TFREQ = FREQ(START)
                FREQ(START) = FREQ(POSNFL)
                FREQ(POSNFL) = FREQ
                WORD = WORD(START)
                WORD(START) = WORD(POSNFL)
                WORD(POSNFL) = WORD
        600     CONTINUE
```

2.3 The Complete Concordance Program

The only remaining step in the original algorithm (Section 2) is "Print the table". The detailed algorithm for this step is obvious:

        Repeat for each line of (reordered) table:
            Print value of WORD and FREQ.

II 2.3 The Concordance Program

The program segment for this task is:

```
      DO 700 LINNBR = 1, LAST, 1
          PRINT, FREQ(LINNBR), WORD(LINNBR)
700       CONTINUE
```

Putting these three program sections together, and adding the necessary declarations and an appropriate title, the complete concordance program is shown below. In addition to the spacing comments that we have been using, comments have been inserted to explain sections of the program. Again, these comments have no effect on the execution of the program, only on its readability. A table size of 75 lines has been chosen in anticipation of the particular text on which the program will be demonstrated. (This is deliberately too small, so that the overflow test and error message will be exercised.)

```
      CHARACTER*100  WORD(75)
      INTEGER   FREQ(75)
      INTEGER   LINNBR, START, NEXT, LAST, NXTLST
      CHARACTER*100  NEWORD
      INTEGER   WRDNBR
      INTEGER   LSOFAR, POSNFL
      INTEGER   TFREQ
      CHARACTER*100  TWORD
      CHARACTER*100  TITLE
C
      READ, TITLE
      LAST = 0
C
      DO 300 WRDNBR = 1, 10000, 1
         READ, NEWORD
         IF(NEWORD .EQ. ')LAST(') GO TO 400
C
C     RECORD WORD IN TABLE
         DO 100 LINNBR = 1, 10000, 1
            IF(LAST .LT. LINNBR) GO TO 150
            IF(NEWORD .NE. WORD(LINNBR)) GO TO 100
               FREQ(LINNBR) = FREQ(LINNBR) + 1
               GO TO 300
100      CONTINUE
150      LAST = LAST + 1
         IF(LAST .LE. 75) GO TO 200
            LAST = 75
            PRINT, 'TABLE OVERFLOW'
            PRINT, 'LAST LINE HAS BEEN OVERLAID'
            PRINT, '   WORD:', WORD(LAST)
            PRINT, '   FREQ:', FREQ(LAST)
            PRINT, ' '
200      WORD(LAST) = NEWORD
         FREQ(LAST) = 1
300   CONTINUE
C
C  SORT TABLE IN DECREASING FREQUENCY ORDER
```

```
  400   NXTLST = LAST - 1
        DO 600 START = 1, NXTLST, 1
           LSOFAR = FREQ(START)
           POSNFL = START
           NEXT = START + 1
           DO 500 LINNBR = NEXT, LAST, 1
              IF(FREQ(LINNBR) .LE. LSOFAR) GO TO 500
                 LSOFAR = FREQ(LINNBR)
                 POSNFL = LINNBR
  500      CONTINUE
C       INTERCHANGE TABLE ENTRIES START AND POSNFL
           TFREQ = FREQ(START)
           FREQ(START) = FREQ(POSNFL)
           FREQ(POSNFL) = TFREQ
           TWORD = WORD(START)
           WORD(START) = WORD(POSNFL)
           WORD(POSNFL) = TWORD
  600   CONTINUE
C
        PRINT, 'WORD USAGE FREQUENCIES IN:', TITLE
        PRINT, ' '
        PRINT, 'FREQUENCY', 'WORD'
        PRINT, ' '
        DO 700 LINNBR = 1, LAST, 1
           PRINT, FREQ(LINNBR), WORD(LINNBR)
  700   CONTINUE
        STOP
        END
```

To illustrate the use of this program, we have run it with the text from the first paragraph of Section 2 as data. In preparing these data all punctuation marks were excluded -- only the words were supplied. The results are the following:

```
TABLE OVERFLOW
LAST LINE HAS BEEN OVERLAID
   WORD: MODEST
   FREQ:            1

WORD USAGE FREQUENCIES IN: PROGRAMMING FOR POETS PART II SECTION 2

FREQUENCY WORD

          7 OF
          7 THE
          4 AN
          4 TO
          3 A
          3 IT
          2 CONCORDANCE
          2 IN
          2 TEXT
          2 WORDS
          2 IS
          2 USED
          2 COMPUTER
          1 AND
          1 SUMMARY
          1 PATTERN
          1 WORD
          1 USAGE
          1 ANALYTICAL
          1 PASSAGE
          1 LITERARY
          1 FREQUENCY
          1 WITH
          1 WHICH
          1 PARTICULAR
          1 RESEARCHER
          1 OCCUR
          1 THEIR
          1 POSITION
          1 RELATIVE
          1 TOOL
          1 OTHER
          1 PRESUMABLY
          1 INDIVIDUAL
          1 WRITERS
          1 HAVE
          1 HIGHLY
          1 CHARACTERISTIC
          1 PATTERNS
          1 THIS
          1 REGARD
```

```
1 HENCE
1 CAN
1 BE
1 ESSENTIALLY
1 ESTABLISH
1 AUTHORSHIP
1 APOCRYPHAL
1 WORK
1 BY
1 COMPARING
1 WORKS
1 KNOWN
1 PROVENANCE
1 TECHNIQUE
1 WAS
1 LONG
1 BEFORE
1 MODERN
1 ANALYSIS
1 BECAME
1 AVAILABLE
1 BUT
1 HAS
1 SUDDENLY
1 MADE
1 POSSIBLE
1 PERFORM
1 MORE
1 DETAILED
1 ANALYSES
1 VOLUMINOUS
1 AT
1 VERY
1 COST
```

II 2.3 The Concordance Program   157

2.3.1 The Program with Input Lines Rather than Words

The program of Section 2.3 assumes the data is given in the form of <u>individual words</u>, each quoted on a separate card. It would undoubtedly be preferable to present the data in terms of full lines, and use a program such as the one given in Section 1.2 to break the lines up into individual words. Essentially this means replacing the statement:

        READ, NEWORD

in the table-building section, by a section similar to the program given in Section 1.2. The resulting program is shown below:

```
        CHARACTER*100   WORD(75)
        INTEGER   FREQ(75)
        INTEGER   LINNBR, START, NEXT, LAST, NXTLST
        CHARACTER*100   NEWORD
        INTEGER   LSOFAR, POSNFL
        INTEGER   TFREQ
        CHARACTER*100   TWORD
        CHARACTER*100   TITLE
C
        INTEGER   LPOSN, RPOSN
        CHARACTER*100   LINE
C
        READ, TITLE
        LAST = 0
        RPOSN = 1
        LINE = ' '
C
        DO 300 WRDNBR =1, 10000, 1
C       EXTRACT NEXT WORD FROM LINE
           IF(LINE(RPOSN:100) .NE. ' ') GO TO 10
              READ, LINE
              RPOSN = 1
  10       DO 20 LPOSN = RPOSN, 100, 1
              IF(LINE(LPOSN:LPOSN) .NE. ' ') GO TO 30
  20       CONTINUE
  30       NEXT = LPOSN + 1
           DO 40 RPOSN = NEXT, 100, 1
              IF(LINE(RPOSN:RPOSN) .EQ. ' ') GO TO 50
  40       CONTINUE
  50       NEWORD = LINE(LPOSN:RPOSN-1)
           RPOSN = RPOSN + 1
           IF(NEWORD .EQ. ')LAST(') GO TO 400
C
C       RECORD WORD IN TABLE
           DO 100 LINNBR = 1, 10000, 1
              IF(LAST .LT. LINNBR) GO TO 150
              IF(NEWORD .NE. WORD(LINNBR)) GO TO 100
                 FREQ(LINNBR) = FREQ(LINNBR) + 1
                 GO TO 300
 100       CONTINUE
```

```
 150      LAST = LAST + 1
          IF(LAST .LE. 75) GO TO 200
             LAST = 75
             PRINT, 'TABLE OVERFLOW'
             PRINT, 'LAST LINE HAS BEEN OVERLAID'
             PRINT, '   WORD:', WORD(LAST)
             PRINT, '   FREQ:', FREQ(LAST)
             PRINT, ' '
 200      WORD(LAST) = NEWORD
          FREQ(LAST) = 1
 300      CONTINUE
C
C   SORT TABLE IN DECREASING FREQUENCY ORDER
 400      NXTLST = LAST - 1
          DO 600 START = 1, NXTLST, 1
             LSOFAR = FREQ(START)
             POSNFL = START
             NEXT = START + 1
             DO 500 LINNBR = NEXT, LAST, 1
                IF(FREQ(LINNBR) .LE. LSOFAR) GO TO 500
                   LSOFAR = FREQ(LINNBR)
                   POSNFL = LINNBR
 500         CONTINUE
C            INTERCHANGE TABLE ENTRIES START AND POSNFL
             TFREQ = FREQ(START)
             FREQ(START) = FREQ(POSNFL)
             FREQ(POSNFL) = TFREQ
             TWORD = WORD(START)
             WORD(START) = WORD(POSNFL)
             WORD(POSNFL) = TWORD
 600      CONTINUE
C
          PRINT, 'WORD USAGE FREQUENCIES IN:', TITLE
          PRINT, ' '
          PRINT, 'FREQUENCY', 'WORD'
          PRINT, ' '
          DO 700 LINNBR = 1, LAST, 1
             PRINT, FREQ(LINNBR), WORD(LINNBR)
 700      CONTINUE
          STOP
          END
```

In actual practice, the program of Section 1.2 would be written as a "subroutine" (see Appendix B.6). Recall the discussion in Section 1.3.2. The result would be the same as the program shown above, but the separation of the line decomposition task into a separate subroutine would make the program easier to understand.

It would also be desirable not to have to enclose each input line in quotes, so that normal text (typed on cards) could be given as input. This is also possible, although not in the subset of FORTRAN we are using. However, the necessary FORTRAN feature is described in Appendix B.3.

Section 2 **Exercises**

1. Modify the program of Section 2.3 so it would *also* report the *length* of the longest word encountered in the passage.

2. Suppose the list of words and frequencies was to be printed in *alphabetical* order of the words (rather than decreasing numerical order of the frequencies). How would the program of Section 2.3 have to be modified to accomplish this?

3. Suppose that some of the "words" presented to the program of Section 2.3 as data included a final blank, and some do not. What would the effect be when the same word sometimes is given with a blank, and sometimes not?

4. Suppose that some of the "words" presented to the program of Section 2.3 as data include a punctuation mark as a final character. What effect will this have on the resulting table? How could the program be modified to improve the situation?

5. What would happen if the program of Section 2.3 were run with a "null" sample of text? That is, suppose the first word of data was ")LAST(". What should the program do in this case? How should the program be modified to make it behave this way?

Section 3   A Statistical System

The examples in Section 1 and 2 have emphasized the use of the computer to manipulate text -- in those programs the only arithmetic operations performed were those incidental to the <u>control</u> of the program. Now we will consider a program for which the data are numeric and the computer is really used to compute.

One of the most common uses of the computer in science is for the analysis of experimental or observational data. Sometimes a special program is written for a specific situation, but very often a scientist can take advantage of an existing program called a "statistical system" or a "statistical package". There are several such systems in widespread use (see Section 3.3). Such a system is actually just a program, written in a language such as FORTRAN, to which the user <u>supplies data</u>. By means of such standard programs, many people <u>use a computer</u>, without having to <u>write a program</u> for it (at least not in the sense of the kind of programming we have been discussing). These "packages" make the computer available and useful to many people who could not justify the time and effort to write their own.

Although it is certainly easier than starting from scratch to write your own program, using such a statistical system is not a trivial task. There is usually a manual or "user's guide" to the system that tells how to prepare the data, how to specify your choice from among the options offered, and how to interpret the output produced. In effect, the manual describes how to write a sort of program in a special statistical programming language -- although, in fact, it is just describing the form of the data to be given to a program already written by someone else. (This phenomenon will be discussed further in Section III.1.)

In the following sections we present a highly simplified version of a statistical system. First we will describe it from the user's point-of-view, much as you would encounter a real statistical system from its user's guide. Then we will present the underlying FORTRAN program that implements this system. Our system is not impressive in the statistical features it offers the user, but it is not intended to be a practical working system. It is designed to be short and simple enough for you to understand the basic idea behind any statistical system.

3.1 User's Guide to PS-PACK

Our system is called "PS-PACK" -- an acronym for the "Poet's Statistical Package". PS-PACK is capable of performing any of the following tasks on a set of numbers presented as data:

1. Print a list of the numbers.

2. Compute the mean (arithmetic average) of the numbers.

3. Determine the maximum value of the numbers.

4. Determine the minimum value of the numbers.

5. Compute the range of the numbers. (The range is the difference between the maximum and the minimum values.)

6. Compute the standard deviation of the numbers.

7. Compute 95 per cent confidence limits on the mean of the population from which these numbers are drawn.

If you are not familiar with "standard deviations" and "confidence limits" -- fear not. Understanding of these terms is not important to understanding the program. But they do illustrate a real danger in using such a statistical package. The user can specify options he does not understand, and then use the results provided without having any comprehension of the significance or interpretation of those results. This danger is discussed further in Section 3.3.

PS-PACK has seven different "commands", corresponding to the seven tasks listed above:

'LIST' to list the numbers

'MEAN' to compute the mean

'MAX' to determine the maximum value

'MIN' to determine the minimum value

'RANGE' to compute the range

'SDEV' to compute the standard deviation

'LIMITS' to compute the confidence limits

Any combination of these commands, in any order, may be specified.

In the data supplied to PS-PACK the commands are given first. The last command is followed by the word

'NUMBERS'

This is followed by an integer specifying how many actual data values follow. For example, if you had the following set of five data values:

13.05   15.1   9.75   10.603   12.0

and wanted the mean and confidence limits for these data, the input could be given as follows:

'MEAN'
'LIMITS'
'NUMBERS'
5
13.05
15.1
9.75
10.603
12.0

The resulting output would be:

```
PS-PACK STATISTICAL ROUTINE

                5 NUMBERS GIVEN

RESULTS:
  MEAN IS:              12.10059000
  95% CONFIDENCE LIMITS ON THE MEAN
        LOWER LIMIT IS:         10.25797000
        UPPER LIMIT IS:         13.94321000

END OF PS-PACK RESULTS
```

II 3.2 The PS-PACK Program

Alternatively, if you wanted to list the values and report their range (for the same five data values) the input to PS-PACK would be:

```
'LIST'
'RANGE'
'NUMBERS'
5
13.05
15.1
9.75
10.603
12.0
```

The resulting output from PS-PACK would be:

```
PS-PACK STATISTICAL ROUTINE

                5 NUMBERS GIVEN
LIST OF DATA VALUES:
                    13.05000000
                    15.10000000
                     9.75000000
                    10.60299000
                    12.00000000
END OF DATA LIST

RESULTS:
  RANGE IS:         5.35000000

END OF PS-PACK RESULTS
```

3.2 The Program for PS-PACK

The program for PS-PACK is somewhat longer than many of those in previous sections, but it is still logically a very simple program. It consists of three parts:

1. Read commands and set control values.

2. Read and process the numeric data.

3. Print the required results.

II 3.2 The PS-PACK Program

In part 2 of the program we have elected to do all of the computations required for all of the options, regardless of whether or not that particular command was given. The program is shorter and clearer this way, and in fact, it is probably also more efficient to do the computations regardless, rather than test for each computation for each item of data to determine whether or not the computation is actually required.

The program follows:

```
      CHARACTER*100  COMAND
      CHARACTER*100  LI, ME, MA, MI, RA, SD, LM
      INTEGER  CNBR, DNBR, QTY
      REAL   VALUE, RANGE
      REAL   SUM, AVG, LARGE, SMALL, DIFF
      REAL   DVSMSQ, DVMNSQ
      REAL   STDDEV, LOWER, UPPER
C
      LI = 'NO'
      ME = 'NO'
      MA = 'NO'
      MI = 'NO'
      RA = 'NO'
      SD = 'NO'
      LM = 'NO'
      DO 100 CNBR = 1, 10000, 1
         READ, COMAND
         IF(COMAND .EQ. 'NUMBERS') GO TO 200
         IF(COMAND .EQ. 'LIST') LI = 'YES'
         IF(COMAND .EQ. 'MEAN') ME = 'YES'
         IF(COMAND .EQ. 'MAX') MA = 'YES'
         IF(COMAND .EQ. 'MIN') MI = 'YES'
         IF(COMAND .EQ. 'RANGE') RA = 'YES'
         IF(COMAND .EQ. 'SDEV') SD = 'YES'
         IF(COMAND .EQ. 'LIMITS') LM = 'YES'
  100 CONTINUE
  200 READ, QTY
C
      SUM = 0
      SUMSQ = 0
      LARGE = -10000
      SMALL = 10000
C
      PRINT, 'PS-PACK STATISTICAL ROUTINE'
      PRINT, ' '
      PRINT, '            ', QTY, 'NUMBERS GIVEN'
      PRINT, ' '
      IF(LI .EQ. 'YES') PRINT, 'LIST OF DATA VALUES:'
C
      DO 300 DNBR = 1, QTY, 1
         READ, VALUE
         IF(LI .EQ. 'YES') PRINT, '            ', VALUE
         SUM = SUM + VALUE
         SUMSQ = SUMSQ + (VALUE*VALUE)
```

II 3.2 The PS-PACK Program

```
            IF(VALUE .GT. LARGE) LARGE = VALUE
            IF(VALUE .LT. SMALL) SMALL = VALUE
300      CONTINUE
      IF(LI .EQ. 'YES') PRINT, 'END OF DATA LIST'
      PRINT, ' '
      PRINT, 'RESULTS:'
      AVG = SUM / QTY
      IF(ME .EQ. 'YES') PRINT, ' ', 'MEAN IS:', AVG
      IF(MA .EQ. 'YES') PRINT, ' ', 'MAXIMUM IS:', LARGE
      IF(MI .EQ. 'YES') PRINT, ' ', 'MINIMUM IS:', SMALL
      DIFF = LARGE - SMALL
      IF(RA .EQ. 'YES') PRINT, ' ', 'RANGE IS:', DIFF
      DVSMSQ = SUMSQ - ((SUM*SUM) / QTY)
      DVSMSQ = DVSMSQ / (QTY - 1)
      STDDEV = SQRT(DVSMSQ)
      IF(SD .EQ. 'YES') PRINT, ' ', 'STQ DEV IS:', STDDEV
      IF(LM .NE. 'YES') GO TO 400
          RANGE = 1.96 * (STDDEV / SQRT(FLOAT(QTY)))
          LOWER = AVG - RANGE
          UPPER = AVG + RANGE
          PRINT, ' ', '95  CONFIDENCE LIMITS ON THE MEAN'
          PRINT, '            ', 'LOWER LIMIT IS:', LOWER
          PRINT, '            ', 'UPPER LIMIT IS:', UPPER
400   PRINT, ' '
      PRINT, 'END OF PS-PACK RESULTS'
      STOP
      END
```

3.3 "Real" Statistical Systems

Two statistical systems that are widely distributed and used are called SPSS and SAS. (Their user's guides are listed in References.) An example of the input that would be supplied to SPSS is given below:

```
RUN NAME         DEFINE, CROSSTABULATE, AND THEN SAVE
                     AN SPSS SYSTEM FILE
FILE NAME        FACSTUDY, SURVEY OF FACULTY PARTY PREFERENCES
VARIABLE LIST    PROF,PARTYPRF,AGE,SEX,RELIGION
INPUT FORMAT     FIXED (F4.0,1X,A1,1X,F2.0,1X,A1,1X,F1.0)
N OF CASES       20
INPUT MEDIUM     CARD
VAR LABELS       PROF,FACULTY MEMBER'S IDENT/
                 PARTYPRF,POLITICAL PARTY PREFERENCE/
                 AGE,AGE IN YEARS
VALUE LABELS     PARTYPRF ('C')CONSERVATIVE ('L')LIBERAL
                          ('S')SOCIAL CREDIT ('N')NEW DEMOCRAT
                          ('R')NOT GIVEN/
                 SEX ('M')MALE ('F')FEMALE/
                 RELIGION (1)PROTESTANT (2)CATHOLIC
                          (3)JEWISH (4)OTHER
MISSING VALUES   PARTYPRF ('R')/ AGE (0)
PRINT FORMATS    PARTYPRF SEX (A)
CROSSTABS        TABLES= SEX BY PARTYPRF
OPTIONS          3,5
STATISTICS       1,3
READ INPUT DATA
1912 C 43 M 1
1834 N 26 M 1
2786 L 35 F 2
2576 R 50 M 1
1633 N 61 F 2
2159 L 31 F 3
2634 L 45 F 3
1582 C 56 M 1
2222 S 37 F 2
1768 N 45 M 4
2651 S 30 M 2
2842 S 44 M 1
1899 N  0 F 2
2011 C 38 M 1
2359 L  0 F 2
1975 L 35 M 1
2488 C 42 M 2
2113 N 36 F 4
1313 L 29 M 4
2296 L 39 F 3
SAVE FILE
FINISH
```

The corresponding output would be the following:

```
DEFINE, CROSSTABULATE, AND THEN SAVE AN SPSS SYSTEM FILE

FILE    FACSTUDY (CREATION DATE = 02/16/74)
               SURVEY OF FACULTY PARTY PREFERENCES

* * * * * * C R O S S T A B U L A T I O N   O F * * * * * *
  SEX BY PARTYPRF   POLITICAL PARTY PREFERENCE
* * * * * * * * * * * * * * * * * * * * * * * * * * * * * *
                 PARTYPRF
         COUNT  I
         COL PCT ISOCIAL C NEW DEMO LIBERAL  CONSERVA    ROW
                IREDIT    CRAT              TIVE       TOTAL
                I  S     I  N      I  L     I  C      I
SEX             --------I--------I--------I--------I
       M        I    2   I    2   I    2   I    4   I    10
    MALE        I  66.7  I  40.0  I  28.6  I 100.0  I  52.6
                -I--------I--------I--------I--------I
       F        I    1   I    3   I    5   I    0   I     9
   FEMALE       I  33.3  I  60.0  I  71.4  I   0.0  I  47.4
                -I--------I--------I--------I--------I
         COLUMN      3         5        7        4        19
         TOTAL     15.8      26.3     36.8     21.1     100.0

CHI SQUARE =   5.78243 WITH  3 DEGREES OF FREEDOM
                    SIGNIFICANCE =  0.1227
CONTINGENCY COEFFICIENT =    0.48304

NUMBER OF MISSING OBSERVATIONS =      1
```

A sample of output from the SAS system is shown below:

```
         S T A T I S T I C A L    A N A L Y S I S    S Y S T E M

NOTE: THE JOB PAGE2 HAS BEEN RUN UNDER RELEASE 76.2 OF SAS

1          DATA:
2          INPUT SSN HIREYEAR SKILL;
3          LENGTH=76-HIREYEAR;
4          CARDS;

NOTE: DATA SET WORK.DATA1 HAS 6 OBSERVATIONS AND 4 VARIABLES
NOTE: THE DATA STATEMENT USED 0.13 SECONDS AND 90K.

11         PROC PRINT;
12         TITLE LIST OF EMPLOYEE DATA;

NOTE: THE PROCEDURE PRINT USED 0.19 SECONDS AND 104K
      AND PRINTED PAGE 1.

13         PROC MEANS; VAR SKILL;
14         TITLE FIND MEAN SKILL RATING;

NOTE: THE PROCEDURE MEANS USED 0.18 SECONDS AND 110K
      AND PRINTED PAGE 2.
NOTE: SAS USED 110K MEMORY.

NOTE: BARR, GOODNIGHT, SALL AND HELWIG
      SAS INSTITUTE INC.
      P.O. BOX 10522
      RALEIGH, N.C. 27605
```

                                                                 1

                       LIST OF EMPLOYEE DATA

OBS	SSN	HIREYEAR	SKILL	LENGTH
1	121334545	71	4	5
2	368445293	51	7	25
3	223666989	75	1	1
4	398742113	67	6	9
5	491337482	69	6	7
6	219334213	73	2	3

                                                                 2

                     FIND MEAN SKILL RATING

VARIABLE	N	MEAN	STANDARD DEVIATION	MINIMUM VALUE	MAXIMUM VALUE	STD ERR OF MEAN
SKILL	6	4.333333	2.422120	1.000000	7.000000	0.988826

II 3.3 "Real" Statistical Systems

The examples above are almost self-explanatory. At least they suggest the simplest kind of use of a statistical package. But elaborate use of one of these systems gets very complicated. As one indication of complexity the user's guide to SPSS is 675 pages long; the guide to SAS is 329 pages. Nevertheless, the use of such a system is significantly easier than writing your own programs for statistical computations in a general-purpose programming languages such as FORTRAN.

Statistical systems such as these are very powerful and convenient. But a consequence of this accessibility is that people can use statistical procedures without being cognizant of their assumptions and limitations. In this regard, the following warning in given in the user's guide to SPSS (page 3):

"The wide dissemination of statistical packages such as SPSS, containing large numbers of complex statistical procedures, have, almost overnight, made these techniques available to the social science community. There is little doubt that social scientists are using them, and there is equally little doubt that in many instances statistical techniques are being utilized by both students and researchers who understand neither the assumptions of the methods nor their statistical or mathematical bases. There can also be little doubt that this situation leads to some "garbage-in, garbage-out" research. The statistical procedures in SPSS have little ability to distinguish between proper and improper applications of the statistical techniques. They are basically blind computational algorithms that apply their formulas to whatever data the user enters."

Section 3 Exercises

1. What would happen if one of the commands in the input to PS-PACK was accidentally repeated? For example, suppose the following was the beginning of the data list:

        'LIST'
        'MEAN'
        'SDEV'
        'MEAN'
        'NUMBERS'
        20
        33.74
        ...

2. What would happen if one of the commands supplied to PS-PACK was misspelled? What if the keyword 'NUMBERS' was misspelled?

3. What would happen if the count specifying the quantity of numbers on the data list for PS-PACK was inconsistent with the actual quantity of data?

4. Are there limits on the quantity or size of numbers that PS-PACK can handle that the user should be warned about? For example, what if some or all of the values are negative? Could the program handle as few as 1 value, or as many as 1000? What if all of the values given were greater than 20,000?

5. What other types of errors might be made in the data supplied to PS-PACK? In each case indicate what effect such an error would have upon the output from the program.

6. Suppose that each of the IF statements following READ, COMAND were rewritten in a form such as the following:

        IF(COMAND(1:2) .EQ. 'ME') ME = 'YES'

What effect would this revision have?

7. Suppose it was required that the optional list of values appear *after* the other results, rather than before. How would the PS-PACK program have to be changed to accomplish this?

Section 4   Translation of Natural Languages

   From the earliest days of modern computing (that is, since the 1950s) people have been intrigued with the possibility of using a computer to translate from one natural language to another. Major research efforts were undertaken to explore this possibility. Early results of this research were quite encouraging and there were soon prototype systems for "mechanical" or "automatic" translation. Those were "cold war" days so that Russian-English and English-Russian translation was the usual subject, and the work was largely funded by the defense establishment on the basis of its potential benefit to the military. Although the translations were somewhat crude, and the sample text had to be rather carefully selected, these initial results were nevertheless impressive and it was generally assumed that the task was possible -- that given computers with sufficient speed and memory capacity, and sufficient research on translation algorithms, there would eventually be practical mechanical translation.

   The economic justification of this effort was never particularly convincing, since translation is neither a large nor a well-paid industry, but the challenge was irresistible. However, despite the inherent interest in the problem and the initial successes, the early optimism about achieving a practical system soon waned. It became apparent that the task was exceedingly difficult. By the mid-1960s the forecasts of eventual success were much more cautious, and there began to appear sober analyses suggesting that, in fact, the task of high-quality mechanical translation was impossible, for all practical purposes.

   Consequently, expectations with regard to the required quality of translation have been lowered. Performance comparable to that of a fairly mediocre human translator is now considered a reasonable standard. The process is now more modestly titled "machine-aided translation" rather than completely "mechanical" translation. The computer is only expected to produce a <u>rough first draft</u> of a translation, which in many cases will require subsequent "polishing" by a skilled human translator.

There are a few places where such machine-aided translation is in actual use today. The U.S. armed forces, the Canadian government, and the European Community in Luxembourg all employ such systems on a production basis. There is even a commercial organization in Los Angeles that offers such a service to the general public. But relatively speaking, translation is not a major area of computer application today. One hears very little about it in either the technical or the popular literature.

The principal difficulty is that even mediocre translation implies a surprising amount of <u>understanding</u> of the <u>meaning</u> of the passage being translated. That is, successful translation is not just a structural or "syntactic" process, but requires substantial "semantic" analysis as well. Progress toward achieving algorithms that perform effective semantic analysis of natural language text has been so slight that there is now a general pessimism about prospects for high-quality mechanical translation. Some research is still going on, but it is now considered basic research in linguistics rather than applied research expected to soon yield an automatic translator.

So this section is basically different from the previous ones. The problems of earlier sections represented (in drastically simplified form) areas in which computers are widely and successfully employed. This section involves an area in which, somewhat surprisingly, computers are <u>not</u> widely used. We include it since it is as important to gain some understanding of the inherent limitations of computers as it is to understand their capability. The discussion begun in this section will be continued in Part III.

In effect, we can parallel the history of research in mechanical translation. We present a very simple program that satisfactorily translates some carefully selected French sentences into reasonable English equivalents. Then we show how limited the capability of this program really is, and how difficult it would be to improve it.

4.1 <u>A Simple "Word-Replacement" Translator</u>

The most obvious difference between two natural languages is their different vocabularies. Hence a first step in translating a passage from language X to language Y would be to look up each word in the X passage in an "X to Y dictionary" and substitute the equivalent Y word in the passage. Our program does simply this and nothing more.

The heart of the program is the dictionary -- implemented by a pair of matched lists. The words of the X language are given in the first list, and the equivalent words of the Y language are given in the second list. In our examples the X language happens to be French and the Y language is English, but there is nothing in the program that is peculiar to either of those langauges. The program replaces French words by an English equivalent simply because those are the word lists supplied to the dictionary in our examples. If the relative order of the data that supplies those dictionary lists were reversed, the program would translate English into French. If the content of those lists were changed the program could translate between two other languages. The names of the variables and lists in the program have been chosen assuming that it will used for French to English translation, but you understand by now that such names are arbitrary and the program would work the same if we had chosen the name "INWORD" instead of "FRWORD" for a word read in the X language input.

A French input sentence to the program is given as individual words, with the end of the sentence denoted by the special word "/END/". We could have specified the input format as sentences rather than words and used a technique such as that described in Section II.1.2 to extract individual words. However, we elected not to do so in order to keep the program shorter and simpler. (This makes it harder to prepare input for the program, but makes the program itself easier to understand.) On the other hand, the output words are composed into lines using a technique similar to that of Section II.1.1.

The algorithm for the program is the following:

    Load the French-English dictionary.
    Print preliminary titles.
    Repeat for each sentence:
        Clear the French sentence.
        Clear the English sentence.
        Repeat for each word of the input sentence:
            Read word from data list.
            Add word to the French sentence.
            Find the word in the French-English dictionary.
            Add the English equivalent word to the English
                sentence.
        Print French and English sentences with titles.
    Print closing message.

The dictionary consists of the two lists VOCAB(30) and TRANS(30). The French words are loaded into VOCAB and the matching English equivalents are loaded into TRANS in matching order. That is, for any value of subscript I, TRANS(I) is the English word equivalent to the French word in VOCAB(I). To translate an individual French word you must search the VOCAB list to find that word. When you have found it -- that is, determined what subscript value locates the word in VOCAB -- then that <u>same subscript value</u> specifies the English equivalent word in the TRANS list.

The program follows:

II 4.1 Word-Replacement Translator

```
      CHARACTER*100   VOCAB(30), TRANS(30)
      CHARACTER*100   FRSNT, ENGSNT
      CHARACTER*100   FRWORD
      INTEGER   WORDS, SNTNCS
      INTEGER   FRPOS, ENGPOS
      INTEGER   I, S, W
C
      READ, WORDS
      DO 10 I = 1, WORDS, 1
         READ, VOCAB(I), TRANS(I)
 10   CONTINUE
C
      PRINT, 'SYNONYM-SUBSTITUTION TRANSLATOR'
      PRINT, '   NUMBER OF WORDS IN VOCABULARY:', WORDS
      PRINT, ' '
      PRINT, ' '
C
      READ, SNTNCS
      DO 100 S = 1, SNTNCS, 1
         FRSNT = ' '
         ENGSNT = ' '
         FRPOS = 4
         ENGPOS = 4
         DO 60 W = 1, 10000, 1
            READ, FRWORD
            IF(FRWORD .EQ. '/END/') GO TO 80
            FRSNT(FRPOS:100) = FRWORD
            FRPOS = FRPOS + LENGTH(FRWORD) + 1
            DO 30 I = 1, WORDS, 1
               IF(FRWORD .NE. VOCAB(I)) GO TO 30
                  ENGSNT(ENGPOS:100) = TRANS(I)
                  ENGSNT = ENGPOS + LENGTH(TRANS(I)) + 1
                  GO TO 60
 30         CONTINUE
            ENGSNT(ENGPOS:ENGPOS) = '*'
            ENGSNT(ENGPOS+1:100) = FRWORD
            ENGPOS = ENGPOS + LENGTH(FRWORD) + 2
 60      CONTINUE
 80      PRINT, 'INPUT SENTENCE:'
         PRINT, FRSNT
         PRINT, ' '
         PRINT, 'TRANSLATED SENTENCE:'
         PRINT, ENGSNT
100   CONTINUE
      PRINT, 'END OF TRANSLATION'
      STOP
      END
```

As an example of the use of this program, suppose we want it to translate the following sentences:

II 4.1 Word-Replacement Translator   175

"Marie apprend la lecon."

"Il lance la balle."

"Le grand bateau est surcharge'."

The corresponding input to the program would be the following:

```
*DATA
 16
 'GRAND'
 'LARGE'
 'BATEAU'
 'BOAT'
 'SURCHARGE'''
 'OVERLOADED'
 'MARIE'
 'MARIE'
 'APPREND'
 'LEARNS'
 'LECON'
 'LESSON'
 'LANCE'
 'THROWS'
 'BALLE'
 'BALL'
 'ME'
 'TO ME'
 'LA'
 'THE'
 'LE'
 'THE'
 'IL'
 'HE'
 'EST'
 'IS'
 'BLEU'
 'BLUE'
 3
 'MARIE'
 'APPREND'
 'LA'
 'LECON'
 '/END/'
 'IL'
 'LANCE'
 'LA'
 'BALLE'
 '/END/'
 'LE'
 'GRAND'
 'BATEAU'
 'EST'
 'SURCHARGE'''
 '/END/'
```

Note that the vocabulary list can be in any order -- it does not have to follow the sentence order. The vocabulary can also include extraneous words that are not needed for the translation of the sentences that follow.

The result of executing the program upon the data given above is the following printed output:

```
SYNONYM-SUBSTITUTION TRANSLATOR
   NUMBER OF WORDS IN VOCABULARY:           14


INPUT SENTENCE:
   MARIE APPREND LA LECON

TRANSLATED SENTENCE:
   MARIE LEARNS THE LESSON


INPUT SENTENCE:
   IL LANCE LA BALLE

TRANSLATED SENTENCE:
   HE THROWS THE BALL


INPUT SENTENCE:
   LE GRAND BATEAU EST SURCHARGE'

TRANSLATED SENTENCE:
   THE LARGE BOAT IS OVERLOADED


END OF TRANSLATION
```

These are, in fact, plausible translations, and the performance of this simple program may at this point be deceptively encouraging.

4.2 Obstacles to Improved Translation

Clearly, the sentences in the example above were carefully chosen so that the French word order is identical to the normal English word order -- so that simple replacement of the French words by their English equivalent is all that is required. However, as any veteran of an introductory French course is sadly aware, that convenient similarity of word order does not hold throughout the language. For example, suppose the following French sentences were to be translated:

"Le bateau bleu est surcharge'."

"Il me lance la balle."

The translation program would produce the following output:

```
SYNONYM-SUBSTITUTION TRANSLATOR
   NUMBER OF WORDS IN VOCABULARY:        14


INPUT SENTENCE:
   LE BATEAU BLEU EST SURCHARGE'

TRANSLATED SENTENCE:
   THE BOAT BLUE IS OVERLOADED


INPUT SENTENCE:
   IL ME LANCE LA BALLE

TRANSLATED SENTENCE:
   HE TO ME THROWS THE BALL


END OF TRANSLATION
```

Although in some cases such translations might be understandable in spite of the improper word order in English, they are not very good, and it would seem that we ought to be able to do better.

The problem of word order in the first example above arises in the peculiarity that certain French adjectives _follow_ the noun, whereas most of them precede the noun. It would certainly be simple enough to include this information in the dictionary. For example, there could be another list called POSITION, containing word order information. Perhaps if POSITION(I) equals 1 then VOCAB(I) is one of those French adjectives that follows its noun, so the program would know that the English word order would have to be different. But determining the proper English word order would not be easy, since in general it could be difficult to identify the correct noun to associate with the adjective in question. Moreover this is obviously just the simplest aspect of the word order question. The word order problem of the second example is even less easily remedied, and this is obviously just the beginning.

A more difficult question concerns words with multiple meanings. When two words in the X language translate to the same word in the Y language, there is no problem. Notice in the data list given above both "le" and "la" translate to "the". But when one word in the X language has several meanings, and hence could be translated into any one of several different words in the Y language, then there is a definite problem. For example, consider the pair of French sentences:

"Il marche vers Cannes."

"La radio marche."

With the addition of several new words to its vocabulary, our translation program would produce the following translations:

HE WALKS TO CANNES

THE RADIO WALKS

It would take a very sophisticated program to be able to choose between "walks" and "works" as alternative meanings for "marche", based upon general context or upon the nature of the subject of the sentence. That is, the program must somehow "know" that radios do not ordinarily walk, so that "walks" is an unlikely translation of "marche".

A classic illustration of the problem of multiple meanings that confronts a translation system is the English sentence:

"Time flies like an arrow."

One could imagine a mechanical translator that would produce an instruction to measure the flight velocity of certain insects, in a manner similar to what might be performed by an arrow. In fact, it is difficult to imagine a translation system sophisticated enough to know that arrows are not generally used as time-measuring instruments, hence this is an unlikely translation. There is also an apocryphal tale of a translation system that rendered the sentence:

"The spirit is willing, but the flesh is weak."

into the equivalent of:

"The liquor is strong, but the meat is rotten."

There are many other problems as well. For example, consider the complication of _idioms_ -- words which in combination assume a special meaning. For example, consider the following French sentences:

"Il jette un coup d' oeil par la fenetre."

"Melez vous de vos oignons."

"Il vient de sortir."

With suitable additions to its vocabulary list our translation program would produce something like the following:

HE THROWS A BLOW OF EYES BY THE WINDOW

MIX YOU OF YOUR ONIONS

HE COMES OF TO EXIT

The following would probably be considered more reasonable translations, but it would take a considerably more complicated program to produce such translations:

"He glanced out the window."

"Mind your own business."

"He just left."

The conclusion is that natural language translation is a very complicated process -- one that may never be performed well by a computer. Then one realizes that it is a process performed very well and very easily by ordinary human beings -- in fact, by small children. This provides an interesting example for discussion of the question of the difference between computer "intelligence" and human intelligence. One issue is whether the two are inherently different in their very nature, or are similar processes that differ only in degree. It is likely that our views on the whole question are very primitive, and will be regarded with amusement by scholars several generations hence.

Section 4 **Exercises**

1. Modify the translation program in Section 4.1 so that a period is added at the end of both the French and English sentences when they are printed in the execution output.

2. Suppose that some of the input words to the translation program of Section 4.1 might possibly include a punctuation character as their final character -- that is, the last character could be a period, a comma, a question mark, etc. This would, of course, prevent the word from being found in the search of the VOCAB list (since this search requires identical values). How could the program be modified to overcome this difficulty? That is, how could the program be modified so that a punctuation mark as the last character is ignored in the dictionary search?

3. How might the translation program of Section 4.1 be modified to provide for the situation that certain French adjectives ("bleu", for example) always follow their nouns, whereas their translated equivalent should precede the noun? (One possibility is suggested in Section 4.2.)

4. What action does the translation program of Section 4.1 take if it is unable to find a word to be translated in the VOCAB list?

5. Consider the possibility of translating from one <u>programming</u> langauge to another. For example, suppose there was a programming language that differed from FORTRAN only in the following respects:

    The word FLOAT is used instead of REAL.

    The word PUT is used instead of PRINT.

    The word FOR is used instead of DO.

How could a translation program similar to the one shown in Section 4.1 be used to translate a <u>program</u> written in FORTRAN to a program written in this new language?

6. How could the translation program of Section 4.1 be modified so that words that are identical in the two languages (such as "Marie" in the example) do not have to be entered in the dictionary.

Section 5 Matching and Selection

   Previous examples have illustrated the computer's power both as a calculator and as a text-processor. However, in reality the type of application that occupies the majority of computers is quite different from these. This dominant type of application primarily exploits the computer's <u>storage</u> capacity. The machine is used to store large quantities of carefully-organized information, and programs are written to <u>selectively retrieve</u> portions of that information. This type of application is introduced in this section, and discussed further in Section 7, and again in Part III.

5.1 <u>The PYS Retrieval System</u>

   We will illustrate this type of application by presenting a storage-retrieval system for a hypothetical business called "Poet's Yacht Sales" -- a broker for used sailboats. Most sales of used sailboats (at least of the larger sizes) are handled through such brokers, who do not own the boats or keep them on the premises (as in the case of used automobiles), but who act as agents for the owners (more like the sale of private homes). A broker maintains a file of descriptions of boats available for sale. A prospective buyer describes his requirements or preferences, and the broker selects candidate boats from the file to match these requirements. For a large brokerage office the file can be of sufficient size that an accurate search by manual methods is a non-trivial task, so the use of a computer is an attractive possibility. Several yacht brokers are already using such a system, but it has not yet become commonplace in this particular industry. Real estate brokers, who operate in an essentially similar manner, are also beginning to use such systems.

   Our sample retrieval system is simplified in two key respects compared to what would actually be required for a practical system. First, we have reduced the number of attributes that constitute the description of an available boat. We consider only the <u>builder</u>, the <u>rig</u>, the overall <u>length</u>, the <u>year</u> built, and the asking <u>price</u>. Our description also includes a "file number" -- presumably a reference to an ordinary file folder containing more complete information and photographs of the boat. In a practical version of such a system, the computer should also store other key dimensions of the boat such as its displacement (weight), sail area, draft (depth), number of bunks, etc. It should also include information on hull material (fiberglass, wood, aluminum), engine type and size, and the types of sails included. But for our purposes a more complete description of the boat would just make the program larger and harder to understand.

The second type of simplification in our program is with respect to the <u>types of query</u> that can be addressed to the system. In the form shown below, our program only permits two types of queries:

<u>Query type 1</u>: Find all boats of a particular model, identified by the name of the builder and the overall length. For example, "find all Hinckley 35s" in the file.

<u>Query type 2</u>: Find all boats with a certain type of rig, within a certain length range. For example, "find all yawls between 35 and 37 feet overall".

There are many other ways in which a client might express his requirements, and to be useful the retrieval system would have to accomodate most of the usual types of queries. We have limited our system to these two types just to keep the program tolerably short. But you will observe that each type of query represents a separate section of the program, and it should be obvious how additional types of queries could be programmed, and where the additional statements would be inserted in the program.

The overall strategy of this program is a little like that of the translation program of Section 4.1. That is, the first stage is to <u>load the file</u> (corresponding to the two dictionary lists); the second stage is to <u>process the queries</u> (corresponding to the sentences to be translated). The initial loading phase is straightforward and should require no special explanation. Processing of the queries is a little less obvious.

The algorithm for processing the queries is the following:

    Repeat for each query:
        Read type of query from data.
        Depending on type, select query routine:
            Routine for type Q1 query.
            Routine for type Q2 query.
                (place for additional query types)
        Print list of yachts selected.

II 5.1 A Retrieval System

The program could have been written so that each query routine would have been self-contained and printed its own list. But the statements to print the list would have been the same for each different type of query -- so this strategy would have involved the duplication of these list-printing statements for each type of query. To avoid this duplication a technique is employed here whereby each query simply "marks" the yachts it selects (by setting a value 1 in a list called SELECT). Then there is a single printing routine, common to all the queries, that prints information for the yachts marked by the query. Note that the printing routine must also "clear the marks" from the file (by resetting the value of SELECT to 0) to prepare for processing of the next query.

The program for the PYS Retrieval System is given below:

```
      CHARACTER*100  BUILD(25), RIG(25)
      INTEGER   FILNBR(25), LENGTH(25), YEAR(25)
      INTEGER   PRICE(25), SELECT(25)
      INTEGER   FILSIZ
      CHARACTER*100  QTYPE, QBUILD, QRIG
      INTEGER   QLEN, QLLEN, QULEN
      INTEGER   I, Q
C
      READ, FILSIZ
      DO 10 I = 1, FILSIZ, 1
         READ, FILNBR(I), BUILD(I), LENGTH(I),
     $        RIG(I), YEAR(I), PRICE(I)
         SELECT(I) = 0
   10 CONTINUE
      PRINT, ' PYS RETRIEVAL SYSTEM'
      PRINT, '    NUMBER OF YACHTS ON FILE:', FILSIZ
      PRINT, ' '
      PRINT, 'SELECTED YACHTS ARE DESCRIBED AS FOLLOWS:'
      PRINT, '    FILE NUMBER, BUILDER'
      PRINT, '    LENGTH, RIG'
      PRINT, '    YEAR BUILT, ASKING PRICE'
      PRINT, ' '
      PRINT, ' '
C
      DO 400 Q = 1, 10000, 1
         READ, QTYPE
      IF(QTYPE .EQ. 'QE') GO TO 500
         PRINT, 'QUERY:'
C
         IF(QTYPE .NE. 'Q1') GO TO 100
            READ, QBUILD, QLEN
            PRINT, '   Q1: SEARCH FOR SPECIFIC MODEL'
            PRINT, '       ', QLEN, QBUILD
            PRINT, ' '
            DO 50 I = 1, FILSIZ, 1
               IF(BUILD(I) .NE. QBUILD) GO TO 50
                  IF(LENGTH(I) .EQ. QLEN) SELECT(I) = 1
   50       CONTINUE
```

```
              GO TO 200
C
  100    IF(QTYPE .NE. 'Q2') GO TO 180
              READ, QRIG, QLLEN, QULEN
              PRINT, '   Q2: SPECIFY RIG WITH MINIMUM',
     $              'AND MAXIMUM LENGTH'
              PRINT, QLLEN, 'TO', QULEN, QRIG
              PRINT, ' '
              DO 150 I = 1, FILSIZ, 1
                 IF(QRIG .NE. RIG(I)) GO TO 150
                    IF(QLLEN .GT. LENGTH(I)) GO TO 150
                       IF(QULEN .GE. LENGTH(I))SELECT(I)=1
  150         CONTINUE
              GO TO 200
C
  180    PRINT, 'IMPROPER QUERY:', QTYPE
         PRINT, ' '
         GO TO 400
C
  200    PRINT, '   SUITABLE YACHTS ON FILE:'
         DO 300 I = 1, FILSIZ, 1
            IF(SELECT(I) .EQ. 0) GO TO 300
               PRINT, '      ', FILNBR(I), BUILD(I)
               PRINT, '      ', LENGTH(I), RIG(I)
               PRINT, '      ', YEAR(I), PRICE(I)
               PRINT, ' '
               SELECT(I) = 0
  300       CONTINUE
         PRINT, ' '
         PRINT, ' '
C
  400    CONTINUE
C
  500    PRINT, ' '
         PRINT, 'END OF QUERIES'
         STOP
         END
```

An example of the use of this program, in which five different queries are processed, is shown below:

II 5.1 A Retrieval System

```
PYS RETRIEVAL SYSTEM
   NUMBER OF YACHTS ON FILE:        12

SELECTED YACHTS ARE DESCRIBED AS FOLLOWS:
   FILE NUMBER, BUILDER
   LENGTH, RIG
   YEAR BUILT, ASKING PRICE


QUERY:
   Q1: SEARCH FOR SPECIFIC MODEL
            35 C & C

   SUITABLE YACHTS ON FILE:
            505 C & C
             35 SLOOP
            1970         33000

                337 C & C
                 35 SLOOP
                1972         37000



QUERY:
   Q2: SPECIFY RIG WITH MINIMUM AND MAXIMUM LENGTH
            35 TO          37 YAWL

   SUITABLE YACHTS ON FILE:
                511 HINCKLEY
                 35 YAWL
                1967         38000

                490 ALBERG
                 35 YAWL
                1966         28000

                373 PALMER JOHNSON
                 35 YAWL
                1971         38000
```

```
QUERY:
  Q2: SPECIFY RIG WITH MINIMUM AND MAXIMUM LENGTH
       30 TO            50 SLOOP

  SUITABLE YACHTS ON FILE:
            505 C & C
             35 SLOOP
           1970           33000

            337 C & C
             35 SLOOP
           1972           37000

            621 GULFSTAR
             37 SLOOP
           1976           60000

            521 PEARSON
             30 SLOOP
           1974           34000

            419 GULFSTAR
             40 SLOOP
           1976           85000

            403 PALMER JOHNSON
             47 SLOOP
           1973          140000

            289 C & C
             39 SLOOP
           1972           60000


QUERY:
  Q2: SPECIFY RIG WITH MINIMUM AND MAXIMUM LENGTH
       10 TO           100 KETCH

  SUITABLE YACHTS ON FILE:
            719 C & C
             36 KETCH
           1969           33500

            972 MORGAN
             41 KETCH
           1973           55000


END OF QUERIES
```

5.2 Limitations on Types of Queries

As mentioned above, additional types of queries could easily be added to this program. For example, consider the following possibilities for additional query types:

> Query type 3: Find all boats whose length is greater than a specified minimum, and whose price is less than a specified maximum. For example, "find all boats of 35 feet or more that cost less than $30,000".
>
> Query type 4: Find the oldest boat in the file.
>
> Query type 5: Find the least expensive boat by a given builder. For example, "find the cheapest available boat by Palmer Johnson".

Each of these types of queries, and many others like them, could be easily programmed and included in the system. In each case, the program section would be similar to the two query sections included in the program given above. That is, there would be a loop to examine each boat in the file, and the body of the loop would be a test that compared certain attributes of the candidate boat to values given in the query (or to values associated with the most appropriate boat selected so far).

But now consider some other types of queries:

> Query type 6: Which boat in the file is the best bargain?
>
> Query type 7: Which boat in the file is the fastest?
>
> Query type 8: Find all boats in the file capable of extended offshore cruising -- that is, all boats that are exceptionally "seaworthy".

These three types of queries are fundamentally different from the previous types. The earlier queries based selection of a yacht upon a simple comparison against attribute values given explicitly in the file. But types 6, 7 and 8 base selection upon some property not given directly in the file. The question is whether the required property can be derived from attributes given in the file. While that might be possible, the examples above were chosen deliberately to make it extremely difficult. That is, neither speed, seaworthiness, nor price-attractiveness is readily computed from measurable attributes of a yacht.

Consider speed, for example. Yacht design has made significant progress in the last decade, and computers are used extensively in the design process, but the overall process is still very much of an art. Sparkman-Stephens 12-meter yachts ("Columbia", "Intrepid", "Courageous", "Enterprise") are fast because Olin Stephens is a remarkable designer, and not because

S & S has a better computer program. While a computer is used at various stages in design (and even in sail design) no racing yacht is "computer designed" in any reasonable sense of the word -- no matter what the newspaper may have reported about the Swedish challenger for the America's Cup. (Consequently, the elimination of "Sverige" does not prove that "men can still design faster boats than computers can".) There simply would be no agreement among yacht designers as to precisely what algorithm should be used to predict boat speed from measurable dimensions of the boat. If there is <u>no algorithm</u>, there can be <u>no program</u>.

There is even less agreement as to how to measure seaworthiness, and obviously, what constitutes a "bargain" in a boat is highly subjective. What is a bargain to one client, with peculiar tastes and objectives, might be unacceptable at any price to a second client. So all three of these queries suffer from essentially the same fatal shortcoming -- there is no generally-accepted algorithm upon which a program could be based.

But suppose some broker was not deterred by our remarks about the state-of-the-art of yacht design, and hired a programmer to write a program for the query "find the fastest yacht". Say that this programmer did a little weekend work in the library (or at the local yacht club bar) and concluded that a reasonable estimate of boat speed could be given by the formula:

$$\text{SPEED} = 1.4 * \text{SQRT}(\text{LWL}) + .2 * \text{SQRT}(\text{SA})$$

where LWL is the length of the boat (in feet) measured at the waterline, and SA is the sail area (given in square feet). Now he has an algorithm, and a program can be written -- with no more difficulty than the earlier types of queries. In fact, this formula does have some relationship to boat speed, and it would in general be able to indicate the difference between a fast boat and a floating cottage. But as a precise measure to distinguish between boats of a similar type -- it is simply laughable. So now the question becomes what the broker will do with these results. It is certainly reasonable to have the program compute this rough estimate of speed capability, and print it out along with other characteristics of the boat. As long as the user of these data keeps in mind that they are based on a very crude and approximate algorithm, then everything is fine. The computer has been used to perform a helpful clerical task. But it is not hard to imagine an over-enthusiastic salesman claiming that he has a computer that can pick the fastest yacht. There is sufficiently little public understanding of computers, and they are regarded with such awe, that such fraudulent representations are not uncommon. (The problem is obviously not peculiar to yacht brokerage.) A knowledgable yachtsman, who would leave laughing if told what the speed-predicting algorithm is, may be impressed when the same nonsense is printed by a computer. It is a common joke (?) among engineers and businessmen that if your case is a little weak, it is worthwhile having the results printed by a computer before presentation to a skeptical audience. The computer provides a certain credibility to even the most flagrant nonsense.

If this seems unlikely and exaggerated, consider the success of the "computer dating" industry. If someone announced to college students that he had a new sociological theory that allowed him to predict "compatability on a date", his reception would be dubious. But if he programs this theory, and masks its shortcomings with the mystery of a computer, these same skeptics will often pay good money for sociological quackery.

5.3 <u>Permanent Files</u>

In practical systems comparable to the retrieval system shown above the files would be of substantial size. It would be inconvenient and costly to maintain these files on punched cards and have to load them each time a query is to be processed. Fortunately this is not necessary. Files such as these can be stored more-or-less permanently on storage devices that are connected to the computer -- usually magnetic tapes or discs. Effectively the program would work like the example shown above except that the file would be copied from tape or disc, rather than from punched cards. (The file would also be copied in small sections, rather than all at once, but that is a detail beyond our immediate needs.)

We should explain why we said such files could be stored "more-or-less" permanently. Storage on tape or disc is <u>permanent</u> -- in comparison to the storage in program variables that we use in our sample programs. That means that tape or disc storage is saved from one execution of a program to another, where the value of program variables is lost after the execution of the program is completed. On the other hand, storage on tape or disc is not so permanent that information in such files cannot be changed. We would have to write special programs (called "file update programs") to read data that represents additions or changes to the file, and whose action would be to alter the information stored in the file on tape or disc. Such programs are not drastically different from the ones we have been discussing, but they would use several additional statement types (types not included in the Poet's subset) to transfer information back and forth between tape or disc and "main" memory. The program is able to read information from tape or disc storage, much as our sample programs read information from an external data list. Programs can also put information on tape or disc, much as our sample programs "put" information on the printer.

Section 5 _Exercises_

1. Write a program for a type 4 query: "Find the oldest boat in the file". Write this in such a way that it can be _inserted_ into the retrieval program given in Section 5.1.

2. Write a program for a type 5 query" "Find the cheapest boat by builder -----". Write this so it can be inserted in the retrieval program given in Section 5.1.

3. Write a retrieval program for a type 3 query: "Find all boats whose length is greater than -----, and whose price is less than -----". Write this so it can be inserted in the retrieval program of Section 5.1.

4. Suppose a system comparable to that shown in Section 5.1 were to be designed for a broker for used autombobiles. What would be appropriate characteristics to store in the file? What would be some sample query types that the system should handle?

Section 6   Random Processes

There is an interesting class of computer programs that involve random processes. In a very special and limited sense, these programs are <u>unpredictable</u> -- they surprise even their authors. There is nothing mysterious about these programs; the computer is still executing a sequence of statements, just as in all the examples we have seen previously, but the control of execution is influenced by the value of certain "random numbers".

To illustrate the basic idea, consider again our original data-listing problem: read and print a data list of strings. Assume a number is given first to specify the number of strings that follow. Recall that the following program can be used:

```
          CHARACTER*100 WORD
          INTEGER COUNT, REPEAT
          READ, REPEAT
          DO 10 COUNT = 1, REPEAT, 1
              READ, WORD
              PRINT, WORD
   10     CONTINUE
          STOP
          END
```

Now suppose that you are required to decide <u>at random</u> whether or not to print each item on the list. The <u>PRINT</u> statement will have to be made conditional:

          IF(condition) PRINT, WORD

and the condition controlling this statement will have to sometimes be true, and sometimes false, at random.

Suppose you tossed a coin, once for each item on the data list. If the coin comes up "heads" the item <u>is</u> to be printed; if it comes up "tails" it <u>is not</u> to be printed. You could record the outcome of these coin tosses on cards, and interleave these data with the original word list. For example, a data list might look as follows:

```
      $ENTRY
      5
      'TAILS'
      'MELVILLE'
      'TAILS'
      'SLOCUM'
      'HEADS'
      'CHICHESTER'
      'TAILS'
      'VERNE'
      'HEADS'
      'BUCKLEY'
```

With these data, the execution output is supposed to be the following:

```
      CHICHESTER
      BUCKLEY
```

A program that will do this is the following:

```
         CHARACTER*100 WORD, TOSS
         INTEGER COUNT, REPEAT
         READ, REPEAT
         DO 10 COUNT = 1, REPEAT, 1
             READ, TOSS, WORD
             IF(TOSS .EQ. 'HEADS') PRINT, WORD
10       CONTINUE
         STOP
         END
```

This program illustrates the basic idea. The <u>results of execution depend upon the random process</u> of tossing a coin. If someone other than the author of the program tossed the coin, and provided that part of the data without showing it to the author, the author could not predict exactly what his program would do. He could not say whether or not it would print any particular word, or how many words would be printed in all. This may not seem like a very profound achievement at this point, but by using it in more complicated ways you can produce very interesting results.

To make this type of program more convenient to use, we incorporate the coin-tossing mechanism into the program, so that we do not have to physically perform the toss, and enter the results by means of the data list. The idea is exactly the same, but the random values are generated within the program by means of the RAND function, described in the next section.

6.1 The RAND Function

The RAND function is a means of generating a <u>sequence of random numbers</u>. Both the argument and result of the function are numbers. The argument gives the <u>last random number</u> obtained from the sequence; the result gives the <u>next</u> random number in the sequence. The RAND function is always used in an assignment statement, such as the following:

            RN = RAND(RN)

RN in this statement is a real variable whose value is the most recently obtained random number. This assignment statement simply replaces the last with the next value from the sequence.

These random numbers are "in the interval from 0 to 1". That is, each value in the sequence is a number greater than 0 and less than 1. To say that the numbers are "random", means that every number in this interval (0 to 1) is <u>equally likely to occur</u> at each value in the sequence. That is, if you are told what the 17th number in the sequence is, this does not help you predict what the 18th number will be.

Strictly speaking, the RAND function cannot generate truly random numbers, because the RAND function is itself a program, and if you knew the algorithm behind this program you could indeed predict the 18th value from the 17th. But it is a very clever algorithm, that disguises its pattern very successfully. The sequences generated by such functions have been tested by statisticians, and found to have remarkably good statistical properties -- essentially what would be expected of true random numbers. Technically, these numbers ought to be called "pseudo-random numbers", but they are random enough for most computational purposes.

The first value in a sequence of random numbers is called the "seed". That is, the first time the RAND function is executed in a program, the value of its argument is the <u>seed of that particular sequence</u>. The seed is generally supplied from the data list. Rules for selecting seeds are the following:

   A seed should be a six digit number greater than .1 and less
   than 1, with no zeros.

That is, all of the following are reasonable seeds:

        .123456   .561278   .975321   .123321

In general, each <u>different seed</u> generates a <u>different sequence</u> of random numbers. For example, a program to generate the first ten numbers from the sequence for each of these seeds is shown below:

II 6.1 The RAND Function

```
      REAL   RN, SEED
      INTEGER  COUNT, NUMBER
      DO 20 COUNT = 1, 4, 1
         READ, SEED
         PRINT, ' '
         PRINT, SEED
         RN = SEED
         DO 10 NUMBER = 1, 10, 1
            RN = RAND(RN)
            PRINT, RN
 10      CONTINUE
 20   CONTINUE
      STOP
      END
```

The results shown below are produced when the four seeds .123456, .561278, .975321 and .123321 are presented to this program: (The results have been arranged in four columns instead of one.)

.123456	.561278	.975321	.123321
.407153	.801258	.761007	.821223
.943817	.368766	.757881	.842461
.868722	.133551	.958325	.172872
.495262	.870266	.436659	.304176
.709470	.475805	.403209	.421422
.493510	.296239	.521757	.249474
.424262	.694384	.317215	.349965
.102978	.586802	.998920	.543897
.474360	.163983	.835832	.566305
.021362	.010241	.019995	.866228

Note that if you were to run this program over again, with the same seeds as data, you would get <u>exactly the same results</u>. That is, the process is effectively random in producing the next number in the sequence, but it is <u>absolutely reproducible</u> -- the same seed will always generate the same sequence.

To illustrate the use of the RAND function, we will rewrite the random list-writing program from the last section. Say that a random number less than .5 represents a "head" -- meaning that the word should be printed. A random number greater than or equal to .5 represents a "tail", so the word should not be printed. The data list now would include a number to serve as the "seed" for the internal random number generator (rather than including the results of an external random process). For example, the data list might be the following:

```
      $ENTRY
       5
       .654321
       'MELVILLE'
       'SLOCUM'
       'CHICHESTER'
       'VERNE'
```

        'BUCKLEY'

The program to process these data would be the following:

        CHARACTER*100 WORD
        INTEGER COUNT, REPEAT
        REAL   SEED, RNBR
        READ, REPEAT, SEED
        RNBR = RAND(SEED)
        DO 10 COUNT = 1, REPEAT, 1
           READ, WORD
           RNBR = RAND(RNBR)
           IF(RNBR .LT. 0.5) PRINT, WORD
 10   CONTINUE
        STOP
        END

With the data list shown above -- that is, with .654321 as the seed -- the resulting execution output would be:

        MELVILLE
        SLOCUM
        VERNE
        BUCKLEY

If a different seed were supplied, say .123456, the results would be:

        CHICHESTER
        BUCKLEY

   What is interesting about this very simple program is that <u>you cannot tell</u>, just by studying the program and the data, <u>what the result of execution will be</u>. We had to actually run this program with the different seeds indicated, in order to shown you what the output would be. (In the second case, since we had already run a previous program to list the numbers generated by this particular seed -- that is, .123456, as shown above -- we could have determined the results by using that list.)

   The RAND function we have been using is not included in FORTRAN, but can be used by including the following after the END statement of any program using it:

```
      REAL FUNCTION RAND(X)
      REAL X
      INTEGER IX
      IX = X * 16777216.
      IX = IX * 452807053
      IF(IX .LT.,0) IX = IX + 2147483647 + 1
      RAND = IX
      RAND = RAND * .456613E-9
      RETURN
      END
```

Note that only one copy of the function is included in the job deck. If more than one different function is included, (e.g. RAND, LENGTH) the order of appearence is unimportant.

6.1.1 The FLOAT Built-in Function

Another built-in function that is useful is the FLOAT function.

The purpose of FLOAT is to convert a value of type INTEGER to type REAL. (REAL variables are said to have a floating decimal point, hence the name FLOAT).

When FORTRAN does arithmetic on values of the type INTEGER, any digits to the right of the decimal point are lost. For example:

      3/2   is 1
      9/10   IS 0

On the other hand, using FLOAT:

      FLOAT(3)/FLOAT(2) is 1.5
      FLOAT(9)/FLOAT(10) is .9

as would be "expected".

6.2 Coin-Tossing Experiments

We used the tossing of a coin to explain the role and purpose of the RAND built-in function -- now we will consider a program whose purpose is to <u>simulate the tossing of a coin</u>. In particular, the program will simulate a series of experiments, in each of which a coin is tossed a certain number of times, and the number of occurrences of "heads" is observed. The user of this program must supply four control values (which are the only data read by the program):

1. the number of experiments to be performed

II 6.2 Coin-Tossing Experiments

2. the number of coin tosses in each experiment

3. the probability that each individual toss yields a "head"

4. the seed for the random number sequence.

An individual toss of the coin is represented by obtaining the next random number from the RAND function. This value is compared to the specified probability for a head, as given in the data. (This need not necessarily be a "fair" coin, with a probability of .5 for a head.) If the random number is less than this specified probability, the outcome is considered a head; otherwise, it is considered a tail. The program statements to perform a single toss and determine the outcome are simply:

```
RN = RAND(RN)
IF(RN .LT. PROBHEAD) toss results in a head
```

This segment is the heart of the program; all of the rest of the program simply controls the number of times this segment is executed, and keeps tracks of the results of its execution.

A complete algorithm for the problem is the following:

```
Program for coin-tossing experiments:
   Create variables.
   Read control values.
   Print titles and control values.
   Repeat for each experiment:
      Repeat for each toss in an experiment:
         Simulate toss of coin.
         Record outcome of toss.
      Report result of experiment.
   Summarize overall results.
   Report overall results.
```

A program obtained by translating this algorithm into FORTRAN is the following:

```
      INTEGER  NBREXP, EXPNBR
      INTEGER  COUNT, EXPLGT
      INTEGER  HEADCT, CUMCNT, TOSSES
      REAL  CUMPRP, PRHEAD, PROP
      REAL  SEED, RN
      READ, NBREXP, EXPLGT, PRHEAD, SEED
C
      PRINT, 'COIN TOSSING EXPERIMENT'
      PRINT, ' '
      PRINT, 'NUMBER OF EXPERIMENTS:', NBREXP
      PRINT, 'LENGTH OF EXPERIMENT:', EXPLGT
      PRINT, 'PROBABILITY OF A HEAD:', PRHEAD
      PRINT, 'SEED OF R.N. SEQUENCE:', SEED
      PRINT, ' '
C
      CUMCNT = 0
      RN = RAND(SEED)
C
      DO 20 EXPNBR = 1, NBREXP, 1
         HEADCT = 0
         DO 10 COUNT = 1, EXPLGT, 1
            RN = RAND(RN)
            IF(RN .LT. PRHEAD) HEADCT = HEADCT+1
10       CONTINUE
         PRINT, 'EXPERIMENT NUMBER:', EXPNBR
         PRINT, ' ', 'NUMBER OF HEADS:', HEADCT
         PROP = FLOAT(HEADCT)/FLOAT(EXPLGT)
         PRINT, ' ', 'PROPORTION OF HEADS:', PROP
         CUMCNT = CUMCNT + HEADCT
20    CONTINUE
C
      TOSSES = NBREXP * EXPLGT
      CUMPRP = FLOAT(CUMCNT)/FLOAT(TOSSES)
      PRINT, ' '
      PRINT, 'CUMULATIVE RESULTS:'
      PRINT, CUMCNT, 'HEADS IN', TOSSES, 'TOSSES'
      PRINT, 'PROPORTION OF HEADS IS:', CUMPRP
      STOP
      END
```

The results of three different executions of this program are shown below. The data lists for each execution are not shown separately, since the program prints the data values at the head of the execution output. For each of these three executions the data were exactly the same except for the seed of the random number sequence. These differences in results are wholly due to the differences in the random numbers produced from the different seeds.

```
COIN TOSSING EXPERIMENT

NUMBER OF EXPERIMENTS:            4
LENGTH OF EXPERIMENT:           250
PROBABILITY OF A HEAD:            0.50000000
SEED OF R.N. SEQUENCE:            0.65432000

EXPERIMENT NUMBER:                1
  NUMBER OF HEADS:              112
  PROPORTION OF HEADS:              0.44799990
EXPERIMENT NUMBER:                2
  NUMBER OF HEADS:              129
  PROPORTION OF HEADS:              0.51599990
EXPERIMENT NUMBER:                3
  NUMBER OF HEADS:              139
  PROPORTION OF HEADS:              0.55599990
EXPERIMENT NUMBER:                4
  NUMBER OF HEADS:              131
  PROPORTION OF HEADS:              0.52399990

CUMULATIVE RESULTS:
        511 HEADS IN       1000 TOSSES
PROPORTION OF HEADS IS:             0.51099990
```

```
COIN TOSSING EXPERIMENT

NUMBER OF EXPERIMENTS:            4
LENGTH OF EXPERIMENT:           250
PROBABILITY OF A HEAD:            0.50000000
SEED OF R.N. SEQUENCE:            0.12378790

EXPERIMENT NUMBER:                1
  NUMBER OF HEADS:              125
  PROPORTION OF HEADS:              0.50000000
EXPERIMENT NUMBER:                2
  NUMBER OF HEADS:              120
  PROPORTION OF HEADS:              0.47999990
EXPERIMENT NUMBER:                3
  NUMBER OF HEADS:              129
  PROPORTION OF HEADS:              0.51599990
EXPERIMENT NUMBER:                4
  NUMBER OF HEADS:              127
  PROPORTION OF HEADS:              0.50799990

CUMULATIVE RESULTS:
        501 HEADS IN       1000 TOSSES
PROPORTION OF HEADS IS:             0.50099990
```

```
COIN TOSSING EXPERIMENT

NUMBER OF EXPERIMENTS:            4
LENGTH OF EXPERIMENT:           250
PROBABILITY OF A HEAD:            0.50000000
SEED OF R.N. SEQUENCE:            0.39485690

EXPERIMENT NUMBER:                1
  NUMBER OF HEADS:              107
  PROPORTION OF HEADS:            0.42799990
EXPERIMENT NUMBER:                2
  NUMBER OF HEADS:              120
  PROPORTION OF HEADS:            0.47999990
EXPERIMENT NUMBER:                3
  NUMBER OF HEADS:              121
  PROPORTION OF HEADS:            0.48399990
EXPERIMENT NUMBER:                4
  NUMBER OF HEADS:              139
  PROPORTION OF HEADS:            0.55599990

CUMULATIVE RESULTS:
        487 HEADS IN           1000 TOSSES
PROPORTION OF HEADS IS:           0.48699990
```

6.2.1 Run-Lengths in a Coin-Tossing Experiment

Another interesting statistic that could be obtained from an experiment such as this would be the maximum "run" of heads -- that is, in each experiment, the greatest number of times that heads occurred in succession. To compute this, a run begins each time a head follows a tail, and continues as long as consecutive heads are observed. The program becomes somewhat more complex since it must keep track of the outcome of the previous toss, the length of the current run, and the maximum run so far. However, this is essentially all at the detail level -- the general structure of the program remains the same. The program follows:

```
      INTEGER   NBREXP, EXPNBR
      INTEGER   COUNT, EXPLGT
      INTEGER   HEADCT, CUMCNT, TOSSES
      REAL   CUMPRP
      REAL   PRHEAD, PROP
      REAL   SEED, RN
      INTEGER   RUN, MAXRUN, ALLMAX
      CHARACTER*100   LAST
C
      READ, NBREXP, EXPLGT, PRHEAD, SEED
      PRINT, 'COIN TOSSING EXPERIMENTS'
```

```
       PRINT, ' '
       PRINT, 'NUMBER OF EXPERIMENTS:', NBREXP
       PRINT, 'LENGTH OF EXPERIMENTS:', EXPLGT
       PRINT, 'PROBABILITY OF HEADS:', PRHEAD
       PRINT, 'SEED OF R.N. SEQUENCE:', SEED
       PRINT, ' '
       CUMCNT = 0
       ALLMAX = 0
       RN = RAND(SEED)
C
C   RUN THE REQUESTED EXPERIMENTS
       DO 30 EXPNBR = 1, NBREXP, 1
           LAST = 'TAIL'
           RUN = 0
           MAXRUN = 0
           HEADCT = 0
           DO 20 COUNT = 1, EXPLGT, 1
               RN = RAND(RN)
               IF(RN .GT. PRHEAD) GO TO 10
                   HEADCT = HEADCT + 1
                   RUN = RUN + 1
                   IF(RUN .GT. MAXRUN) MAXRUN = RUN
                   LAST = 'HEAD'
                   GO TO 20
  10           LAST = 'TAIL'
               RUN = 0
  20       CONTINUE
C
C      PRINT THE RESULTS OF EXPERIMENT
           PRINT, 'EXPERIMENT NBR:', EXPNBR
           PRINT, ' ', 'NUMBER OF HEADS:', HEADCT
           PROP = FLOAT(HEADCT)/FLOAT(EXPLGT)
           PRINT, ' ', 'PROPORTION OF HEADS:', PROP
           PRINT, ' ', 'MAXIMUM RUN OF HEADS:', MAXRUN
           CUMCNT = CUMCNT + HEADCT
           IF(MAXRUN .GT. ALLMAX) ALLMAX = MAXRUN
  30   CONTINUE
C
C   CALCULATE AND PRINT SUMMARY STATISTICS
       TOSSES = NBREXP * EXPLGT
       CUMPRP = FLOAT(CUMCNT)/FLOAT(TOSSES)
       PRINT, ' '
       PRINT, 'CUMULATIVE RESULTS:'
       PRINT, CUMCNT, 'HEADS IN', TOSSES, 'TOSSES'
       PRINT, 'PROPORTION OF HEADS IS:', CUMPRP
       PRINT, 'LONGEST RUN OF HEADS OBSERVED:', ALLMAX
       STOP
       END
```

The results of three different executions of this program are shown below. As in the previous version, the program prints the data values at the head of the output. Note that in this case different probabilities of tossing a head were used in the different runs.

```
COIN TOSSING EXPERIMENTS

   NUMBER OF EXPERIMENTS:           4
   LENGTH OF EXPERIMENTS:         250
   PROBABILITY OF HEADS:           0.50000000
   SEED OF R.N. SEQUENCE:          0.45678800

   EXPERIMENT NBR:           1
      NUMBER OF HEADS:     116
      PROPORTION OF HEADS:            0.46399990
      MAXIMUM RUN OF HEADS:           7
   EXPERIMENT NBR:           2
      NUMBER OF HEADS:     117
      PROPORTION OF HEADS:            0.46799990
      MAXIMUM RUN OF HEADS:           5
   EXPERIMENT NBR:           3
      NUMBER OF HEADS:     120
      PROPORTION OF HEADS:            0.47999990
      MAXIMUM RUN OF HEADS:           8
   EXPERIMENT NBR:           4
      NUMBER OF HEADS:     121
      PROPORTION OF HEADS:            0.48399990
      MAXIMUM RUN OF HEADS:           7

   CUMULATIVE RESULTS:
         474 HEADS IN        1000 TOSSES
   PROPORTION OF HEADS IS:            0.47399990
   LONGEST RUN OF HEADS OBSERVED:            8
```

```
COIN TOSSING EXPERIMENTS

   NUMBER OF EXPERIMENTS:           4
   LENGTH OF EXPERIMENTS:         250
   PROBABILITY OF HEADS:           0.75000000
   SEED OF R.N. SEQUENCE:          0.98321490

   EXPERIMENT NBR:           1
      NUMBER OF HEADS:     193
      PROPORTION OF HEADS:            0.77199990
      MAXIMUM RUN OF HEADS:          20
   EXPERIMENT NBR:           2
      NUMBER OF HEADS:     194
      PROPORTION OF HEADS:            0.77599990
      MAXIMUM RUN OF HEADS:          16
   EXPERIMENT NBR:           3
      NUMBER OF HEADS:     175
      PROPORTION OF HEADS:            0.69999990
      MAXIMUM RUN OF HEADS:          20
   EXPERIMENT NBR:           4
      NUMBER OF HEADS:     182
      PROPORTION OF HEADS:            0.72799990
      MAXIMUM RUN OF HEADS:          18

   CUMULATIVE RESULTS:
         744 HEADS IN        1000 TOSSES
   PROPORTION OF HEADS IS:            0.74399990
   LONGEST RUN OF HEADS OBSERVED:           20
```

```
COIN TOSSING EXPERIMENTS

NUMBER OF EXPERIMENTS:           4
LENGTH OF EXPERIMENTS:           250
PROBABILITY OF HEADS:            0.39999900
SEED OF R.N. SEQUENCE:           0.12378790

EXPERIMENT NBR:                  1
  NUMBER OF HEADS:               104
  PROPORTION OF HEADS:           0.41599990
  MAXIMUM RUN OF HEADS:          7
EXPERIMENT NBR:                  2
  NUMBER OF HEADS:               96
  PROPORTION OF HEADS:           0.38399990
  MAXIMUM RUN OF HEADS:          4
EXPERIMENT NBR:                  3
  NUMBER OF HEADS:               105
  PROPORTION OF HEADS:           0.41999990
  MAXIMUM RUN OF HEADS:          4
EXPERIMENT NBR:                  4
  NUMBER OF HEADS:               94
  PROPORTION OF HEADS:           0.37599990
  MAXIMUM RUN OF HEADS:          5

CUMULATIVE RESULTS:
         399 HEADS IN            1000 TOSSES
PROPORTION OF HEADS IS:          0.39899990
LONGEST RUN OF HEADS OBSERVED:   7
```

6.3 A Turtle Race

A "turtle race" is a contest in which two turtles, presumably specially trained for racing, are placed in the middle of a "ring" -- that is, a circle drawn on the ground. The first turtle to sprint (or wander) across the ring at any point wins the race. Whether or not anyone really indulges in such an entertainment, it provides a good illustration of a random process. Presumably the turtles are either nearsighted, or do not precisely understand the object of the exercise, for it is well-known that they do not move purposefully from the center to the perimeter of the ring -- they are inclined to wander about until eventually one of them happens to cross the line. In any event, that is the process -- real or imaginary -- that we will attempt to simulate by a computer program.

Our program will use the RAND function to generate steps that are supposed to represent "aimless wandering" by the turtles. The program will keep track of each turtle's position in terms of map coordinates. That is, in terms of its distance (North, South, East or West) from the center of the ring. Its position will be assumed to be a distinct point -- say, the exact tip of its nose. We will assume that somehow both turtles can be placed exactly at the center of the ring at the beginning of the race. We will simplify the situation slightly by making the ring a square (just to avoid dealing with the equation for a circle), but will continue to refer to it as a ring.

The algorithm for this program is the following:

```
Simulate a turtle race:
    Create variables.
    Read control values.
    Print title and control values.
    Repeat moves until one turtle reaches ring:
        Generate random move for each turtle.
        Compute new position for each turtle.
        Print position for each turtle.
        Check position relative to ring.
    Report outcome of race.
```

A program developed from this algorithm is shown below:

```
      REAL    RINGSZ
      REAL    REDSTP, BLKSTP
      REAL    RN, SEED
      REAL    REDNS, REPEW, BLKNS, BLKEW
      REAL    NORTH, SOUTH, EAST, WEST
      INTEGER MOVE
      INTEGER WINNER
C
      READ, RINGSZ, REDSTP, BLKSTP
      IF(RINGSZ .GE. 2) GO TO 10
          PRINT, 'RING TOO SMALL'
          RINGSZ = 2
   10 NORTH = RINGSZ/2
      SOUTH = -RINGSZ/2
      EAST = RINGSZ/2
      WEST = -RINGSZ/2
      REDNS = 0
      REDEW = 0
      BLKNS = 0
      BLKEW = 0
      WINNER = 0
C
      READ, SEED
      RN = RAND(SEED)
C
      PRINT, 'A TURTLE RACE'
      PRINT, ' '
      PRINT, 'RED AND BLACK BOTH START AT 0.0'
      PRINT, 'RING IS', RINGSZ, 'ONE EACH SIDE'
      PRINT, 'RED STEP IS:', REDSTP, 'BLACK STEP IS:', BLKSTP
      PRINT, ' '
C
      DO 20 MOVE = 1, 1000, 1
C
C         CALCULATE MOVES FOR EACH TURTLE
          RN = RAND(RN)
          REDNS = REDNS + (2*(RN-.5))*REDSTP
```

II 6.3 A Turtle Race

```
            RN = RAND(RN)
            REDEW = REDEW + (2*(RN-.5))*REDSTP
            RN = RAND(RN)
            BLKNS = BLKNS + (2*(RN-.5))*BLKSTP
            RN = RAND(RN)
            BLKEW = BLKEW + (2*(RN-.5))*BLKSTP
C
            PRINT, 'MOVE NUMBER:', MOVE
            PRINT, ' ', 'RED IS AT:  ', REDNS, REDEW
            PRINT, ' ', 'BLACK IS AT:', BLKNS, BLKEW
C
C     DETERMINE WINNER
            IF(REDNS .GT. NORTH) WINNER = 3
            IF(REDNS .LT. SOUTH) WINNER = 3
            IF(REDEW .GT. EAST) WINNER = 3
            IF(REDEW .LT. WEST) WINNER = 3
            IF(BLKNS .GT. NORTH) WINNER = WINNER + 1
            IF(BLKNS .LT. SOUTH) WINNER = WINNER + 1
            IF(BLKEW .GT. EAST) WINNER = WINNER + 1
            IF(BLKEW .LT. WEST) WINNER = WINNER + 1
            IF(WINNER .GT. 0) GO TO 30
  20        CONTINUE
C
C   PRINT OUTCOME
  30        PRINT, ' '
            IF (WINNER .LE. 3) GO TO 40
            PRINT, 'RACE IS A TIE'
            GO TO 60
  40        IF(WINNER .EQ. 3) GO TO 50
            PRINT, 'THE BLACK TURTLE WINS'
            GO TO 60
  50        PRINT, 'THE RED TURTLE WINS'
  60        STOP
            END
```

The output from two different executions of this program is shown below:

```
A TURTLE RACE

RED AND BLACK BOTH START AT 0.0
RING IS          10.00000000 ONE EACH SIDE
RED STEP IS:          2.00000000 BLACK STEP IS:          2.00000000
MOVE NUMBER:          1
  RED IS AT:          -0.86545130          -1.58536600
  BLACK IS AT:         1.21057400          -1.34958200
MOVE NUMBER:          2
  RED IS AT:          -1.41589900          -2.99029400
  BLACK IS AT:         2.46629000          -1.77206000
MOVE NUMBER:          3
  RED IS AT:           0.56587310          -3.95595300
  BLACK IS AT:         2.24688800          -1.34140400
MOVE NUMBER:          4
  RED IS AT:          -1.42956100          -5.85844400
  BLACK IS AT:         3.37941800           0.57911490

THE RED TURTLE WINS
```

```
A TURTLE RACE

RED AND BLACK BOTH START AT 0.0
RING IS          10.00000000 ONE EACH SIDE
RED STEP IS:          2.00000000 BLACK STEP IS:          3.00000000
MOVE NUMBER:          1
  RED IS AT:          -1.95405100          -1.69082000
  BLACK IS AT:         1.24701600          -0.67514630
MOVE NUMBER:          2
  RED IS AT:          -2.67362700          -2.50671500
  BLACK IS AT:        -1.15519100          -2.80561200
MOVE NUMBER:          3
  RED IS AT:          -2.80280900          -3.94494200
  BLACK IS AT:        -4.14927800          -3.23495800
MOVE NUMBER:          4
  RED IS AT:          -4.67883800          -5.43988800
  BLACK IS AT:        -6.63358900          -5.19287900

RACE.IS A TIE
```

II 6.3 A Turtle Race

The turtle race program is probably simpler in overall concept than many of the previous examples, yet it is surprisingly elaborate in detail. It takes quite a few statements to initialize the race, and quite a few to perform a move for each turtle and to compare their positions to the perimeter of the ring. Moreover, there is a curious way of determining which turtle won and announcing the results. If you cannot see why it was done this way you might find a hint in Exercise 6.

6.4 Poetry Composition

The next step is almost inevitable. Having described various text-processing programs in earlier sections, and now having described a means for making random choices in a program, it is obvious that eventually we would get around to a program that choses text at random and attempts to compose something. While such programs are not eminently useful, they are a good deal of fun, and quite thought-provoking. We explore the fun here, and provoke the thoughts in Part III.

Program of this sort have been written to compose music, write stories and write various forms of poetry. Considering the title of this opus, we thought it most appropriate to exhibit a program to write a form of free verse. Our program, named POET, is long compared to previous examples, but not really more complicated. Once you understand the general manner in which it operates, it would not be too difficult for you to create a poet of your own.

The algorithm for POET, at the highest level, is the following:

```
Create variables.
Load control values and phrases.
Print title.
Repeat for required number of stanzas:
    Repeat for required number of lines:
        Repeat for each phrase:
            Select phrase.
            Add phrase to partial line.
Print closing.
```

The algorithm could be written in more detail, as follows:

```
Create variables:
    stanza controls
    line controls
    phrase controls
    line-under-construction
        last character used in line
    list of phrases
    list of phrase lengths
    random number and seed
    probability controls
Load and test control values.
Load phrases,
    compute lengths.
Initialize.
Print title.
Repeat stanza section req'd number of times:
    Repeat line section:
        Initialize line.
        Set initial line indentation.
        Repeat phrase section:
```

II 6.4 Poetry Composition

```
            Check for repetition.
            Choose next phrase.
            Add phrase to partial line.
            Check for comma.
            Check for line termination.
         Print line.
         Check for stanza termination.
   Print closing.
   Print control values.
```

There are still many details not clear at this level. For example, the punctuation given at the end of phrases is significant in that it can cause the line or the stanza to be terminated, but this isn't described in the algorithm at this level. Similarly, the list of phrases is not treated as a single homogeneous list of twenty phrases -- it is considered to be four groups of five phrases each. These groups affect the manner in which phrases are selected, but that is not described at this level. If you were writing the program, it would be worthwhile to refine the algorithm at least one more level, in order to specify how to handle these details. For purposes of reading the program, we will leave the algorithm at this level.

Another help in understanding a program is to have a precise understanding of the role of each variable. For POET, this is given by the following description:

```
    STZNBR -- the number of the current stanza
    NBRSTZ -- the number of stanzas to be generated
    LINNBR -- the number of the current line (within a stanza)
    MAXLIN -- the maximum number of lines in a stanza
    PHRCNT -- the number of the current phrase (within a line)
    PHRNBR -- the number of the current phrase
              (refers to position in the list)
    GROUP  -- the group number of PHRNBR
    PHRGRP -- number of the current phrase (within its group)
    LINE   -- the line under construction
    LSTCHR -- the last character used in LINE
    PHR(20) -- the list of user-supplied phrases
    PHRLEN(20) -- the length of the corresponding PHR
    RN     -- the current random number
    SEED   -- the user-supplied initial value of RN sequence
    PREPT  -- the probablity that a phrase is repeated
    PIN2   -- the probability that a line is indented 2 spaces
    PIN5   -- the probability that a line is indented 5 spaces
    PSKIP  -- the probability that a line is skipped
              within a stanza
    PCOMMA -- the probability a comma is added,
              after a phrase
    PTRMLN -- the probability that the current
              phrase ends the line
    PTRMST -- the probability the current line
              ends the stanza.
```

In studying POET you should refer back to this list, to recall the <u>exact role</u> of each variable, as it appears in the program.

One more useful preliminary, before presenting the actual program, is a "hybrid" form -- part algorithm and part program. The portions in capital letters are segments that have already been translated to FORTRAN. The segments in lower-case letters are still in algorithmic form. This hybrid version should help you identify the key control phrases in the program:

```
Create
    STZNBR number of current stanza
    NBRSTZ total number of stanzas
    LINNBR number of current line
    MAXLIN maximum lines in stanza
    PHRCNT phrase number within line
    PHRNBR phrase number within list
    PHRGRP phrase number within group
    LINE line under construction
    LSTCHR last character used in LINE
    PHR(20) list of phrases
    PHRLEN(20) list of PHR lengths
    RN current random number
    SEED initial random number
    PREP prob of phrase repeat
    PIN2 prob of line indent 2
    PIN5 prob of line indent 5
    PSKIP prob of line skip
    PCOMMA prob of comma after phrase
    PTRMLN prob of end of line
    PTRMST prob of end of stanza

READ, SEED, NBRSTZ, MAXLIN
Test control values.
READ, PREP, PCOMMA. PTRMLN, PTRMST
READ, PIN2, PIN5, PSKIP
DO phrases PHRNBR = 1, 20, 1
    Read phrases and set lengths.
Initialize RN and GROUP.
Select random title and print the title.

DO stanzas STZNBR = 1, NBRSTZ, 1

    DO lines LINNBR = 1, MAXLIN, 1
        Initialize LINE and LSTCHR.
        If not first line in stanza
            Check for random indentation.

        DO phrases PHRCNT = 1, until jump out.
            If first phrase skip over Repetition.
            Check for random repetition; if repeat
                skip over phrase selection.
            Random phrase selection.
            Check for random comma.
            Check for random line termination.
```

II 6.4 Poetry Composition

```
      phrases     CONTINUE
                  PRINT line.
                  Check for random stanza termination.
                  Check for random line skip.
      lines       CONTINUE
                  Insert blank lines between stanzas.
      stanzas CONTINUE

         Print closing.
         Print control values.
         STOP
         END
```

With all this preparation it should be a relatively straightforward task to read the program, even though it is 120 lines long. Essentially all you have to do in reading the program is figure out in detail exactly _how_ each one of the sub-tasks described in the hybrid program _is_ actually performed. Each of these segments is only a few statements. The overall program may be formidable in size -- but you already understand its overall structure. All that remains is to understand its local details. Keep referring back to the hybrid form to keep clear _what_ each section is doing; refer back to the annotated list of variables to recall what each variable represents.

```
            INTEGER   STZNBR
            INTEGER   NBRSTZ
            INTEGER   LINNBR
            INTEGER   MAXLIN
            INTEGER   PHRCNT
            INTEGER   PHRNBR
            INTEGER   GROUP
            INTEGER   PHRGRP
            CHARACTER*100   LINE
            INTEGER LSTCHR
            CHARACTER*100   PHR(20)
            INTEGER   PHRLEN(20)
            REAL   RN
            REAL   PIN2
            REAL   PIN5
            REAL   SEED
            REAL   PREP
            REAL   PSKIP
            REAL   PCOMMA
            REAL   PTRMLN
            REAL   TRMST
C
            READ, SEED, NBRSTZ, MAXLIN
            IF(NBRSTZ .LE. 30) GO TO 10
               PRINT, 'TOO MANY STANZAS'
               NBRSTZ = 30
C
   10       IF(NBRSTZ .GT. 0) GO TO 20
               PRINT, 'NO STANZAS'
```

```
              NBRSTZ = 1
C
 20    IF(MAXLIN .LE. 10) GO TO 30
           PRINT, 'TOO MANY LINES'
           MAXLIN = 10
C
 30    IF(MAXLIN .GE. 1) GO TO 40
           PRINT, 'NOT ENOUGH LINES'
           MAXLIN = 1
C
 40    SEED = ABS(SEED)
       IF(SEED .GT. 1) SEED = 1/SEED
       IF(SEED .LT. 0.1) SEED = SEED+0.1
       READ, PREP, PCOMMA, PTRMLN, PTRMST
       READ, PIN2, PIN5, PSKIP
       DO 100 PHRNBR = 1, 20, 1
           READ, PHR(PHRNBR)
           PHRLEN(PHRNBR) = LENGTH(PHR(PHRNBR))
 100       CONTINUE
       RN = RAND(SEED)
       GROUP = 0
C
C   CHOOSE TITLE
       RN = RAND(RN)
       PHRNBR = 1 + 10*RN
       PRINT, ' ', PHR(PHRNBR)
       PRINT, '     A POEM'
       PRINT, ' '
C
C   GENERATE NBRSTZ STANZAS
       DO 550 STZNBR = 1, NBRSTZ, 1
           DO 450 LINNBR = 1, MAXLIN, 1
               LINE = ' '
               LSTCHR = 0
               IF(LINNBR .EQ. 1) GO TO 150
                   RN = RAND(RN)
                   IF(RN .LT. PIN2) LSTCHR = 2
                   IF(RN .LT. PIN5) LSTCHR = 5
C
C           CHOOSE PHRASES AND ADD TO LINE
 150           DO 350 PHRCNT = 1, 10000, 1
                   IF(PHRCNT .EQ. 1) GO TO 250
                   RN = RAND(RN)
                   IF(RN .GE. PREP) GO TO 250
C                   PHRASE REPETITION
                       IF(PHRLEN(PHRNBR) + LSTCHR .GT. 97) GO TO 400
                       LSTCHR = LSTCHR - 1
                       IF(LINE(LSTCHR:LSTCHR) .LT. 'A') GO TO 200
                           LSTCHR = LSTCHR + 1
                           LINE(LSTCHR:LSTCHR) = ','
 200                   LINE(LSTCHR+2:100) = PHR(PHRNBR)
                       LSTCHR = LSTCHR + 1 + PHRLEN(PHRNBR)
                       GO TO 400
C                   RANDOM PHRASE SELECTION
 250                   RN = RAND(RN)
```

II 6.4 Poetry Composition

```
                  GROUP = GROUP + 1 + (2*RN)
                  IF(GROUP .GT. 3) GROUP = GROUP - 4
                  RN = RAND(RN)
                  PHRGRP = 1 + (5*RN)
                  PHRNBR = (5*GROUP) + PHRGRP
                  IF(PHRLEN(PHRNBR) +LSTCHR .GT. 98) GO TO 400
                      LINE(LSTCHR+1:100) = PHR(PHRNBR)
                      LSTCHR = LSTCHR + PHRLEN(PHRNBR)
C
C                 PUNCTUATION PROCESSING
                  IF(LINE(LSTCHR:LSTCHR) .LT. 'A') GO TO 400
                     RN = RAND(RN)
                     IF(RN .GT. PCOMMA) GO TO 300
                        LSTCHR = LSTCHR + 1
                        LINE(LSTCHR:LSTCHR) = ','
  300                RN = RAND(RN)
                     IF(RN .LT. PTRMLN) GO TO 400
                        LSTCHR = LSTCHR + 1
  350             CONTINUE
  400         PRINT, LINE
C         STANZA TERMINATION
C
              IF(LINE(LSTCHR:LSTCHR) .EQ. '.') GO TO 500
              RN = RAND(RN)
              IF(RN .LT. PTRMST) GO TO 500
              RN = RAND(RN)
              IF(RN .LT. PSKIP) PRINT, ' '
  450         CONTINUE
  500     PRINT, ' '
  550     CONTINUE
C
      PRINT, '                           ', '-ANON.'
      PRINT, ' '
      PRINT, ' '
      PRINT, SEED, NBRSTZ, MAXLIN, PREP, PCOMMA
      PRINT, PTRMLN, PTRMST, PIN2, PIN5, PSKIP
      STOP
      END
```

Someone could <u>use</u> this program without reading or understanding it. In fact, one could use the program without having any idea of how a program is written, how it is executed, or even what the letters "FORTRAN" stand for. Instructions for such a user might look something like the following:

> POET is a machine for automatically generating poems in a somewhat random manner. You can control the subject and, to a certain extent, the form of the poetry. Input to POET consists of <u>ten numbers</u> and <u>twenty phrases</u>, as described below. Output from POET is a printed copy of a poem.
>
> The first input to POET is ten numbers, in the following order:

1. An "inspirational number" -- some number greater than .1 and less than 1.0. Each different inspirational number produces a different poem.

2. The number of stanzas in the poem; should be at least 1 and not more than 30.

3. The maximum number of lines in a stanza; should be at least 1 and not more than 10. (Some stanzas will have fewer lines than this maximum number.)

4 through 10 are probabilities -- in effect, long-run proportions. Each is a number between 0 and 1. These values "guide" the random decisions made during the construction of a poem.

4. The probability of a phrase being repeated. (When this happens the repetition also ends the line.)

5. The probability of a comma being inserted after a phrase.

6. The probability of terminating the line after a phrase.

7. The probability of terminating the stanza after a line.

8. The probability of indenting a line (except for the first line of a stanza) by two spaces.

9. The probability of indenting a line (except the first line of a stanza) by five spaces.

10. The probability of skipping a line -- that is, leaving a blank line -- within a stanza.

Following these control numbers are twenty phrases from which the poem is generated. Phrases can be almost anything -- one word, a group of words, or a complete line. Punctuation of any sort is permitted, with the following effect:

1. If a phrase ends with a period, when this phrase occurs, it will always end the stanza.

2. If a phrase ends with any other punctuation mark, when this phrase occurs, it will end the line.

3. Internal punctuation -- that is, in any position except the last -- has no effect on the construction of the poem.

The phrases are given in four groups of five phrases each. The groups are significant in the selection of phrases as the poem is constructed: that is, two consecutive phrases are never drawn from the same group (although once selected, there is a chance that a certain phrase will be repeated).

6.4.1 Sample Results from POET

POET is an amusing toy. By supplying clever sets of phrases, grouping them ingeniously, and tinkering with the control numbers, you can produce some intriguing free verse. It requires patience, since not all of POET's efforts are inspired, but sometimes the results are rather remarkable. If you can face the task of keypunching the three pages of program, you will probably enjoy experimenting with POET yourself.

To demonstrate POET's ability, three different phrase sets were used. These are listed below:

```
OH PROGRAM, MY PROGRAM,
OH, MIGHTY MAIN PROCEDURE
LOOPS AND CONDITIONS
READS AND PRINTS, GO TOS AND DOS
DECLARATIONS -- NOT SPECULATIONS
NESTING EVER DEEPER
ONE AFTER ANOTHER
STEP BY PATIENT STEP
PAGE AFTER PAGE AFTER PAGE
ALWAYS SO PERFECTLY PRECISE
CRAFTED WITH LOVING CARE
WITH NEVER AN ERROR
PROSE OF SUCH BEAUTY
AN ELEGANT STRUCTURE
AH -- FORM BEYOND COMPARE.
TO EXECUTE FOREVER --
PROGRAMMER'S JOY
WHAT CAN YOU NOT DO?
CORRECT BEYOND QUESTION
A CLASSIC CONSTRUCTION
```

```
MIDNIGHT DREARY
FIERY EYES
BIRD OR FIEND
THING OF EVIL
PROPHET
BEGUILING ME
THRILLED ME
STILL BURNING ...
BURNED.
NEVER FLITTING
SIGN OF PARTING
AND MY SOUL
DARKNESS THERE
SHALL BE LIFTED
QUOTH THE RAVEN
NOTHING MORE
YET AGAIN
SLOWLY CREEPING
... NEVERMORE,
EVERMORE


SEA AFTER SEA
ENDLESS OCEAN
GTEY SEAS ROLLING
WIND IS WAILING
SPINDRIFT FLYING
NEVER EVER ENDING.
RISING HIGHER,
CRASHING TUMULT
DARKER, BLACKER
ALMIGHTY FURY
TIS SAILOR'S PERIL
TIS SEAMAN'S CHALLENGE
NIGHT WITHOUT END
ENDLESS VOYAGE
WHY ARE WE HERE?
HOLD HER STEADY --
RISE TO MEET THEM
SLOWLY ONWARD
TO OVERCOME
FLEE THE LEE SHORE
```

The following are samples of POET's poems, produced from one of the phrase lists shown above. The control values for each run are printed at the bottom of the output. We must admit that these are not the first samples obtained, but were selected from many different runs.

```
    NESTING EVER DEEPER
         A POEM

STEP BY PATIENT STEP,
   AN ELEGANT STRUCTURE
   CORRECT BEYOND QUESTION,
   DECLARATIONS -- NOT SPECULATIONS,

NESTING EVER DEEPER,
   AN ELEGANT STRUCTURE,
   READS AND PRINTS, GO TOS AND DOS
   STEP BY PATIENT STEP,

TO EXECUTE FOREVER --
   PAGE AFTER PAGE AFTER PAGE,
   AH -- FORM BEYOND COMPARE.

A CLASSIC CONSTRUCTION
   LOOPS AND CONDITIONS
   ONE AFTER ANOTHER
   TO EXECUTE FOREVER --

NESTING EVER DEEPER,
   CRAFTED WITH LOVING CARE
   A CLASSIC CONSTRUCTION
   NESTING EVER DEEPER,

CRAFTED WITH LOVING CARE,
   READS AND PRINTS, GO TOS AND DOS,
   ALWAYS SO PERFECTLY PRECISE
   AN ELEGANT STRUCTURE

A CLASSIC CONSTRUCTION
   DECLARATIONS -- NOT SPECULATIONS
   WITH NEVER AN ERROR
   READS AND PRINTS, GO TOS AND DOS,

ALWAYS SO PERFECTLY PRECISE
   WHAT CAN YOU NOT DO?
   NESTING EVER DEEPER
   PROSE OF SUCH BEAUTY

              -ANON.


   0.5265631E 00            8            4    0.0000000E 00    0.5000000E 00
   0.1000000E 01    0.0000000E 00    0.1000000E 01    0.0000000E 00    0.0000000E 00
```

```
            ENDLESS OCEAN
                 A POEM

NEVER EVER ENDING.

ENDLESS VOYAGE, FLEE THE LEE SHORE NEVER EVER ENDING.

ENDLESS VOYAGE, RISE TO MEET THEM,
DARKER, BLACKER, TO OVERCOME RISING HIGHER,
TIS SAILOR'S PERIL
     HOLD HER STEADY --
     NEVER EVER ENDING.

RISE TO MEET THEM SPINDRIFT FLYING ENDLESS VOYAGE, SLOWLY ONWARD
    GREY SEAS ROLLING
     TIS SEAMAN'S CHALLENGE FLEE THE LEE SHORE, FLEE THE LEE SHORE
SPINDRIFT FLYING TIS SEAMAN'S CHALLENGE,
SPINDRIFT FLYING, SPINDRIFT FLYING
    TIS SAILOR'S PERIL, ENDLESS OCEAN ENDLESS VOYAGE,

SLOWLY ONWARD WIND IS WAILING,
    NIGHT WITHOUT END HOLD HER STEADY --
         ALMIGHTY FURY, WHY ARE WE HERE?
    HOLD HER STEADY --
ALMIGHTY FURY
SLOWLY ONWARD,

ENDLESS OCEAN,
TIS SEAMAN'S CHALLENGE,
      ENDLESS OCEAN CRASHING TUMULT TO OVERCOME
WIND IS WAILING, WIND IS WAILING
      TIS SEAMAN'S CHALLENGE RISE TO MEET THEM,
   NEVER EVER ENDING.

                 -ANON.


  0.5814731E 00           6           6   0.1499990E 00    0.3999990E 00
  0.3999990E 00    0.0000000E 00   0.6999990E 00    0.1999990E 00   0.0000000E 00
```

II 6.4 Poetry Composition

```
       SEA AFTER SEA
           A POEM

TIS SAILOR'S PERIL
   TO OVERCOME,
RISING HIGHER,
   TIS SAILOR'S PERIL FLEE THE LEE SHORE, CRASHING TUMULT,
     WHY ARE WE HERE?
        SEA AFTER SEA, CRASHING TUMULT TO OVERCOME, WIND IS WAILING DARKER, BLACKER,

SEA AFTER SEA
       TIS SEAMAN'S CHALLENGE
GREY SEAS ROLLING, NIGHT WITHOUT END
       SEA AFTER SEA NIGHT WITHOUT END, NIGHT WITHOUT END
   RISE TO MEET THEM ALMIGHTY FURY TIS SAILOR'S PERIL
      ENDLESS OCEAN ALMIGHTY FURY

SLOWLY ONWARD DARKER, BLACKER ENDLESS VOYAGE
   RISE TO MEET THEM SEA AFTER SEA DARKER, BLACKER, DARKER, BLACKER
   RISE TO MEET THEM,
ENDLESS OCEAN NIGHT WITHOUT END SEA AFTER SEA,
   NIGHT WITHOUT END
SEA AFTER SEA, CRASHING TUMULT, TO OVERCOME

DARKER, BLACKER,
TO OVERCOME, RISING HIGHER,
   TIS SEAMAN'S CHALLENGE RISE TO MEET THEM, RISE TO MEET THEM
RISING HIGHER,
TIS SEAMAN'S CHALLENGE RISE TO MEET THEM DARKER, BLACKER,
   ENDLESS VOYAGE, ENDLESS VOYAGE

SEA AFTER SEA,
NEVER EVER ENDING.

WHY ARE WE HERE?
   WIND IS WAILING
NIGHT WITHOUT END, GREY SEAS ROLLING, GREY SEAS ROLLING
   NEVER EVER ENDING.

SLOWLY ONWARD,
   NEVER EVER ENDING.

TIS SAILOR'S PERIL
       RISE TO MEET THEM RISING HIGHER,
TIS SEAMAN'S CHALLENGE, TIS SEAMAN'S CHALLENGE
   RISE TO MEET THEM
    CRASHING TUMULT ENDLESS VOYAGE, HOLD HER STEADY --
SPINDRIFT FLYING, DARKER, BLACKER TIS SAILOR'S PERIL

                 -ANON.


    0.5814710E 00          8            6     0.1499990E 00     0.3000000E 00
    0.3999990E 00   0.0000000E 00    0.6999990E 00    0.1999990E 00    0.0000000E 00
```

BEGUILING ME
       A POEM

STILL BURNING ...

QUOTH THE RAVEN ... NEVERMORE,
      PROPHET, DARKNESS THERE, FIERY EYES, BEGUILING ME
      SHALL BE LIFTED MIDNIGHT DREARY QUOTH THE RAVEN YET AGAIN
      FIERY EYES, BEGUILING ME QUOTH THE RAVEN THING OF EVIL QUOTH THE RAVEN
      SLOWLY CREEPING STILL BURNING ...

SIGN OF PARTING, SIGN OF PARTING

NOTHING MORE
      MIDNIGHT DREARY QUOTH THE RAVEN ... NEVERMORE,
      FIERY EYES
      SIGN OF PARTING BIRD OR FIEND, BIRD OR FIEND
SIGN OF PARTING, BIRD OR FIEND DARKNESS THERE SLOWLY CREEPING THING OF EVIL DARKNESS THERE
SLOWLY CREEPING,

THRILLED ME
      SLOWLY CREEPING, SLOWLY CREEPING
      MIDNIGHT DREARY, DARKNESS THERE ... NEVERMORE,
BURNED.
NOTHING MORE BEGUILING ME
      SIGN OF PARTING, SIGN OF PARTING
      BIRD OR FIEND, BIRD OR FIEND
NEVER FLITTING, DARKNESS THERE FIERY EYES, AND MY SOUL, FIERY EYES, BEGUILING ME,
SLOWLY CREEPING,
      PROPHET

DARKNESS THERE, DARKNESS THERE
      PROPHET, SHALL BE LIFTED

EVERMORE, BIRD OR FIEND, BURNED.

                    -ANON.

   0.5265631E 00   8   6   0.1499990E 00   0.3499990E 00
   0.2500000E 00   0.4999990E-01   0.1999990E 00   0.6999990E 00   0.4999990E-01

6.5 Simulation of a Queuing System

If we quit at this point, the previous examples would leave the impression that the only use of programs for random processes was for fun and games. This is not the case. Such programs are often used to simulate complicated systems. Engineers can perform experiments with such programmed models of real systems, and use the results to predict the performance of the counterpart real system. For example, airlines have used such programs to study ways to improve the scheduling of aircraft and flight crews, and have found ways to achieve better utilization of both. Traffic engineers can study the capacity of various traffic control and interchange mechanisms, and as a result, pour actual concrete with greater confidence. Industrial engineers often use this technique in the design of complex materials handling systems for a factory or warehouse, and in the choice of decision rules to schedule production.

Many of the systems that are simulated are some form of "queuing system". They are characterized by the unscheduled arrival of "customers", who must then wait in "queue" to be "served". For example, the customers could be aircraft, and the service could be use of a runway for landing. Or the customers might really be "customers", and the service might be a teller's window at a bank. These and many other situations are examples of queuing systems. Some of the interesting characteristics of a queuing system are the size of the queue, the length of time that individual customers have to wait, and the activity pattern of the server. For certain special (and simple) forms of queuing systems, these properties can be predicted by means of probability theory, but there are many situations where the theory does not apply, and a simulation program must be used.

The simplest kind of queuing system has a single server, and the customers are processed in the order of their arrival. A program to simulate such a system is given below. The program represents the _state_ of the system by noting the number of customers in queue (NBRINQ), and the number of customers being served (NBRINS). The _events_, when one of these values changes, are the arrival of a new customer, and the completion of service of a customer. At each such event the program adjusts the values of NBRINQ and NBRINS to reflect an arrival, a departure, or a move from queue to service. The program reports the average number of customers in queue, and the proportion of time that the server is idle.

II 6.5 Simulation of a Queue

At the highest level of description, the algorithm for this problem is the following:

>Simulate single-server queuing system:
>   Create variables.
>   Read control values.
>   Repeat for each event until time limit:
>   Accumulate statistics.
>   Process the event -- either an arrival
>   or a service completion.
>   Compute averages.
>   Print results.

The section of program to "process an arrival event" is quite straightforward -- the number of customers waiting (NBRINQ) is increased by 1, and the time of the next random arrival (NXTARV) is determined. The program section to "process a service completion" is more complicated, since there are two possibilities -- either there are customers waiting, or the queue is empty. We leave it to you to figure out the scheme by which the server is "set idle", and then reactivated when there is work to do. You might also examine the situation at the very beginning of the run, and satisfy yourself that the simulation starts off properly. We should warn you that this is probably the most difficult of all the examples we present. The program follows:

```
      REAL   NXTARV, NXTCMP, TIMLIM
C            NEXT ARRIVAL, COMPLETION, TIME LIMIT
      INTEGER  NBRINQ, NBR
C            NUMBER IN QUEUE, NUMBER IN SERVICE
      REAL   CUMST, IDLTIM, LSTEVN
C            CUMULATIVE STATE, IDLE TIME, LAST EVENT
      REAL   MEANST, FRCIDL
C            MEAN STATE, FRACTION IDLE
      REAL   RN, SEED
      REAL   ARVMN, SERVMN
C            ARRIVAL MEAN, SERVICE MEAN
      INTEGER  EVENT
C
      READ, TIMLIM, ARVMN, SERVMN, SEED
      RN = RAND(SEED)
      NXTARV = 0
      NXTCMP = 0
      NBRINQ = 0
      NBRINS = 0
      CUMST = 0
      IDLTIM = 0
      LSTEVN = 0
C
      DO 100 EVENT = 1, 10000, 1
         IF(NXTARV .GT. TIMLIM) GO TO 200
         IF(NXTARV .GE. NXTCMP) GO TO 10
C        NEXT EVENT IS AN ARRIVAL
```

II 6.5 Simulation of a Queue

```
              CUMST = CUMST+(NBRINQ+NBRINS) * (NXTARV-LSTEVN)
              LSTEVN = NXTARV
    10        IF(NXTARV .LT. NXTCMP) GO TO 20
C             NEXT EVENT IS A COMPLETION
              CUMST = CUMST+(NBRINQ+NBRINS) * (NXTCMP-LSTEVN)
              LSTEVN = NXTCMP
    20        IF(NXTARV .GT. NXTCMP) GO TO 30
C             ADD PERSON TO QUEUE
              NBRINQ = NBRINQ + 1
              RN = RAND(RN)
              NXTARV = NXTARV+(2*ARVMN*RN)
              GO TO 100
    30        IF(NBRINQ .EQ. 0) GO TO 40
C             REMOVE PERSON FROM QUEUE
              NBRINQ = NBRINQ - 1
              NBRINS = 1
              RN = RAND(RN)
              NXTCMP = NXTCMP+(2*SERVMN*RN)
              GO TO 100
    40        NBRINS = 0
              IDLTIM = IDLTIM+(NXTARV-NXTCMP)
              NXTCMP = NXTARV
   100        CONTINUE
C
C      CALCULATE AND PRINT SUMMARY STATISTICS
   200        MEANST = CUMST/TIMLIM
              FRCIDL = IDLTIM/TIMLIM
              PRINT, 'SINGLE SERVER QUEUE SIMULATOR'
              PRINT, 'RUN LENGTH:', TIMLIM
              PRINT, 'MEAN TIME BETWEEN INTERVALS;', ARVMN
              PRINT, 'RANDOM NUMBER SEED:', SEED
              PRINT, 'MEAN NBR IN SYSTEM:', MEANST
              PRINT, 'FRACTION OF TIME IDLE:', FRCIDL
              STOP
              END
```

The output from four different executions of this queue simulator is shown below:

II 6.5 Simulation of a Queue

```
SINGLE SERVER QUEUE SIMULATOR
RUN LENGTH:          200.00000000
MEAN TIME BETWEEN INTERVALS:       10.00000000
RANDOM NUMBER SEED:    0.78912190
MEAN NBR IN SYSTEM:    1.80590500
FRACTION OF TIME IDLE:    0.02894424
```

```
SINGLE SERVER QUEUE SIMULATOR
RUN LENGTH:          200.00000000
MEAN TIME BETWEEN INTERVALS:       10.00000000
RANDOM NUMBER SEED:    0.65432000
MEAN NBR IN SYSTEM:    2.45205100
FRACTION OF TIME IDLE:    0.01634605
```

```
SINGLE SERVER QUEUE SIMULATOR
RUN LENGTH:          200.00000000
MEAN TIME BETWEEN INTERVALS:       10.00000000
RANDOM NUMBER SEED:    0.12378790
MEAN NBR IN SYSTEM:    1.16386900
FRACTION OF TIME IDLE:    0.20514680
```

```
SINGLE SERVER QUEUE SIMULATOR
RUN LENGTH:         2000.00000000
MEAN TIME BETWEEN INTERVALS:       10.00000000
RANDOM NUMBER SEED:    0.57575600
MEAN NBR IN SYSTEM:    4.12167300
FRACTION OF TIME IDLE:    0.05059637
```

Section 6 **Exercises**

The following questions pertain to the coin-tossing programs of Section 6.2:

1. How would the second program of 6.2 be modified to report the position of the first head in each experiment? For example, if an experiment began with TTTH, the answer reported would be 4.

2. How would the second program of 6.2 be modified to report the position of the last head in each experiment?

3. Would the first program of 6.2 work correctly if the first item of data (the value for NBREXP) given is 1? What would happen if the first item is 0?

4. How would the first program of 6.2 be modified so that for each experiment it simply reports whether there were more heads or more tails?

The following questions pertain to the turtle-race program of Section 6.3:

5. How would the program be modified to have the turtles race in a circular ring instead of a square one?

6. The program has a problem of "fairness" between the two turtles. Presumably they should move simultaneously, but in the program red moves before black. To compensate for this, the program lets both turtles complete each move before checking for a winner, and it admits the possibility of a tie. Alternatively, suppose fairness is provided by randomly deciding which turtle goes first on each move, and ruling out ties. How would be program be modified to implement this scheme?

7. Suppose that during the race, a tape recording of very attractive turtle music is played to the East of the ring. How could the program be modified to impose an "Eastward-bias" in the turtles' movements?

The following questions pertain to the POET program of Section 6.4:

8. POET will never start a line with the same phrase that ended the preceding line. How is this restriction implemented in the program?

9. What would happen in POET if one of the control probabilities, say the probability of phrase repetition, was accidentally given as a negative number?

10. How is the title for a poem selected?

11. Suppose that in a particular phrase set, every phrase that ended in a period had a blank added after the period -- so that it ended in ". ". What effect would this have on the action of POET?

12. Suppose one phrase in a phrase set consisted entirely of blanks. What effect would this have?

13. How would you modify POET to ensure that every stanza begins with a phrase from group 1?

14. Describe POET's punctuation rules, whenever a particular phrase is to be repeated.

15. Suppose you wanted poems in which each stanza is exactly 5 lines long, and the format of a stanza is always the following:

       first line ...
          second line ...
          third line ...
          fourth line ...
          fifth line ...

    How would input be given be achieve this?

16. Suppose the probability of phrase repetition (fourth control value) was given as 1. What form of poem would be produced?

17. How would the program be modified to cause phrase selection to move strictly from group 1 to group 2, to 3, to 4, to 1, etc.?

18. Describe the exact role of "groups" in POET's phrase selection process.

Section 7   Interactive Computing Systems

All of the programs of the preceding sections have assumed that the computer processing will be performed under a form of supervisory system called a "batch processor". The key characteristic of such a system is that the complete <u>execution</u> of the program takes place in a way that is <u>inaccessible</u> to the user. In effect, in this conventional batch processing there are three separate phases to the use of a program:

1. The user prepares all of the input that will be required for the complete execution of the program, and loads all of these data into the computer at once, in advance of execution.

2. The computer executes the program, reading data prepared in advance, and preparing lines of output -- but not actually printing the lines until execution is completed.

3. The output lines are printed and delivered to the user.

Note that <u>all</u> of the data are irrevocably prepared and loaded before execution even begins, and that <u>none</u> of the output can be seen until executed has been completed. This obviously means that the user <u>cannot be influenced by</u> the contents of early portions of the <u>output</u> in deciding <u>what input</u> to supply.

For most purposes this three-stage processing is tolerable for the user, and since it is also very efficient from the computer's point-of-view this is generally regarded as the normal mode of processing. Most academic computing centers provide this as the standard mode of service (since it permits more jobs to be run by a given computer than does the alternative form described below).

However, there is an interesting and useful alternative to this batch processing. There are supervisory systems that execute a program in a single stage -- so that the user sees the lines of output immediately upon execution of each PRINT statement, and supplies data as it is required for execution of each READ statement. Such systems are said to be "interactive" because the user can <u>interact</u> with the program <u>during its execution</u>. That is, the user can see partial results of execution, and use this information in deciding what further data to supply to the program.

An interactive system uses a different type of device for input and output, rather than a card-reader and a line-printer. The device is either a machine similar to an electric typewriter, or one with a typewriter keyboard and a cathode-ray-tube (that is, a television screen) to display results. The point is, a single device is used for <u>both input and output</u> and the user is physically present and active at the device while the program is being executed.

Ordinarily, interactive systems are designed to serve a number of devices (users) simultaneously. The users are said to "time-share" the services of the computer. The computer must execute many programs at once by jumping back and forth very rapidly from one to another. This is done in such a way that each user has the impression that his is the only program being executed. This requires some complicated control action by the computer, and consequently it is more costly to run a program this way, but it does allow certain types of use of the computer that are simply not possible with a batch system. These are illustrated in the following sections.

Time-sharing is currently necessary for practical interactive use of a computer simply because current computers are too expensive to allow one user to monopolize the services of a computer for a significant period of time. (It takes only a fraction of a second to process most student jobs in a batch system; it might take the best part of an hour in a single-user interactive system.) But this situation is rapidly changing. The cost of a computer of a given amount of power has been reduced by a factor of 100 in the last ten years, and a reduction of another factor of 10 is clearly in prospect. At that point, a small computer may be sufficiently inexpensive (and sufficiently small) that it can be built right into the input-output device, and powerful "personal" computing will be a reality. It seems clear that except for the current economic deterrent, interactive computing is preferable to batch processing. Hence it is a reasonable forecast that the mode of computing described in this section will become increasingly important as the cost of computers is reduced.

There is a version of WATFIV that can be used interactively. From the user's point-of-view the FORTRAN programming is identical to that in normal batch WATFIV, but changes have been made to permit interactive execution. An interactive FORTRAN may or may not be available at your computer installation, but the following examples illustrate the kinds of things that can be done only with such an interactive system.

7.1 An Interactive Version of the PYS Retrieval System

First we present an interactive version of the yacht brokerage retrieval system that was given in conventional form in Section 5.1. The objectives of this interactive version are exactly the same as before -- only the mode of execution has been altered.

A practical interactive version of the retrieval system would necessarily use a permanent file system for the list of available yachts (see Section 5.3), since it would be unreasonable to have to re-enter the entire file from the typewriter keyboard each time the retrieval system was to be used. The program would copy the file from secondary storage into main memory, rather than read it from external data each time. Since we don't want to have to explain in detail exactly how this is done, we replace that section of the program by an English description (given in lower-case rather than capital letters).

A second difference in the interactive program is that each READ statement requesting data input from the user at the terminal is immediately preceded by a PRINT statement that provides instructions to the user. The output produced by these statements are called "prompting messages". In a conventional non-interactive system, user instructions must be provided separately, and be available before execution of the program begins, since nothing printed by the program itself can be seen by the user in time to help him prepare the data. However, in the interactive system the instructions can be delivered to the user, step by step, exactly when they are needed.

The most important difference in the interactive system, and the reason why such a version would be used, is that the number and nature of the user queries can be determined during execution, based upon results obtained from previous queries. The expected pattern of use would be to enter a query, look at the results for that query, and then to enter another query representing some modification of the first. This "dialog" could continue until the user is satisfied that he has obtained the information he wants (at least to the extent that it is present in the file). At that point the user can either terminate the execution, or continue with some new query.

The program is given below:

```
      CHARACTER*100  BUILD(25), RIG(25)
      INTEGER    FILNBR(25), LENGTH(25), YEAR(25)
      INTEGER    PRICE(25), SELECT(25)
      INTEGER    FILSIZ
      CHARACTER*100  QTYPE
      CHARACTER*100  QBUILD, QRIG
      INTEGER    QLEN, QLLEN, QULEN
      INTEGER    I, Q
```

Read in values from permanent file.

```
C
      PRINT, ' PYS RETRIEVAL SYSTEM'
      PRINT, '   NUMBER OF YACHTS ON FILE:', FILSIZ
      PRINT, ' '
      PRINT, 'SELECTED YACHTS ARE DESCRIBED AS FOLLOWS:'
      PRINT, '   FILE NUMBER, BUILDER'
      PRINT, '   LENGTH, RIG'
      PRINT, '   YEAR BUILT, ASKING PRICE'
      PRINT, ' '
      PRINT, ' '
C
      DO 400 Q = 1, 10000, 1
         PRINT, 'DO YOU HAVE A QUERY?'
         PRINT, '(ANSWER "YES" OR "NO")'
         READ, QTYPE
         IF(QTYPE .EQ. 'NO') GO TO 500
         PRINT, 'WHAT TYPE OF QUERY?'
         READ, QTYPE
C
         IF(QTYPE .NE. 'Q1') GO TO 100
            PRINT, '   Q1: SEARCH FOR SPECIFIC MODEL'
            PRINT, 'WHAT BUILDER?'
            READ, QBUILD
            PRINT, 'WHAT LENGTH?'
            READ, QLEN
            PRINT, '     ', QLEN, QBUILD
            PRINT, ' '
            DO 50 I = 1, FILSIZ, 1
               IF(BUILD(I) .NE. QBUILD) GO TO 50
                  IF(LENGTH(I) .EQ. QLEN) SELECT(I) = 1
   50       CONTINUE
            GO TO 200
C
  100    IF(QTYPE .NE. 'Q2') GO TO 180
            PRINT, '   Q2: SPECIFY RIG WITH MINIMUM',
     $             'AND MAXIMUM LENGTH'
            PRINT, 'WHAT RIG?'
            READ, QRIG
            PRINT, 'WHAT MINIMUM LENGTH?'
            READ, QLLEN
            PRINT, 'WHAT MAXIMUM LENGTH?'
            READ, QULEN
            PRINT, 'SEARCHING FOR', QLLEN, 'TO', QULEN, QRIG
            PRINT, ' '
            DO 150 I = 1, FILSIZ, 1
               IF(QRIG .NE. RIG(I)) GO TO 150
                  IF(QLLEN .GT. LENGTH(I)) GO TO 150
                     IF(QULEN .GE. LENGTH(I)) SELECT(I) = 1
  150       CONTINUE
            GO TO 200
```

II 7.1 An Interactive Retrieval System

```
C
 180      PRINT, 'IMPROPER QUERY:', QTYPE
          PRINT, ' '
          GO TO 400
C
 200      PRINT, '   SUITABLE YACHTS ON FILE:'
          DO 300 I = 1, FILSIZ, 1
             IF(SELECT(I) .EQ. 0) GO TO 300
                PRINT, '      ', FILNBR(I), BUILD(I)
                PRINT, '      ', LENGTH(I), RIG(I)
                PRINT, '      ', YEAR(I), PRICE(I)
                PRINT, ' '
             SELECT(I) = 0
 300      CONTINUE
          PRINT, ' '
          PRINT, ' '
C
 400      CONTINUE
C
 500      PRINT, ' '
          PRINT, 'END OF QUERIES'
          STOP
          END
```

A sample of the use of this program is shown below. This is a copy of what would be printed at a typewriter terminal if this program was executed using WATFIV. This represents both <u>input to</u> and <u>output from</u> the program. The lower case lines are the input and the upper case the output. If you were actually sitting at a terminal executing this program it would be obvious which lines you entered and which lines are typed by the system, but when you read the page later the difference is not obvious.

```
   PYS RETRIEVAL SYSTEM
      NUMBER OF YACHTS ON FILE:            12

SELECTED YACHTS ARE DESCRIBED AS FOLLOWS:
     FILE NUMBER, BUILDER
     LENGTH, RIG
     YEAR BUILT, ASKING PRICE


DO YOU HAVE A QUERY?
(ANSWER "YES" OR "NO")
>'yes'
WHAT TYPE OF QUERY?
>'q1'
     Q1: SEARCH FOR SPECIFIC MODEL
WHAT BUILDER?
>'alberg'
WHAT LENGTH?
>35
                35 ALBERG

     SUITABLE YACHTS ON FILE:
                490 ALBERG
                 35 YAWL
                1966         28000



DO YOU HAVE A QUERY?
(ANSWER "YES" OR "NO")
>'yes'
WHAT TYPE OF QUERY?
>'q2'
     Q2: SPECIFY RIG WITH MINIMUM AND MAXIMUM LENGTH
WHAT RIG?
>'ketch'
WHAT MINIMUM LENGTH?
>30
WHAT MAXIMUM LENGTH?
>50
SEARCHING FOR           30 TO          50
KETCH

     SUITABLE YACHTS ON FILE:
                719 C & C
                 36 KETCH
                1969         33500

                972 MORGAN
                 41 KETCH
                1973         55000



DO YOU HAVE A QUERY?
(ANSWER "YES" OR "NO")
>'no'

END OF QUERIES
```

The ability to use the output in choosing further input makes this version of the retrieval system more convenient than the previous one. It would require several separate executions of the conventional batch version to provide information comparable to what could be obtained from a single execution of the interactive version. If you know in advance, with complete certainty, exactly what queries you want to ask, then the two systems are equivalent. But very often certain queries would not occur to you until you had seen the results from some initial queries. In these cases the interactive system is clearly advantageous.

7.2 Competitive Programs

One interesting way to exploit the capability of an interactive system is with programs that compete with the user. For example, programs can be written to "play games" where the program represents one player and the user is the other player. Each play by the program is reported to the user. The user considers the program's move and chooses some appropriate countermove, which is entered as data input. The ability to interact during execution is obviously essential to such competition -- it would be very slow and clumsy to play a game against a conventional batch-processed program (many separate executions would be required).

We will illustrate the idea of a competitive interactive program with a simple variation of a venerable game called NIM. This variation is just complex enough to be interesting, yet it is simple enough to describe and program.

We call the game "Match-Snatch". There are two players. Our program will represent one player and the user at the keyboard will be the other player, but we will initially describe the game as it would be played by two people.

Some number of matchsticks are placed in a pile between the two players. A "move" is for a player to remove some number of matches from those remaining in the pile. To make a valid move he must take at least one match, and not more than some number agreed upon as a move-limit before the game begins. The players alternate moves, and the object of the game is to avoid being the player who has to take the last mactch. (Obviously, without the move-limit the game would be trivial since faced with a pile of n matches the first player would immediately take n-1 matches and the second player would lose on his first move.) A typical game might start with a pile of fifteen matches and have a move-limit of three.

In the computer version of Match-Snatch there will, of course, not actually be any physical pile of matches. A variable, say MATCHS, will represent the number of matches in the imagined pile. The removal of matches from the pile will be simulated by announcing a number representing the number to be removed. This number will be subtracted from MATCHS and the game will terminated when the value of MATCHS becomes zero.

There is an algorithm for playing this game which will allow the first player to assure himself victory <u>if he unfailingly follows the algorithm</u>. If he lapses on even one move, then this same algorithm becomes available to his opponent, and allows the opponent to assure himself victory -- unless he in turn errs and returns the advantage to the first player.

It is not difficult to discover what this winning algorithm is. Suppose the move-limit is k matches. If you can take enough matches to leave just one in the pile your opponent will lose on his next move. So obviously, if the pile presented to you on some move contains n matches, where $2 \leq n \leq k+1$, you will simply take n-1 matches and leave your opponent with 1. But if n > k+1 it is not that simple, since you cannot take enough matches to leave only 1. However, if you manage to leave k+2 matches in the pile after your move, then no matter how many matches your opponent takes in his next move he cannot leave you with 1, and you will be able to leave him with 1 on your next move. By repeating this reasoning, you will discover that if you leave 2k+3 matches after some move you will surely be able to leave k+2 after the next move, and leave 1 on the move after that. So in general, if you can arrange to leave m(k+1)+1 matches in the pile after your move, for m=0,1,2,..., you will be able to win the game in m more moves. But if you ever fail to leave exactly m(k+1)+1 matches after your move, then your opponent can move so as to leave you with m(k+1)+1. Thereafter he is in the driver's seat, unless he gets careless (or unless he doesn't understand the game).

Our Match-Snatch program uses this algorithm for the computer's moves -- and the program will never be careless. Hence if the user grants the computer the first move the user will always lose (unless he has been clever enough to chose initial values for the number of matches and the move-limit so that the number of matches is m(k+1)+1 when the program makes its first move). If the user claims the first move he <u>can</u> win, but if he slips up just once the computer will seize the opportunity and go on to win the game.

In addition to acting as one player the Match-Snatch program also operates the game. It negotiates the initial conditions with the user, keeps track of the number of matches and announces the outcome. (It is a little unusual to have one player of a game also serve as the referee and scorekeeper, but this particular program is impeccably honest so it works out all right.)

The algorithm for this program is the following:

    Obtain initial number of matches.
    Obtain a number to serve as a move-limit.

II 7.2 Competitive Programs

          Obtain choice for who moves first.
          Alternate moves until someone wins:
              If user's turn, obtain valid move.
              If program's turn, make move.
          Report outcome.

Each time the algorithm specifies the action "obtain" the program is going to get input from the user at the terminal. This involves a prompting message to let the user know what is required, and a READ statement to read his response. But in this program we also illustrate the opportunity that an interactive system provides to <u>check the validity</u> of the user's responses. The value read by the READ statement is immediately checked, and if it is not proper the whole input cycle is repeated. The program is very patient, and will continue prompting the user indefinitely until a valid response is obtained.

   A complete program to play Match-Snatch on an interactive system is given below:

```
         INTEGER   MATCHS, LIMIT, MOVE
         CHARACTER*100   WHOSE
         INTEGER   I, J
         INTEGER   MAT, MLIM
C
         PRINT, 'WELCOME TO MATCH-SNATCH'
         PRINT, ' '
C
         DO 10 I = 1, 10000, 1
            PRINT, 'HOW MANY MATCHES TO START?'
            READ, MATCHS
            IF(MATCHS .GE. 1) GO TO 20
            PRINT, 'MUST HAVE AT LEAST 1'
  10     CONTINUE
C
  20     DO 40 I = 1, 10000, 1
            PRINT, 'HOW MANY IN ONE MOVE?'
            READ, LIMIT
            IF(LIMIT .GE. 1) GO TO 30
               PRINT, 'MUST BE AT LEAST 1'
               GO TO 40
  30        IF(LIMIT .LE. MATCHS) GO TO 50
               PRINT, 'NOT THAT MANY MATCHES'
  40     CONTINUE
C
  50     DO 60 I = 1, 10000, 1
            PRINT, 'WHO MOVES FIRST? "YOU" OR "ME"'
            READ, WHOSE
            IF(WHOSE .EQ. 'YOU') GO TO 70
            IF(WHOSE .EQ. 'ME') GO TO 70
  60     CONTINUE
  70     DO 200 I = 1, 10000, 1
            IF(WHOSE .EQ. 'ME') GO TO 100
```

```
                MAT = MATCHS - 1
                MLIM = LIMIT + 1
                DO 80 J = 1, 1000, 1
                    MOVE = MAT - MLIM
                    IF(MOVE .LT. MLIM) GO TO 90
                    MAT = MOVE
   80           CONTINUE
   90      IF(MOVE .LE. 0) MOVE = 1
           PRINT, 'I TAKE', MOVE, 'MATCHS'
           GO TO 150
C
  100      DO 130 J = 1, 10000, 1
               PRINT, 'HOW MANY DO YOU TAKE?'
               READ, MOVE
               IF(MOVE .GE. 1) GO TO 110
                   PRINT, 'MUST TAKE AT LEAST 1'
                   GO TO 130
  110          IF(MOVE .LE. LIMIT) GO TO 120
                   PRINT, 'THAT''S MORE THAN WE AGREED ON'
                   GO TO 130
  120          IF(MOVE .LE. MATCHS) GO TO 150
                   PRINT, 'THERE AREN''T THAT MANY'
  130      CONTINUE
  150      MATCHS = MATCHS - MOVE
           IF(MATCHS .EQ. 0) GO TO 300
           PRINT, 'THERE ARE', MATCHS, 'LEFT'
           IF(WHOSE .EQ. 'ME') GO TO 160
               WHOSE = 'ME'
               GO TO 200
  160      WHOSE = 'YOU'
  200      CONTINUE
  300      PRINT, ' '
           IF(WHOSE .EQ. 'YOU') PRINT, 'YOU WON, NICE GOING.'
           IF(WHOSE .EQ. 'ME') PRINT, 'I WON, TOUGH LUCK.'
           STOP
           END
```

If a game of Match-Snatch were played by executing this program on an interactive system the output would look roughly like the lines shown below. We have indented the lines that represent input from the user to distinguish them from lines of output printed by the program.

II 7.2 Competitive Programs

```
WELCOME TO MATCH-SNATCH

HOW MANY MATCHES TO START?
>25
HOW MANY IN ONE MOVE?
>4
WHO MOVES FIRST? "YOU" OR "ME"
>'you'
I TAKE             4 MATCHES
THERE ARE          21 LEFT
HOW MANY DO YOU TAKE?
>5
THAT'S MORE THAN WE AGREED ON
HOW MANY DO YOU TAKE?
>0
MUST TAKE AT LEAST 1
HOW MANY DO YOU TAKE?
>3
THERE ARE          18 LEFT
I TAKE             2 MATCHES
THERE ARE          16 LEFT
HOW MANY DO YOU TAKE?
>4
THERE ARE          12 LEFT
I TAKE             1 MATCHES
THERE ARE          11 LEFT
HOW MANY DO YOU TAKE?
>3
THERE ARE           8 LEFT
I TAKE             2 MATCHES
THERE ARE           6 LEFT
HOW MANY DO YOU TAKE?
>1
THERE ARE           5 LEFT
I TAKE             1 MATCHES
THERE ARE           4 LEFT
HOW MANY DO YOU TAKE?
>3
THERE ARE           1 LEFT
I TAKE             1 MATCHES

YOU WON, NICE GOING.
```

Match-Snatch is not a particularly exciting or demanding game, but it is short and simple enough to permit us to show the entire program, and for you to readily understand just what is going on. It should at least suggest what the possibilities of this type of competition might be. Generally, whenever an interactive computing system is available, a great deal of time and ingenuity goes into devising various game-playing programs. (This is often true in the business world, as well as at universities.) It may seem like a frivolous use of the computer, but the ideas in programming can be learned just as well on problems that are fun as on those that are serious.

For interactive systems that use a typewriter terminal, the games of Tic-tac-toe and Blackjack ("21") are old favorites. A new game called Othello should also become popular on computers. On the other hand, whenever the computing system has terminals using a display screen (instead of a printer) many more possibilities are available. Most such systems have variations of "space war" programs in which the players control space vehicles and missiles, and the program plots and displays their trajectories (with suitably spectacular displays for a "hit").

Systems can be set up so that two or more terminals can communicate with the same program -- in which case programs can be written to permit two users to compete against each other, with the program just running the game rather than participating in it. In effect, the popular "TV-games" ("TV-Pong", "Super-Pong", "TV-Hockey", etc.) are examples of such systems. The usual current versions are just special-purpose computers pre-programmed to offer a certain repertoire of games, but programmable "micro-computers" are becoming available that will allow you to device such games on your own.

The classic game is of course Chess, which has challenged computer game-players from the beginning. A great deal of serious research has been done on programs to play Chess and considerable success has been achieved. There are many different programs today that play play Chess quite effectively. While none has yet achieved the "grand master" level, there are many that can beat casual human players. Computer-Chess is intrinsically interesting for its own sake, but research on Chess-playing programs also contributes to our general understanding of strategies used to solve compex problems.

We have described computer game-playing in terms of pitting a computer against a human opponent, but obviously one computer program can be pitted against another program. For example, for several years now there has been an annual national Chess tournament in which the competitors are all computer programs. The current "champion" (1977) is a program written at Northwestern University.

Competitive programs can be used for more serious purposes. Programs similar in principle to the one shown above are sometimes used to train personnel to perform complex competitive tasks. For example, part of a commercial pilot's training takes place in a computer-driven "simulator", in which the computer presents the neophyte pilot with an emergency situation, and then tracks the pilot's response -- perhaps further complicating the situation. The system is said to be so realistic that most participants soon forget they are actually safe on the ground and really feel the tension of a flight emergency. Similarly, competitive programs are used to play "war games" -- to permit evaluation of alternative strategies, and to train personnel to react to situations one hopes they will never actually face.

7.3 A Conversational Program

In both the PYS-Retrieval and the Match-Snatch programs of the previous sections the prompting messages and the user responses give the impression of a dialog between the user and the computer. But in both of these examples the dialog is incidental to the main purpose of the program. It is used simply to elicit proper input values from the user. However, programs can be written whose primary purpose is to <u>conduct such a dialog</u>, and in particular, to imitate the responses that a person might make in a conversation. One of the earliest and best-known programs of this type was written by Weizenbaum (see References). The program is named ELIZA, after the heroine of <u>Pygmalion</u>, but she sounds more like a psychiatrist than a flower girl.

Teitelbaum has written a simplified version of ELIZA for use in an introductory programming course. This version is not much longer or more complicated than POET, and uses ideas already suggested in Sections 1 and 4. It has to decompose the user's responses into individual words, and scan those words for certain "keywords". Each individual keyword specifies a certain pattern of reply for the computer, with phrases copied from the user's input. This involves searching a "dictionary" and making substitutions similar to our translation program in Section 4. Although the algorithm is really quite simple, the overall effect is impressive.

The following is a sample dialog from Teitlebaum's version of ELIZA. The user has entered the lines marked "PATIENT". ELIZA's responses are marked "DOCTOR". (The program is written in such a way that the input strings need not be quoted -- see Appendix B.3.)

```
PATIENT: HELLO
DOCTOR:  HOW DO YOU DO.  PLEASE STATE YOUR PROBLEM.

PATIENT: MEN ARE ALL ALIKE.
DOCTOR:  IN WHAT WAY.

PATIENT: THEY ARE ALWAYS BUGGING US ABOUT SOMETHING
         OR OTHER.
```

DOCTOR: CAN YOU THINK OF A SPECIFIC EXAMPLE.

PATIENT: WELL, MY BOYFRIEND MADE ME COME HERE.
DOCTOR: YOUR BOYFRIEND MADE YOU COME HERE.

PATIENT: HE SAYS I AM DEPRESSED MUCH OF THE TIME.
DOCTOR: I AM SORRY TO HEAR YOU ARE DEPRESSED.

PATIENT: IT IS TRUE, I AM UNHAPPY.
DOCTOR: DO YOU THINK COMING HERE WILL HELP YOU NOT TO BE UNHAPPY.

PATIENT: I NEED SOME HELP.
DOCTOR: WHAT WOULD IT MEAN TO YOU IF YOU GOT SOME HELP.

PATIENT: PERHAPS I COULD LEARN TO GET ALONG WITH MY MOTHER.
DOCTOR: TELL ME MORE ABOUT YOUR FAMILY.

PATIENT: MY MOTHER TAKES CARE OF ME.
DOCTOR: WHO ELSE IN YOUR FAMILY TAKES CARE OF YOU.

PATIENT: MY FATHER
DOCTOR: I WOULD LIKE TO KNOW MORE ABOUT YOUR FATHER.

PATIENT: YOU ARE LIKE MY FATHER IN SOME WAYS.
DOCTOR: WHAT RESEMBLANCE DO YOU SEE.

PATIENT: YOU ARE NOT VERY AGRESSIVE.
DOCTOR: WHAT MAKES YOU THINK I AM NOT VERY AGRESSIVE.

PATIENT: YOU DON'T ARGUE WITH ME.
DOCTOR: WE WERE DISCUSSING YOU - NOT ME.

PATIENT: BECAUSE YOU ARE JUST A COMPUTER.
DOCTOR: DO COMPUTERS WORRY YOU.

PATIENT: I AM AFRAID OF THEM.
DOCTOR: IS IT BECAUSE YOU ARE AFRAID OF THEM THAT YOU CAME TO ME.

PATIENT: NO, BECAUSE THEY MADE ME TAKE CS-100.
DOCTOR: IS THAT THE REAL REASON.

Section 7 Exercises

1. The Match-Snatch program given in Section 7.2 doesn't know how to alter its responses for singular and plural objects. Note in the sample game that the program reports the number of matches remaining by the line:

    THERE ARE 4 LEFT

This is all right, but when there is only one match left the program prints:

    THERE ARE 1 LEFT

This is crude and tends to make the computer look rather illiterate (when actually the fault is that of a lazy programmer). Indicate how the program should be modified so that

    THERE IS ONLY 1 LEFT

will be printed when only one match remains.

2. Modify the retrieval program of Section 7.1 to improve the readability of the output by providing the message

    NO SUCH YACHTS ON FILE

in response to any query that does not select at least one suitable candidate.

3. Modify the retrieval system of Section 7.1 to provide a "persistent prompt" for the question "Do you have a query?" That is, the program should insist that the answer be either 'YES' or 'NO' in a manner similar to that used in the Match-Snatch program of Section 7.2.

4. Modify the retrieval system of Section 7.1 to check the length specified in queries to be sure that it is not less than 25 nor greater than 70. If a length outside of this range is specified by the user, the system should prompt the user for a more appropriate value.

5. Write an interactive program (comparable to Match-Snatch of Section 7.2) to play a game of matching coins. Two players each toss a coin. They agree in advance which player will win if the two coins match (are both "heads" or both "tails"), with the other player winning if the two coins come up different (one head and one tail). The program should "manage" the game (as in Match-Snatch) and represent one player. Use the RAND function (see Section 6.1) to simulate the toss of a coin by the program.

6. The Match-Snatch program given in Section 7.2 is almost infinitely patient with an inept user (or with one who tries to cheat on the rules). Modify the program so that it appears to "lose patience" and changes its response if the user continues to give improper responses.

PART III   THE NATURE AND LIMITS OF PROGRAMMING

Section 1   Users and Programmers

By now we have developed sufficient background to permit a more meaningful discussion of our initial question "What is a program?" Consider the following answer:

A <u>program</u> is a <u>sequence of statements</u>, written in some <u>programming language</u>, by which a <u>computer is instructed</u> to solve some particular problem.

We want to concentrate for the moment on the phrase "written in some programming language". Such a language is presumably a language <u>intelligible to a computer</u>. That means that an algorithm is not a program, simply because it is written in English and not in a programming language. An algorithm is a sequence of statements to solve a problem, but it is not in a form that can be interpreted by a computer.

We have explained and used one particular programming language -- FORTRAN -- but there are many others. Most are somewhat like FORTRAN, differing only in various details. And a few languages are quite different. What all programming languages have in common is simply that they are intelligible to some computer. This suggests some interesting questions:

1. Why are there so many different programming languages? (In fact, there are thousands of them.)

2. Can one particular computer understand more than one language?

3. Why do we need special languages? Why isn't English a satisfactory programming language? That is, why can't a computer understand instructions in ordinary English?

4. Does everyone who uses a computer, "program it"?

None of these questions is easy to answer, and our attempts will be neither complete nor rigorous, but perhaps they will help you achieve some insight into some interesting issues.

Let us carefully review and summarize the programming process we have been describing since Part I. Faced with a certain type of <u>problem</u>, we devised an <u>algorithm</u> -- a sequence of actions, whose performance would constitute a solution to the problem. We translated the actions of this algorithm into the statements of a <u>programming language</u> to produce a <u>program</u>. We loaded the program into a computer and caused it to be executed. During its execution, the program read <u>data</u> and produced <u>results</u>.

Recall that, in general, we tried to keep our algorithms flexible, so they would be useful for many similar problems, rather than one specific problem. For example, our very first program to print a value was designed to print <u>any value given</u> as data, and not just one specific value. Our program to print a list of values was designed to accommodate lists of any length, and not just lists of one particular length. Consequently, the program derived from such an algorithm will accommodate some particular "class" of problem; each individual execution of the program involves one specific example of a problem from that class. That is, each set of input data represents one particular instance of the problem type for which the program was designed. The resulting output is an "answer" applicable to that specific problem.

On this basis, we might try to distinguish between a <u>programmer</u> -- one who writes a program to solve some class of problem, and a <u>user</u> -- one who executes a program to solve one specific example of that class of problem.

In general, the user need not understand the programming language in which the program he uses has been written. He will be given some "operating instructions" for the program, which will specify the form in which input is to be presented to the program. This should seem fairly natural and obvious. It parallels other situations in our experience -- some people <u>build</u> automobiles, many more people <u>drive</u> automobiles, and drivers do not need to know much about building them. They only need <u>operating instructions</u>.

Essentially, this is true in computing, and represents a fair description of how the business operates. There are professional programmers who write programs (in languages such as FORTRAN). There are many other people who use those programs, directly or indirectly, and need to know nothing about how the program was written -- indeed, in many cases they are unaware that a program is involved. For example, modern telephone systems are largely computer-controlled, so every time you dial a long distance telephone call you are <u>using a program</u> -- that is, you are supplying data to a program, and obtaining output from the program. (In this case, "output" is both a "connection" and billing for that connection.)

III 1.1 A Language for Lists   245

  While this is a satisfactory explanation from a practical
point-of-view, it is interesting to examine it more carefully.
We will approach this by exploiting our trusty value-listing
problem.

1.1 **A Programming Language for Lists**

  Suppose we felt that value-listing was such an important
class of problem that it would be useful to have a special
programming language just for value-listing. We will call our
new language PLL (for "Programming Language for Lists"). The
syntax (grammar) of PLL might be the following:

  1. The first statement of every PLL program is:

        'LISTING PROGRAM'

  2. The second statement is:

        'VALUES ARE'
            value-type-specification

    where value-type-specification is either 'NUMBERS' or
    'STRINGS'.

  3. The third statement is:

        'THE NUMBER OF VALUES IS'
            integer

  4. The fourth statement is:

        'VALUES FOLLOW:'

A sample PLL program, with its data, might be the following:

        'LISTING PROGRAM'
        'VALUES ARE'
          'STRINGS'
        'THE NUMBER OF VALUES IS'
          5
        'VALUES FOLLOW:'
          'QUICKS'
          'ROBINSONS'
          'CANAPITSIT'
          'CUTTYHUNK'
          'PENIKESE'

Now forget PLL for a moment and consider the following FORTRAN program:

```
      CHARACTER*100   TEXT, TYPE
      INTEGER   COUNT, LENGTH
      REAL   NUMBER
      CHARACTER*100   STRING
C
      READ, TEXT
      IF(TEXT .NE. 'LISTING PROGRAM') PRINT, 'SYNTAX ERROR'
      READ, TEXT
      IF(TEXT .NE. 'VALUES ARE') PRINT, 'SYNTAX ERROR'
      READ, TYPE, TEXT
      IF(TEXT .NE. 'THE NUMBER OF VALUES IS')
     $   PRINT, 'SYNTAX ERROR'
      READ, LENGTH, TEXT
      IF(TEXT .NE. 'VALUES FOLLOW:') PRINT, 'SYNTAX ERROR'
C
      DO 100 COUNT = 1, LENGTH, 1
         IF(TYPE .NE. 'NUMBERS') GO TO 20
            READ, NUMBER
            PRINT, NUMBER
            GO TO 100
  20     IF(TYPE .NE. 'STRINGS') GO TO 100
            READ, STRING
            PRINT, STRING
 100     CONTINUE
      STOP
      END
```

If you had seen this FORTRAN program without the preceding discussion you would just consider it a slight generalization of the list program we developed back in Section I.3. It has more elaborate preliminary control values that allow it to be used for a list of either string or number values. But having described PLL, you should have realized in reading the FORTRAN program, that the <u>data for this FORTRAN program</u> would look just like the <u>program and data</u> for the preceding PLL program. That is, if you supplied the PLL program and its data to this FORTRAN program as data, the execution of the FORTRAN program would <u>effectively be executing the PLL program</u>.

Consider the implications of this program. Suppose you taught someone the PLL language -- but nothing at all about FORTRAN. After he had written a program in PLL and wanted to execute it on the computer you would give him a copy of the FORTRAN program shown above, and tell him that these are "control cards" that have to precede his program. He would not realize that his program isn't really a program at all, but just the beginning of the <u>data input to the FORTRAN program</u>. Nevertheless, he could proceed to write listing "programs" in PLL, and only you would know that these programs were really just data. Note that the PLL programs might be <u>used</u> by others who knew nothing of the details of PLL (much less, of FORTRAN) -- they would just follow the operating instructions associated with a particular PLL program.

The interesting thing is that for all practical purposes <u>PLL has become a real programming language</u> -- simply because we wrote a program (in FORTRAN) that is capable of reading a PLL program (as data) and <u>doing what the PLL statements specify</u>. The existence of FORTRAN program means that PLL is effectively <u>intelligible</u> to a computer. In fact, any computer that understands FORTRAN could also understand PLL.

Obviously, PLL is not much of a programming language. But we could have made it more elaborate -- adding statements to control the format of input and output, and provide various error checks -- and eventually we could have defined a reasonably plausible special-purpose programming language for this particular class of problem. (Of course, our FORTRAN program to read PLL programs would also have to be made more elaborate.)

1.2 A Programming Language for Poems

Let us emphasize the point by constructing another example. Consider the operating instructions for the program called POET in Section II.6.4. These instructions describe the control values and phrases that must be supplied as data to POET. We could have dressed these instructions up, and described them as a "Programming Language for Poets" -- PLP, of course. An example of a PLP "statement" might be the following:

```
'GENERATE'
   number
'STANZAS.'
```

You should be able to envision the changes to the POET program that would allow it to read this expanded form of input, and extract from these "statements" the control values it needs. The twenty phrases that constitute the second part of POET's input would be the "data" to the PLP program. In other words, with only superficial changes in the POET program and in the operating instructions for POET, the <u>user of the POET program</u> just became a <u>programmer in the programming language called PLP</u>. This programmer could, in turn, write programs in PLP -- to compose limericks, for example -- that would be used by other people who knew nothing of PLP or FORTRAN.

A third example of a highly specialized programming language has already been presented -- in the "statistical packages" described in Section II.3. These are effectively programming languages developed specifically for statistical problems, although they are usually described as "packages" or "systems" rather than as languages. But for all practical purposes the users of these systems are really writing programs in a very specialized language.

There are a number of conclusions that can be drawn:

1. The distinction between a <u>programmer</u> and a <u>user</u> is not really as sharp and clear as we implied previously.

The distinction must rest on the definition of a <u>programming language</u>, and that is very difficult to provide -- what are apparently statements of a programming language at one level can turn out to be just data to some program at a higher level.

2. We can invent new programming languages without having to physically build a computer to understand the new language. A language can become a "programming" language just by having someone write a program in some other programming language that is capable of interpreting and executing statements in the new language. The difficulty of this implementation task depends entirely on the complexity of the prospective programming language.

3. Obviously, a single computer can "understand" many languages, since any language it understands can in turn give birth to others -- just as FORTRAN programs in our examples created the PLL and PLP languages.

4. Apparently the complexity of a programming language is related to the flexibility it provides the programmer. For example, FORTRAN is more complex and harder to learn than PLL, but FORTRAN can be used over a broad range of problems, while PLL has very limited capability.

5. The converse of point 4 is that anytime one is willing to sacrifice generality, it should be possible to invent a specialized programming language that would be much easier to use. This is, in fact, frequently done; various examples are described below.

1.3 <u>The Real Nature of FORTRAN</u>

Now we have a confession to make (which you might have suspected was soon to come). That is, <u>FORTRAN itself is a programming lauguage only in the same sense as PLL and PLP</u>. It is an entirely artifical language, not native to any computer, and it qualifies as a programming language only because there is a program (called a "FORTRAN Compiler") that reads FORTRAN statements as its data.

You might wonder how much deeper this deception can go. Be reassured that this is the end of it. The FORTRAN compiler is written in a <u>real</u> programming language -- that is, it is written in a language that is physically built into the structure of the computer. This is the native language of the IBM 370 family of

III 1.3 The Real Nature of FORTRAN

computers. It is called the "370 Machine Language", or sometimes "370 Assembly Language", or "Basic Assembly Language for the 370" (abbreviated "370 BAL").

To restate the situation, the FORTRAN compiler is a program written in 370 Machine Language, which reads FORTRAN statements as data. The compiler program analyzes these statements, and in effect, <u>translates</u> them into the equivalent machine language instructions that will cause the computer to perform the actions you expect from the definition of the meaning of the FORTRAN statement.

Our deception with regard to FORTRAN was harmless and practical. It was harmless because the basic ideas about programming that we have discussed and illustrated in terms of FORTRAN are essentially independent of the particular programming language used. The same concepts -- looping, conditional execution, branching, use of memory -- are present in machine language, but in that form they are somewhat harder to understand and to use. Our use of FORTRAN is practical in the sense that this is the <u>type</u> of programming language that is most widely used today. That is, most programs are written in languages that are very much like FORTRAN. The only programs written in real machine language are the compilers that make it possible to use languages like FORTRAN for everything else. When most people speak of computer programming today, they are thinking of programs similar to what we have been presenting, written in languages that are much like FORTRAN.

In many places in the text we have referred to the "WATFIV language" -- in most respects identical to FORTRAN, but with various differences of detail. Now we can explain that, in fact, the difference rests in the <u>compiler</u>. A group of computer scientists at the University of Waterloo produced a different compiler for the FORTRAN language. The "WATFIV Compiler" was designed to serve a different group of programmers than most FORTRAN compilers. The WATFIV Compiler is more efficient for short programs, and more helpful in response to programming errors, but essentially the two compilers process the same statements as data. The only differences are that WATFIV has omitted a few FORTRAN statements which were considered unnecessary for instructional purposes, and has added a few features (such as character variables) that are very convenient in instruction.

1.4 Other Programming Languages

Other programming languages you may have heard of -- for example, PL/I, BASIC, APL and COBOL -- are also all <u>translated</u> languages, in the same sense as FORTRAN. None is really a native machine language.

In fact, there are many hundreds of different programming languages in use today -- almost all of them translated languages. Each different type of computer has its own native "machine language", but there are many more languages than there are types of computers. There are several reasons why there are so many programming languages. The best reason is that it has been found useful to develop <u>special-purpose languages</u> for specific types of problems -- much as we suggested with PLL and PLP in Section 1.2. But there are also different programming languages just because there are differences of opinion as to exactly how the details of problem specification should be expressed. All these programming languages have much in common -- although you would never suspect this to hear programmers argue the merits of their favorite language. These matters are debated with a fervor that would do credit to religious zealots -- with perhaps an equal chance of achieving agreement. Nevertheless, the fact of the matter is that general-purpose programming languages have much in common and differ largely in details.

There is a fine encyclopedia of programming languages (by Sammet, see References), but perhaps it would be useful to give a brief (and biased) description of the most widely used languages. The following paragraphs describe FORTRAN, COBOL, ALGOL, PL/I, PASCAL, APL and BASIC.

FORTRAN is an ancient language, dating back to the Stone Age of computing (circa 1956). It was not, as is commonly believed, the first of its kind, but it is certainly the only survivor of the era. It was designed to perform numerical computations for scientists and engineers, but has come to be used much more broadly. In terms of availability on many different types of computers, FORTRAN is the closest thing that exists to a "universal programming language". FORTRAN has now been "standardized" (American National Standards Institute) and that will slow the already glacial pace at which the language is evolving. Other languages have emerged that are at least marginally better than FORTRAN in every respect except the number and tenacity of its users. The problem is basically that FORTRAN was too good an early development. None of its would-be successors has been able to demonstrate a sufficient superiority to convince a majority of FORTRAN users to undertake the task of converting their skills and their program libraries.

COBOL was created in 1959 by a committee of programmers concerned with business data-processing. Envious of the facility that FORTRAN had brought to numerical computation, they devised a comparable language with additional features to process string data, and handle data in large structured files. The result was very successful, and COBOL has also become a National Standard. The language is generally scorned by computer scientists, and is seldom taught in universities, but the fact remains that COBOL is by far the most widely used of all general-purpose programming languages.

ALGOL is actually a series of languages, developed by an international committee of computer scientists, beginning in the late 1950's. In the United States the ALGOL languages have been influential, but not widely used. Unfortunately, ALGOL has become a symbol of a communication gap between the academic computer science community and the professional programmers, both groups feeling (with considerable justification) that the other is nearsighted and parochial.

PL/I was created in the mid-sixties by a joint committee consisting of IBM representatives, and users of IBM equipment. The new language was intended to serve both the numerical and business communities, and thereby replace both FORTRAN and COBOL. It was also to incorporate some of the ideas (and the elegance) represented by ALGOL. The committee had an impossibly short time for its design task, but in spite of this they defined a language that could serve both FORTRAN and COBOL users. (Perhaps given more time, their design might have been more elegant, but it was nevertheless a remarkable achievement.) However, any hope that adherents of FORTRAN, COBOL or ALGOL would desert their prior tongues in significant numbers was doomed to disappointment. Instead of consolidating the programming language situation, PL/I just added a fourth major general-purpose language to the Babel.

These four -- COBOL, FORTRAN, PL/I and ALGOL -- are the major general-purpose programming languages in use today. Their similarities are really more important than their differences, and historians will surely regard them as members of the same family of languages. There are several other, more specialized languages that deserve honorable mention:

PASCAL is an early-seventies derivative of ALGOL. Unlike the committee efforts that led to the languages described above, PASCAL was at least initially a one-man effort. Its author is Professor Niklaus Wirth of the Federal Institute of Technology in Zurich. PASCAL is not yet widely used outside of the academic community, but its use there has grown rapidly in the last year. It is still a minor dialect, but it has many attractive aspects and will bear watching.

APL is another one-man effort -- in this case, by Dr. Kenneth Iverson of IBM. Long a language crying in the wilderness, APL has finally caught on, and has gained a substantial following. In fact, APL advocates seem to be the most zealous of all programming partisans. The language is most suitable for relatively small, short-lived problems (its proponents would be outraged at this narrow characterization) but in fact it has achieved use far beyond this type of problem. It has benefitted from the fact that it is part of an effective interactive system, and many of the virtues ascribed to APL are more accurately attributed to its interactive nature. (More precisely, some of APL's popularity arises from the fact that FORTRAN and PL/I are usually available only in a non-interactive batch-processing form, and the interactive APL is attractive by comparison.)

BASIC is another programming language that has benefitted from an interactive environment. Developed at Dartmouth College in the mid-sixties, this very simple and limited language has achieved wide use as an instructional language in secondary schools. In many respects the complete BASIC language is similar to the Poet's subset of FORTRAN that we are using. (The subset approach has the advantage that it can later be expanded if you continue on in programming.)

Finally, PL/C is an alternative compiler for the PL/I language, developed at Cornell. It is efficient for short programs, and provides an extensive, forgiving and persistent diagnostic capability. This diagnostic facility alerts the programmer to both syntax and execution errors and continues processing in order to provide as much help as possible. In effect, PL/C bears a relation to PL/I similar to that between WATFIV and FORTRAN.

1.5 English as a Programming Language

This brings us to the question of why special programming languages are required -- why not use ordinary English to instruct a computer? The answer is surprisingly simple -- <u>no one has been able to produce a compiler for English</u>, or for any other comparable natural language. This has been an obvious objective for some time, and it has received considerable attention, but no realistic observer has much optimism that it will soon be achieved.

Certain special-purpose languages have achieved a remarkably <u>readable</u> English-like syntax. For example, the following are programs written in a data-processing language called ASAP:

FOR ALL BOATS WITH BUILDER = 'HINCKLEY' AND LENGTH = 35, PRINT A LIST OF FILENBR, BUILDER, LENGTH, RIG, YEAR, PRICE, ORDERED BY PRICE.

FOR ALL BOATS WITH RIG = 'YAWL' AND LENGTH >= 35 AND LENGTH <= 37, PRINT A LIST OF FILENBR, BUILDER, LENGTH, RIG, YEAR, PRICE, ORDERED BY LENGTH, ORDERED BY YEAR, ORDERED BY PRICE.

Compare these "programs" to their FORTRAN counterparts in Section II.5.1 and it is apparent that these are significantly more readable -- in fact, they seem to be comparable to the <u>algorithms</u> we have been using to explain our programs. But this impression is somewhat deceptive. In the first place, ASAP is a very specialized language -- useful only for updating and retrieving information from a file stored on tape or disc. For that particular type of program it is very easy to use, but on the other hand, it would be impossible to write most of the programs from other sections of this book in ASAP. Moreover, while these query programs are <u>readable</u> and understandable as English-like text (without any knowledge of the ASAP language) ASAP is a long way from being able to accept <u>any</u> English text as a program. ASAP is rigidly structured, with syntax rules just as strict as those of FORTRAN. The ASAP syntax happens to have been designed to emphasize readability, but the similarity to English is more apparent than real.

It is not inconceivable that someday a strictly-defined and highly-structured subset of English -- perhaps somewhat like what we have been using for algorithms -- could be used directly as a programming language. However, by the time enough detail had been included to describe precisely each action to be performed, it is not at all clear that it would be an easier language to learn and use than FORTRAN. You should realize that in our examples, the algorithms have been shorter and easier to understand than the corresponding programs -- not primarily because they are written in an English-like language, but because they <u>omit most of the details</u>. If these algorithms were to be used directly as programs, they would necessarily have to be precise and unambiguous. Describing that kind of detail in proper English prose is tediously verbose, and you would soon long for the concise precision of a language like FORTRAN.

We might note in this regard that English-like readability was one of the design goals of COBOL, way back in the late fifties, and considerable extra verbiage was woven into the COBOL syntax to enhance this aspect of its programs. This turned out not to constitute a compelling advantage, and COBOL's widespread use is attributable to other reasons.

One other interesting development is that English is already <u>legally</u> a programming language. Very recently one small computer firm developed a new programming language (similar to ASAP in many respects). They shrewdly named their language "English", <u>trademarked that name</u>, and now advertise that their computer is the only one that can be "programmed in English". That may have been a clever marketing gimmick, but it doesn't really alter the situation described above.

1.6 Future Programming Languages

It would be appropriate to conclude this section with some astute prediction as to future directions in programming languages, but our crystal ball is very cloudy in this regard. There will certainly be increasing interest in the development of specialized languages for certain types of problems -- each obtaining greater ease of use by surrendering flexibility. Languages such as ASAP, or the statistical systems described in Section II.3, offer the user such a tremendous advantage -- as long as his problems fall within their limited scope -- that their use will certainly expand. But the question of future directions for general-purpose languages is much more difficult.

We hate to forecast that our grandchildren will be programming in FORTRAN -- it seems comparable to saying they will be driving Model-A Fords -- but every obituary for FORTRAN has turned out to be ludicrously premature. PL/I apparently didn't possess enough advantage to displace FORTRAN, and it may well turn out that PASCAL's advantages relative to PL/I are insufficient. Each of these languages has represented an <u>evolutionary</u> improvement, and there is a very strong economic argument favoring stability in this matter. A "break-through" language could appear at any time, but there is no sign of it yet, and forecasting the arrival of break-throughs in any field is a hazardous occupation.

It should be obvious after all this discussion that there really is no clear and sharp distinction betweens <u>users</u> and <u>programmers</u>. The extreme situations are clear. Anyone writing statements in machine-language or FORTRAN is certainly "programming", and anyone supplying straightforward data to a program is hardly programming. But as soon as some of those data provide control values, and thereby exercise some choice and control over the program's actions -- then the distinction starts to blur.

Our intention has been to exhibit a wide variety of different ways in which a computer's power can be brought to bear on a problem. Some of these ways could reasonably be called "programming languages", and their users could be said to be "programming", but the distinction is not important. What is important is the following.

First, you should realize that it is relatively easy to develop new programming languages for new classes of problems. For a particular type of problem a specialized programming language may well permit individual problems to be described for computation much more easily than could be done in FORTRAN.

However, the significance of FORTRAN and comparable languages (such as PL/I or ALGOL) is that these languages, although still themselves not true machine languages, nevertheless <u>reflect actual machine operations</u> sufficiently closely that one can obtain real insight into the inherent nature and capability of the computer. That is, the variables, loops and statements of FORTRAN are sufficiently representative of what is actually going on in the computer that you can really understand what a computer is capable of doing. You can begin to understand that <u>only tasks that can be reduced to a sequence of such operations</u> can be effectively computed.

The special-purpose languages, such as statistical packages or ASAP, work very hard to disguise these basic operations, and consequently such languages tend to exaggerate the mysterious workings of the computer. It helps to keep in mind that <u>every program in such a specialized language</u> is actually just <u>data to some program written in FORTRAN</u> (or some similar language). The underlying FORTRAN program is reading the "statements" of the apparent user language, and interpreting these commands to control the assignment of values to variables, the executions of loops, etc. -- all the operations we have described in numerous examples. The computing process inherently consists of such operations -- somehow or other the user's tasks must be described in terms of such a sequence.

The remarkable convenience of various special-purpose languages is actually a tribute to the ingenuity of the people who devise the underlying programs that implement these languages. Through these languages the computer can appear to wear many hats, but underneath this exotic millinery, the basic computing process is still the same as we have been describing since Part I.

Section 2   Some Limits on Programming

Now that you have some understanding of how a computer's actions are controlled, and some experience in reading programs to solve given problems, it is worthwhile exploring the limits of the programming process. However, attempting to identify what can and what cannot be done by today's computers is very difficult, and if you try to forecast where the dividing line will fall some years in the future, it is all but impossible.

To a certain extent the limits on what is computable depend upon how much effort one is willing to expend, and what kind of performance one demands as a result. The projection for the future depends on the rate at which machine capacity will increase (which is somewhat predictable in the short run), and the rate at which progress will be made in the development of more powerful programming languages, which is very unclear.

Much has been written on the question, but a fair amount of that is self-aggrandizing and less than objective. Many computer specialists have written extravagant descriptions of what will be achieved (or at least what could be achieved if only research support was forthcoming). But even well-informed non-specialists give enthusiastic projections. For example, Kahn and Wiener (who are not computer specialists) summarize the situation as follows (The Year 2000, MacMillan, 1967):

> "As a result, when one specialist declares that 'the computer gives signs of becoming the contemporary counterpart of the steam engine that brought on the industrial revolution' (McCarthy, Scientific American, Sept. 1966) and another argues that the computer represents 'an advance in man's thinking process as radical as the invention of writing' (Simon, Time, April 2, 1965) one is not irritated by the grandiosity of the claim, but only by what has become its obviousness. The capacity of the computer ultimately to effect a dramatic extension of man's power over his environment, as well as many other social and economic changes, is by now obvious to all."

In general, if one reviews the accuracy of forecasts concerning computers over the brief period for which the results are known, one does not acquire great confidence in current predictions. There has at least been a pattern in the errors in past forecasts. They have consistently <u>underestimated</u> the rapidity of growth of relatively <u>unsophisticated applications</u>, and at the same time consistently <u>overestimated</u> the rate of progress toward more exotic, quasi-intellectual uses. The very rapid growth of the field is largely explained by increases in the speed and memory size of computers, and a reduction in their cost. Relatively little can be attributed to progress in programming languages or programming methodology.

The preceding sections may suggest a general long-range optimism (or pessimism, depending on your point-of-view) about the prospects for computing. At least they fail to give any solid limits on the prospects. However, there are limits of several different kinds. This section briefly suggests three different types of problems that are impossible to compute -- no approach will yield an effective program. Sections 2.1 and 2.2 concern problems that are too vague or too large to be effectively computable. Such problems occur frequently and the programmer must be wary of them. Section 2.3 describes a curious type of problem for which it can be proved that no completely effective program can be written.

2.1 <u>Ill-Defined Problems</u>

Many problems are just not understood well enough to be programmed. Sometimes we can write what is apparently an algorithm, but then be unable to convert this to a program. For example, in an algorithm we can use English commands and phrases, such as "solve", "find", "create", etc. This is useful, but it can lead to unwarranted optimism about the kinds of problems that can be programmed. Eventually, each of these commands must be translated into the statements of a programming language. The program development process breaks down if, at any point, you encounter a command that cannot be reasonably translated into actual program statements. For example, it is easy to write "solve", but it is sometimes impossible to figure out any way to go about "solving". You can write "find", and then discover that you don't even know where to look.

It is often easy to disguise the inability to refine such a command. For example, in developing a program to select potential companions for an applicant to a "computer dating" service, one must at some point refine the meaning of the term "appropriate date" into program statements. No algorithm capable of doing this in an effective way has yet been discovered. Nevertheless, scores of different programs have been written to "perform" this task. Unfortunately, the use of a computer sometimes lends respectability and credibility to an algorithm that would be laughable if used by a human.

This is not to suggest that it is not sometimes necessary to use algorithms that only approximate the required results -- this is often all that is possible. But the ethics of programming demand that approximations be clearly identified as such. A program must not be allowed to pretend to greater authenticity and validity than it really possesses.

Recall that we raised this issue in Section II.5.2 with regard to certain queries addressed to the yacht broker's retrieval system. We argued then that the exact manner in which a boat's speed or seaworthiness depends upon measurable dimensions of the boat is not completely understood. Hence it is not possible to write a program to "select the fastest boat" from among those on file.

By now you should thoroughly appreciate the fact that one does not just "feed a problem to a computer" -- not even a trivial problem, let alone nuclear proliferation, pollution control and economic development. Problems require programs; programs require algorithms; and algorithms imply that the problem is precisely stated, and a method of solution is known. Relatively speaking, computers still work on simple problems, and progressing toward solving really complex problems is going to be painfully slow. No breakthrough in the development of programming languages, or increase in the speed of computers, is going to change the fundamental fact that we must thoroughly understand a problem in order to program a solution to it.

2.2 Impossibly-Long Programs

Most neophyte programmers are somewhat awed by the computer's speed. Programs that take hours to write are executed in a fraction of a second, and one begins to regard the computer's speed as essentially infinite. Therefore, it is surprising and a bit disillusioning to discover how easy it is to suggest problems that are just too long to be computed. There are numerous problems that can be clearly and precisely stated, and can be easily programmed, but that would require so much execution time that they are effectively impossible.

Many such problems are essentially "combinatorial" in nature -- they involve trying "all possible combinations" of a number of factors. These problems increase in size very rapidly with an increase in the number of factors that must be considered.

For example, suppose you worked for an international oil company that decided it needed a new consistent logo for its world-wide operations. In addition to a contest among employees to think up a new name, you are asked to produce a list of <u>all possible names</u>, in order to make sure that no good possibilities are overlooked.

III 2.2 Impossibly-Long Programs

A program to produce such a list is easily written. Suppose you decide to work with an alphabet of 28 characters -- the 26 letters plus the blank and the hyphen. A simple program to produce all possible five-character names from this alphabet is shown below:

```
      CHARACTER*100  L(28)
      CHARACTER*100  WORD
      INTEGER   I1, I1, I3, I4, I5
      L(1) = ' '
      L(2) = '-'
      L(3) = 'A'
      L(4) = 'B'
      L(5) = 'C'
      L(6) = 'D'
      L(7) = 'E'
      L(8) = 'F'
      L(9) = 'G'
      L(10) = 'H'
      L(11) = 'I'
      L(12) = 'J'
      L(13) = 'K'
      L(14) = 'L'
      L(15) = 'M'
      L(16) = 'N'
      L(17) = 'O'
      L(18) = 'P'
      L(19) = 'Q'
      L(20) = 'R'
      L(21) = 'S'
      L(22) = 'T'
      L(23) = 'U'
      L(24) = 'V'
      L(25) = 'W'
      L(26) = 'X'
      L(27) = 'Y'
      L(28) = 'Z'
      WORD = ' '
      DO 50 I1 = 1, 28, 1
         DO 40 I2 = 1, 28, 1
            DO 30 I3 = 1, 28, 1
               DO 20 I4 = 1, 28, 1
                  DO 10 I5 = 1, 28, 1
                     WORD(1:1) = L(I1:I1)
                     WORD(2:2) = L(I2:I2)
                     WORD(3:3) = L(I3:I3)
                     WORD(4:4) = L(I4:I4)
                     WORD(5:5) = L(I5:I5)
                     PRINT, WORD
10                CONTINUE
20             CONTINUE
30          CONTINUE
40       CONTINUE
50    CONTINUE
```

```
STOP
END
```

In due course the list will be produced (the printing will take a while), and indeed, it will provide some excellent possibilities -- names such as:

EXXON, ESSO, KODAK, XEROX, IBM, GM, FORD

But suppose the Logo Committee decides that all the good names from the five-character list have already been used, so it would be better to work from a list of ten-character names so as not to miss any possibilities comparable to, say, COCA-COLA or KLEENEX.

The program to do this is not quite twice as long as the five-character generator shown above, and as easily written. But while you are waiting for the results to come back from the computing center you might make some rough calculations as to how long its execution will take. As a simple basis for estimate, consider only the assignment statements in the innermost loop. They will have to be executed 28^{10} times. That is obviously a large number, but then computers are very fast. But consider the number a bit further. 28^{10} is roughly 3×10^{14}. Suppose we had a computer capable of executing one million such sets of statements per second. (That is roughly ten times the speed of the fastest computer that exists today, and probably more than 100 times the speed of whatever computer you have been using.) It would take this super-computer just over 200 years to execute the required number of assignment statements. (Printing the actual list will take a little longer, since it takes something like 50,000 times as long to execute a PRINT statement as an assignment statement.)

Our example is whimsical, but comparable problems are not at all uncommon. People often suggest that a computer be used to "enumerate all the possibilities" (even people who ought to know better). Such combinatorial problems increase in length incredibly rapidly, and are computationally impossible for surprisingly small dimensions. Moreover, they will remain impossible no matter what progress computing technology may make.

2.3 "Undecidable" Problems

For certain problems it can be <u>proved</u> that <u>no</u> effective program can be written. It is not just a matter of not yet having found an efficient algorithm, or not yet having computers that are fast enough -- it can be rigorously <u>proved that no program is possible</u>. One important branch of computer science is concerned with classifying problems according to degree of difficulty (rate at which execution time increases with some key dimension of the problem) and, in particular, identifying such non-computable problems. In most cases rather sophisticated mathematical arguments are involved, but the following example will suggest the general nature of the problems and proofs.

Suppose you were asked to write a program called "Truthtest" that will be able to determine the truth or falsity of some special class of English statements. Assume each statement submitted would have an identifying label prefix. For example, the following might be submitted to Truthtest:

'STATEMENT23: STARBOARD IS THE RIGHT SIDE.'

Truthtest would "process" such a statement and then print one of the following results:

      either   STATEMENT23 IS FALSE

      or   STATEMENT23 IS TRUE

The question is whether or not it would be <u>possible</u> to write a program that would meet these requirements.

The answer depends upon how rich a class of statements Truthtest must be able to handle. Trivial versions are obviously feasible. For example, suppose there were exactly ten different statements that constituted the set of possible input statements. You could decide in advance which were true and which were false, so the program would simply have to "recognize" which statement had been given and look up the proper pre-programmed answer. In effect, the program would be like the retrieval program shown in Section II.5. This simple-minded strategy could be expanded to handle hundreds or even thousands of different statements -- but it is clearly not an interesting program. So consider a strategy where the statements are not listed in advance, but rather a program is written that is capable of analyzing arbitrary sentences. It could have a fixed vocabulary, and the input sentences would have to be constructed from that vocabulary. It could also have a limited area of discourse, and the input sentences would have to be interpretable within that area. Would it be possible to write such a version of Truthtest?

Again, the answer is obviously "yes". The program SAM, described in Section III.5, is an example of just such a program. The catch comes when you try to describe precisely the class of statements that Truthtest will be able to classify -- or equivalently, to assess the accuracy of its classifications.

To illustrate the difficulty, suppose Truthtest were presented with the following statement to classify:

'STATEMENT9: STATEMENT9 IS FALSE.'

If Truthtest reports:

STATEMENT9 IS FALSE

it will be confirming the truth of the statement it is declaring to be false. This would be a contradiction, so Truthtest would be considered to have made a mistake. On the other hand, if it reported:

STATEMENT9 IS TRUE

it would be contradicting the statement it claims to be true. So the only two answers available to the program are both wrong. The only resolution of this paradox is to conclude that it is impossible to produce any program to do what Truthtest is supposed to do. But note that this is not an inherent limitation of a computer -- given the same problem requirements, you would face the same dilemma. It is the problem that is impossible, not the machine that is incapable.

The difficulty of the problem does not lie in the definition of truth and falsity; that is, this is not just a disguised example of an "ill-defined" problem, such as those cited in Section 2.1. The following example should clarify the distinction. It is similar to the Truthtest problem, but its task is more precisely defined. Nevertheless, it leads to the same type of paradox and the same conclusion of impossibility.

Suppose you are asked to devise a program that can scan the statements of another program and decide whether or not that program contains any errors of a type called an "infinite iterative loop". For example, the following would be an infinite iterative loop (let us abbreviate this as an "iil"):

```
         DO 100 I = 1, 5, 1
            I = I - 1
100      CONTINUE
```

If a program contains any iil it will never complete its execution, so large amounts of computer time might be wasted before the user abandoned the attempt to execute the program. Hence it would certainly be useful to have such a testing program, and our objective is not at all artificial. Note that there is no way to test for the presence of iils empirically, because you could not distinguish between programs that would never terminate, and those that are just impossibly long, as described in Section 2.2. Of course, the distinction between

III 2.3 "Undecidable" Problems

the two is not of any great practical consequence.

So your objective is to write a program that will read <u>any</u> program as data, and decide whether or not it contains any construction that is effectively an iil. To be precise, suppose we say that your program (let's call it "Testiil") should report the result "NOHALT" if the program being analyzed contains an iil, and report the result "HALT" if the program contains no iil and will therefore eventually come to a halt. Whether or not a program halts may depend upon the data it is processing, so Testiil will have to consider the data as well as the program. So the <u>data</u> supplied to Testiil will consist of the statements of the subject program and the data for that program. For example, the data supplied to Testiil could be something like the following:

```
          INTEGER I, X
          READ, X
          DO 100 I = 1, 5, 1
            I = I -X
100       CONTINUE
          STOP
          END
     $ENTRY
          0
```

Testiil should read this data and decide that it does not contain an iil, so it should print the result "HALT". However, if the last line of this data had been 1 instead of 0, then Testiil should report the result "NOHALT".

It can be convincingly shown that it is impossible to produce any program that will do what Testiil is supposed to do. The detailed argument is a little more complicated than is appropriate for this book, but essentially it comes down to examining what would happen if we <u>could</u> construct a Testiil program -- and then <u>fed it a copy of itself</u> as the program to be tested. This leads to the same kind of paradox that faces the Truthtest program, and hence the same conclusion that it is impossible to produce a program such as Testiil. (The argument is given in either the Conway-Gries <u>Introduction</u> or the <u>Primer</u>, see References.)

To restate the conclusion -- no matter how hard you worked, or how clever you were, or what programming language you used, there simply is <u>no way to write a program that will do what Testiil is supposed to do</u>.

Note that it is obviously not impossible to write a program that tests other programs for <u>some kinds of errors</u> -- the WATFIV Compiler is, in fact, an example of such a program. Recall that we did not claim it was impossible to write a Truthtest program that would correctly classify <u>some</u> statements. But there are certain types of errors, such as infinite iterative loops, that cannot always be detected. That is, it is not just for lack of

III 2.3 "Undecidable" Problems

ingenuity on the part of the University of Waterloo programmers that WATFIV does not detect all infinite loops -- it is <u>provable</u> that no one could produce a version of WATFIV that would be able to detect all infinite loops.

This is an example of a phenomenon called "undecidability". The problem of determining whether program P processing data D will ever halt is said to be "undecidable". This particular problem was first proved undecidable by a British mathematician Alan Turing in 1936 (ten years before the first modern computer). The most readable contemporary exposition of the idea is Chapter 8 of Minsky's <u>Computation</u> (Prentice-Hall, 1967). One does not exactly stumble on undecidable problems every day in the course of programming, but it is nevertheless interesting to know that such absolute limits on the computing process do exist.

Section 3   Errors in the Computing Process

The most serious flaw in the computer's public reputation is its supposed susceptibility to errors. The newspapers delight in reporting its lapses. Innumerable clerks and bureaucrats have learned to blame every clumsiness and delay on a "computer foulup". This calumny is undeserved since the computer is actually one of the most reliable devices man has constructed. But the public sees not the computer alone, but a complete data processing system, of which the computer is just one component. Unfortunately, such systems have too often earned a reputation for questionable reliability. The following sections discuss this problem, and assign responsibility where it belongs.

3.1 Types of Errors

Assuming that by now you have written and executed several programs you have undoubtedly had some experience with errors in the computing process. Thinking back over your experience you can probably identify errors of several different kinds. For example:

1. Errors of misunderstanding the precise requirements of the problem.

2. Errors of misunderstanding how some feature of FORTRAN works -- that is, exactly what some FORTRAN statement means.

3. Errors that are simply accidents -- keypunch mistakes, misspellings, omissions, etc.

But it is exceedingly unlikely that you will have encountered a bona fide "computer error". These presumably do occasionally happen, but you are probably more likely to be struck by lightning while walking to the computer center than to experience a real computer error.

This same pattern holds for the field in general -- computers rarely make errors, but people often do. Compared to people, computers are essentially infallible. But computers must depend upon people to write their programs and to supply their data, so this cooperative venture called the computing process is subject to many errors.

This does not necessarily mean that the process must yield to those errors and perform unreliably for its users. It just means that systems must be designed with the error-proneness of the human participants in mind, so that appropriate precautions can be provided.

3.2 Errors in the Data

In a classroom situation, when you are just learning to write programs, you _may_ be able to assume that the data for your programs are prepared so carefully that they will precisely satisfy all the requirements of the problem. But except for these special circumstances, _real_ programs to solve real problems must contend with data errors. There are a number of different "attitudes" a program can take with regard to data errors, which we can illustrate using the PS-PACK program from Section II.3.

Recall that PS-PACK read a sequence of words representing statistical commands, followed by the sequence of numbers to be processed. Consider the portion of the program that read the command words. It consists of the following statements:

```
      DO 100 CNBR = 1, 10000, 1
         READ, COMAND
         IF(COMAND .EQ. 'NUMBERS') GO TO 200
         IF(COMAND .EQ. 'LIST') LI = 'YES'
         IF(COMAND .EQ. 'MEAN') ME = 'YES'
         IF(COMAND .EQ. 'MAX') MA = 'YES'
         IF(COMAND .EQ. 'MIN') MI = 'YES'
         IF(COMAND .EQ. 'RANGE') RA = 'YES'
         IF(COMAND .EQ. 'SDEV') SD = 'YES'
         IF(COMAND .EQ. 'LIMITS') LM = 'YES'
  100 CONTINUE
  200 ...
```

The question is how well this program responds to possible errors in this portion of the data. For example, what happens if one of the commands is misspelled? In particular, what if the command 'NUMBERS' is misspelled?

This routine is not upset by misspelled commands -- it just ignores them. If the word read does not satisfy any of the sequence of tests it is simply discarded. That is, it has no effect on the values of the control variables (LI, ME, MA, etc.) and it is overwritten on the next repetition of the loop. If the final command 'NUMBERS' is misspelled (or omitted altogether) then the numbers will be read by the command loop, rather than by the subsequent number-processing loop. In this case FORTRAN will automatically provide a warning that something is wrong, since the numeric data will be incompatible with the string-valued variable COMAND. But for the misspelling of any command other than 'NUMBERS', <u>there will be no indication to the user</u> that any error has occurred. The program will simply proceed without performing the required action that should have been specified by the misspelled command.

The following is an alternative version of this section of the program:

```
        DO 100 CNBR = 1, 10000, 1
            READ, COMAND
            IF(COMAND .EQ. 'NUMBERS') GO TO 200
            IF(COMAND .NE. 'LIST') GO TO 10
                LI = 'YES'
                GO TO 100
10          IF(COMAND .NE. 'MEAN') GO TO 20
                ME = 'YES'
                GO TO 100
20          IF(COMAND .NE. 'MAX') GO TO 30
                MA = 'YES'
                GO TO 100
30          IF(COMAND .NE. 'MIN') GO TO 40
                MI = 'YES'
                GO TO 100
40          IF(COMAND .NE. 'RANGE') GO TO 50
                RA = 'YES'
                GO TO 100
50          IF(COMAND .NE. 'SDEV') GO TO 60
                SD = 'YES'
                GO TO 100
60          IF(COMAND .NE. 'LIMITS') GO TO 90
                LM = 'YES'
                GO TO 100
90          PRINT, 'IMPROPER COMMAND:', COMAND
            PRINT, '    THIS COMMAND IS IGNORED.'
100     CONTINUE
200     ...
```

This version is functionally equivalent to the first version <u>if all of the commands are given in perfect form</u>, but if there is a mistake in a command this version <u>warns the user</u>.

Consider still another version of this section of the program:

```
        DO 100 CNBR = 1, 10000, 1
            READ, COMAND
            IF(COMAND(1:1) .EQ. 'N') GO TO 200
            IF(COMAND(1:3) .NE. 'LIS') GO TO 10
```

```
              LI = 'YES'
              GO TO 100
     10       IF(COMAND(1:2) .NE. 'ME') GO TO 20
              ME = 'YES'
              GO TO 100
     20       IF(COMAND(1:2) .NE. 'MA') GO TO 30
              MA = 'YES'
              GO TO 100
     30       IF(COMAND(1:2) .NE. 'MI') GO TO 40
              MI = 'YES'
              GO TO 100
     40       IF(COMAND(1:1) .NE. 'R') GO TO 50
              RA = 'YES'
              GO TO 100
     60       IF(COMAND(1:1) .NE. 'S') GO TO 60
              SD = 'YES'
              GO TO 100
     60       IF(COMAND(1:3) .NE. 'LIM') GO TO 90
              LM = 'YES'
              GO TO 100
     90       PRINT, 'IMPROPER COMMAND:', COMAND
              PRINT, '    THIS COMMAND IS IGNORED.'
    100       CONTINUE
    200       ...
```

In this version each test considers <u>just enough characters</u> from the string read from data to <u>distinguish each command</u> from the others. In effect, only the first few characters of each command are significant to the program -- misspellings involving only the final characters are irrelevant. As in the second version, the user is warned if a valid command is not found.

The point is that all three of these versions solve the required problem <u>if the data are perfect</u>. But the second and third versions are better programs because they take into consideration the fact that the data may well not be perfect. This is a much more realistic assumption. In fact, if a program involves a substantial quantity of data it must be assumed that some errors will be present.

The third version is better than the second because it is <u>more tolerant</u> of errors on the part of the user. It recognizes that completely perfect spelling is not required to distinguish between the commands, so it does not demand more of the user than the problem really requires.

Note that once you decide that a program of the third type will be used, it would be preferable to choose the command words for the system to be as dissimilar as possible. For example, if the command word 'PRINT' had been chosen instead of 'LIST', it would be just as mnemonic for the user and there would be less overlap with the command word 'LIMITS'.

The WATFIV compiler is a good example of a program that is realistic about the quality of the data that it will receive. It makes extensive checks to detect errors in its data (your program is WATFIV's data) and warns the user (you) when errors are found. The PL/C compiler (the WATFIV for PL/I mentioned in 1.4) even goes further than this and attempts to <u>repair</u> minor errors. At least in some cases these repairs achieve what the user intended, so the program can be successfully executed.

It takes more effort to design and write a program that is tolerant of errors, but it is the only reasonable and realistic strategy. Any program that demands absolute perfection of its data is of limited utility in a world where perfection is a rare commodity.

3.3 <u>Program Errors</u>

Programming demands an attention to detail and a degree of perfection that is rarely required in human activity. Moreover, the demand for programmers is large enough that the profession cannot be extremely selective in choosing its practitioners. Most programs are not written by dedicated programming artists, who take great pride in their craft -- they are written by very ordinary people, just doing a job to earn a living.

The only thing that makes the whole process practical at all is that a program <u>does not have to be perfect on the first try</u>. The programmer can work over his creation, refining it, finding and removing errors one by one, until eventually he is satisfied with its correctness. This is a major part of the programming process. In general, as much time and effort is spent on testing and refining programs as is spent writing them in the first place.

This book is not the place to describe the testing process in great detail, since we are not trying to make you into a programmer. But it is the place to candidly admit that these techniques are not entirely successful. Even conscientiously applied they do not guarantee the correctness of a large program. In fact, it is a reasonable conjecture that <u>every large program contains latent errors</u> in spite of the best efforts of its authors.

The problem lies in deciding when the testing and refining phase is finished. Unfortunately there is no completely satisfactory way of knowing when the <u>last error</u> in a program has been found and eliminated. It is human nature to be optimistic in this regard, so inevitably programmers often terminate testing prematurely and announce that a program is finished when, in fact, errors still remain. As a consequence there is always some risk that a program that has been running satisfactorily for years will suddenly be confronted with a set of circumstances that never happen to have occurred before (either in testing or in production) and that a latent flaw will be revealed.

So the reliability of the computing process _is_ suspect -- because of latent _program errors_, rather than lapses by the machine in executing the program -- but we can't expect the general public to appreciate that distinction. But what is important is to realize that the computing process is _extremely reliable in repetition_. If it has done something once successfully, it will continue to do the same thing successfully. When confronted with something new a flaw in the program may be revealed -- but if it is, when that error is repaired it will remain repaired and the new event will be added to the repertoire of reliable tasks. _Programs don't wear out_. They don't rust or deteriorate. They can be damaged by a programmer trying to make a change to meet some new variation in the problem requirements, but left alone they will repeat their action with endless reliability.

The problem of program errors is perhaps the most serious facing the computing profession. Programming managers in industry seek to minimize the occurrence of errors in the first place by training, and by disciplining the way in which programs are written. They also try to maximize the effectiveness of the testing process -- but neither effort can be entirely successful. This situation is currently the topic of considerable research in computer science. There is work on developing programming languages that are less susceptible to errors, and on developing new tools to aid in the testing process.

In summary, the next time you read about some computer writing a check for $6,000,000 when the amount should have been $600, you should understand that the difficulty may have originated in a faulty item of data, or a latent program error, or some combination of the two. Some curious combination of circumstances could have caused the program to take a path that had not been adequately tested, and that is now revealed to have contained an error all along. It is also obvious that the programmer neglected to include checks on "reasonableness" in the program. That is, some "common sense" _can_ be built into a program to enable it to recognize unusual situations. In this case, the program might test for negative amounts, and for amounts greater than some specified upper limit, and take some special action if either occurs.

While it may not be clear exactly what did cause the erroneous value to appear on the check, it should be clear _what did not cause the problem_. It is exceedingly unlikely that some random electronic gremlin choose to add four zeros to the value of some variable. It is equally certain that those actually responsible for the error will be happy to assign full credit for the problem to their faithful servant, the computer.

Section 4   Abuses of the Computer

It is not clear whether this section should be titled "Abuses of the Computer" or "Abuses by the Computer". We are not particularly concerned here with physical abuse of computers by humans -- although this sometimes occurs. There have been a number of incidents where computers have been shot, stabbed, burned or bludgeoned by people who had been pushed beyond their limit, and who attributed some of the shoving to the computer. The computer has also become something of a symbol of the "system", so that the occupation of, and sometimes the destruction of, the campus computing center was not an infrequent event when students sought to redirect the course of national affairs. (Many universities came to regret the "fish-bowl" architecture with which they showed off their new toy.)

What we are concerned with here is abusive use of the computer. This may sometimes lead to retaliatory abuse of the machine, but our point is that this would be mis-directed revenge, since responsibility for abuse will always rest in the hands of some programmer or user. The computer is an essentially guileless tool in the employ of some human malefactor.

Like most machines, the purpose of a computer is to amplify some human capability. Inevitably, some users will use it to amplify actions that are less than admirable. In some respects the computer is just like other machines in this regard -- for example, automobiles, airplanes, or rifles. It can be used for good or otherwise. But because the computer is more flexible than other machines, and is used in so many different ways, the risks of abuse are correspondingly greater.

To a certain extent these abuses are possible because of general ignorance of both the capabilities and limitations of the computer. Abuse is also invited because of serious weaknesses in current legislation. On these grounds one might be optimistic that some of the problems are transitory and will diminish as the computer age matures. But on the other hand, certain of the risks seem to be inherent in the expanding use of computers and should be a source of serious and active concern.

4.1 The Impersonal Touch

The complaint is often voiced that business or government or the university is becoming cold, impersonal and rigid in the treatment of individuals. Since this perceived trend has paralleled the increasing use of computers by those organizations, the computer is regarded as both the symbol and the agent of this deterioration in the humaneness of our society.

Superficially the indictment is obviously accurate. The computer is, by definition, "impersonal". The computer is, by construction, "rigid", in the sense that it follows its instructions with precise and absolute faithfulness. But if the overall effect of those instructions is perceived to be unreasonable and inflexible, then whoever specified the algorithm for the program did not do an entirely effective job and did not take full advantage of the capabilities of the computer.

The underlying assumption that if humans performed the task instead of a computer, one would be treated more "humanely" is very dubious. The interminable repetition of some simple task is not a stimulating occupation for a human, and in the long run is not likely to produce innovative or sympathetic actions. The notion that low-level clerks and bureaucrats will often waive the rules and use "common sense" is hardly supportable by experience. A computer is at least consistent, and does not become irritable late in the day.

A well-designed program "knows" its own limitations. That is to say, a program should be written so that input is checked for exceptional conditions. When conditions occurs that have not been explicitly provided for in the processing actions of the program, then the program should refer the problem to some human backup service.

The frequent stories in newspapers about endless arguments between an aggrieved customer and a computer over some discrepancy in a "charge account" have conditioned much of the public's image of the computer. These stories are at once both reassuring (the computer isn't perfect after all) and alarming (the individual appears helpless). To the extent that these stories are factual, they reveal a poorly designed program, or inept users who operate the system (or both). In either case, the abuse is being perpetrated by a fellow human. One might suspect that similar difficulties existed in days before computers, but without the involvement of a computer they were not newsworthy.

The real significance of the computer in this situation is that it has made possible a tremendous growth in the consumer-credit business. The popular bank charge-card systems would not be economically viable without computers to perform the processing. The volume of such transactions has increased tremendously, and individuals can now exercise their credit in places where they are not known personally. In effect, the computer has allowed expansion of the credit business to an extent and in a way that the newspaper stories were inevitable, but presumably this is a service the public wants and not one forced upon it by computers.

Another example is the direct-mail advertising business. The computer is widely used to manipulate mailing lists and to generate much of the "junk mail" that innundates us. It is interesting that the computer is sometimes used to "personalize" this mail. What previously came addressed to "occupant" now often bears a specific name. Moreover, the name is often repeated somewhere in the body of the text to enhance the impression that the "letter" was personally typed. (See the program in Exercise 7 in Section II.1.) The computer is neither more nor less impersonal than the printing press it has replaced -- the insertion of names notwithstanding. But the computer has made the direct-mail process more selective, and hence more effective -- hence the technique is more widely used and the volume of such mail has increased.

As this is written an ominous transition is taking place in the direct-solicitation industry. The contrast between rising postage rates and relatively stable telephone costs is shifting the industry toward automatic telephone-solicitation systems. A computer is programmed to systematically step through all telephone numbers within a certain range. The output is connected into an automatic dialing device and a recording system to deliver the advertising message (and to take a order, if the message is successful). The computer portion of this system can even record numbers that did not answer (or that "hung up" prematurely) for subsequent recall. Unless new legislation intervenes, such systems may be expected to spread rapidly, and the computer is again going to be involved in what many will consider an abusive activity.

4.2 The Invasion of Privacy

The inherent "right to privacy" is much discussed these days. It may not be quite clear where this right originates, or how much privacy an individual is entitled to, but there is a widespread feeling that privacy is gradually being eroded, and that the computer is somehow involved. There is considerable merit to the charge.

The privacy issue really gained public attention when a consolidated federal "data bank" was proposed. The justification was increased processing efficiency, to be gained by collecting all of the information about each individual from various different government files into one single consolidated file system. There was little argument that such a system would be more efficient -- in fact, the problem was that it threatened to be too efficient. It would make it significantly easier for various government agencies to pool and cross-check information. While this would permit the detection of certain abuses of the system by individuals, it would also make possible very serious abuses of individuals by the system. For example, the "enemies list" compiled by the White House staff not too long ago could have been much more effective had there been a consolidated data bank. Fortunately, Congress decided that the risks of abuse outweighed the potential benefits, and that specific proposal has been at least temporarily postponed. But there is an inexorable trend toward consolidation of data files, and toward inter-connection of systems that maintain such files. This is taking place both in government and in private business, so the net effect of the proposed federal data bank may be achieved gradually and quietly without any announcement or public debate.

One technical problem involved in such large files is that the programming systems that manage large files are not yet sufficiently selective in granting access to that information. For example, if several federal agencies shared a common data bank there is not yet any effective way to <u>limit the portion of information</u> that would be available to each separate agency. Systems that can selectively control dissemination can presumably be developed, but none is available yet.

Even when the technology is available to enforce restrictions so that each user of a shared data bank can access only that information for which there is a legitimate "need to know", there will be the difficult question of <u>who is to decide</u> who gets what information. The computing literature talks about a new job called a "data base administrator", and considers the technical problem to be the <u>enforcement</u> of this administrator's decisions. But who he is, and how he makes those decisions is another matter. One might well worry that the agency in charge of "dissemination policy" might be precisely the agency that represents the greatest threat to individual privacy. Recent Washington history is not greatly reassuring in this regard.

Consequently there is a certain comfort in the present somewhat chaotic data processing systems where information about a single individual is dispersed over many different files, so that it would take considerable effort (and might attract some attention) to collect a complete dossier about a particular individual. But this is at best a temporary reprieve, and the time should be used to prepare for the consolidated systems that are sure to come.

The computer plays a central role in this development. While in principal the same information could be collected and interchanged using old-fashioned paper files, in practice it would just be too expensive and inconvenient to do it this way. For example, the personal "credit investigation" is not a new phenomenon, but the widespread application of computers to this task has turned it into enough of a problem to require additional legal controls. The ability of computer systems to assemble voluminous information, which may include some of dubious authenticity and questionable relevance, has led to legislation establishing the rights of disclosure and challenge. But these are essentially minor adjustments in the process, and the fundamental questions of the rights to accumulate and distribute information about individuals have not yet been seriously addressed.

There is just no question that the computer has reduced the cloak of anonymity that was afforded by less effective information processing mechanisms. The eventual result could be very significant and very unfortunate.

4.3 An Accessory to Fraud

In several previous sections (II.5.2, III.2.1) we have noted how the computer can be used to deceive. An unscrupulous user can trade upon the general ignorance of the real limitations on the power of a computer in order to cloak some dubious algorithm with a mantle of authority. For example, the pseudo-science of astrology often exploits such computer-supplied image-enhancement.

In its mildest form, this enhancement is widely practiced in business and engineering to make some estimate seem a little more precise than it really is, or make some designer's choice seem a little more rational. This is beginning to become a common phenomenon in product advertising -- a computer is in some way cited as an authority to endorse a particular product. For example, General Motors advertised that the suspensions of its 1977-model cars were "computer designed". This was presumably intended to suggest that these coil-springs were somehow better than others. It is a reasonable guess that GM suspension engineers have been using computers in their work for years, so it is anybody's guess precisely what innovation (if any) lies behind the advertising claim.

Anyone who understands the nature of programming is aware of how meaningless such claims of computer-enhanced authority are, and in fact, becomes especially suspicious of those who seek to depend on such support. So this phenomenon should fade from the scene as the novelty of computer use wears off and the general understanding of computing increases.

Deception involving computers can be carried to the point of criminal fraud, and there is growing evidence that "computer crime" is becoming a serious problem. A series by Thomas Whiteside in the New Yorker magazine (August 22 and 29, 1977) gives an excellent survey of the situation. Most of the examples he cites amount to computer-aided-embezzlement. Some insider -- a programmer or a sophisticated user -- exploits detailed knowledge of the internal structure of some business accounting system to divert funds to his advantage. The exact techniques vary from example to example, but a common pattern becomes very clear.

None of the techniques described in Whiteside's examples involves particularly sophisticated programming, and one cannot help but wonder whether more subtle examples are lacking simply because they have not been <u>detected</u>, and not because they do not exist.

It is apparent that the traditional auditing techniques that kept embezzlement in pre-computer accounting systems to a tolerable level, are inadequate for computer-based systems. In fact, the efficacy of standard auditing is diminishing rapidly as computer systems are interconnected into networks, and as transactions are directly entered into on-line terminal systems without any use of paper source-documents.

In many of Whiteside's examples, the management of the programming process itself is revealed to have been incredibly naive. Banks who monitor their tellers with extreme care often seem to regard their programmers as incorruptible -- although the latter have access to far larger sums and far better opportunities for diversion.

Furthermore, there is apparently little effective deterrent to computer crime. In many cases the legal statutes that define crimes and classify their severity are hopelessly obsolete. For example, in many cases computer time is not recognized as a valuable commodity, so its misappropriation is not a significant offense. The <u>copying</u> of information is not considered theft in itself, since the legitimate owner of the information is not deprived of it. Whiteside cites one case in which the theft of a magnetic tape representing millions of dollars of financial transactions could only be prosecuted for the value of the physical tape (about $30). Neither the typical prosecutor nor the typical jury is likely to have enough technical background to understand the details of a computer-aided-crime, and the resulting confusion works to the benefit of the defendant. Moreover, since these crimes are generally non-violent, rather impersonal, and have an engaging man-against-the-system flavor, in those rare cases where conviction actually occurs, punishment is exceedingly light.

One ironic aspect of the situation is that the publicity attendant upon detection and conviction of a computer crime can turn out to be professionally rewarding. In two separate incidents in California recently, the perpetrators of significant incursions into computer systems were apprehended, convicted and subjected to minor punishment. However, subsequently both became "consultants on computer security".

Cornell had a comparable incident several years ago, and we suspect that similar events have occurred on many other campuses. A student "cracked" the computer center's security barriers and gained access to the most sacrosanct of its privileged files. The incursion was detected (quite by accident), and the campus judicial system proved to be entirely helpless. The computing center publicly decried such reprehensible conduct -- but then hired the miscreant to its systems programming staff.

Overall, it is obvious that the rewards for computer crime are frequently generous and the risks are minimal. Unless it turns out that undetected computer crime is far more widespread than is believed to be the case, then one would have to conclude that programmers on the whole have resisted temptation quite admirably. But for a major industry to be so dependent on the voluntary good behavior of its workers is an uncomfortable state of affairs.

It is, after all, not just a game -- man against a machine. The cost of computer crime is a cost of business. Each successful incursion and embezzlement inevitably is reflected in higher insurance premiums for business and higher prices for consumers. These are society's mechanisms for distributing the cost of such abuse. Presumably the legal system will someday catch up and realistically classify, prosecute and punish these modern crimes, but this is not likely to happen until there is much wider understanding of the nature of the computer.

Even more important, the data processing community must gradually "harden" its systems -- make them less vulnerable to assault. This applies both to monitoring of the programming process itself, and to strengthening the defenses built into the actual programs. These are not simple tasks, but they merit high priority as the field matures. Until this is done the growing business dependence upon computer processing of financial information is in a precarious state.

4.4 The Second Industrial Revolution

The term "second industrial revolution" appeared in the Introduction of the book <u>Cybernetics</u>, by Norbert Wiener (Wiley, 1947). One paragraph of this Introduction sounded an ominous warning:

> "Perhaps I may clarify the historical background of the present situation if I say that the first industrial revolution, the revolution of the dark satanic mills, was the devaluation of the human arm by the competition of machinery. There is no rate of pay at which a United States pick-and-shovel laborer can live which is low enough to compete with the work of a steam shovel as an excavator. The modern industrial revolution is similarly bound to devalue the human brain at least in its simpler and more routine decisions. Of course, just as the skilled carpenter, the skilled mechanic, the skilled dressmaker have in some degree survived the first industrial revolution, so

the skilled scientist and the skilled administrator may survive the second. However, taking the second revolution as accomplished, the average human being of mediocre attainments or less has nothing to sell that it is worth anyone's money to buy."

This remarkable book was published just a year or so after the first computer was operating in a university laboratory. By today's standards that was an incredibly crude and limited machine, and Wiener's insight as to the possible long-term implications is very impressive. Needless to say, it gained considerable attention and launched a debate that still continues.

The term "automation" was coined soon after that to refer to highly-automatic equipment, and economists and sociologists and labor union leaders began to worry publicly about the implications of fully-automatic factories. The computer was what made such an event a possibility, and if it turned out that this led to a serious disruption of society it would, indeed, be an abuse by the computer.

Now, thirty years into the computer age, the crisis forecast by Wiener has not yet occurred. But it seems too soon to be greatly reassured. We could just be in the position of the man who jumped from the top of a tall building and when questioned halfway down reported that everything was going well -- that the predictions of disaster had been greatly exaggerated.

The computer has already had major impact on employment patterns, although so far the displacement has more generally been clerical rather than production workers. At least todate, the displacements seem to have been offset by growth in the computer industry itself, and by increases in business volume that the efficiency of automatic processing has permitted. But predictions that this delicate balance will continue indefinitely are not entirely convincing. The use of computers might accelerate to the point where an economic society based on the sale of an individual's services would no longer be viable. None of the arguments, on either side of the issue, is particularly convincing, so the accuracy of Wiener's conjecture is still an open question.

The computer also figures importantly in most apocalyptic forecasts of a totalitarian world. If any of these is close to accurate it will be the ultimate computer abuse. One might wish that the computer had never been created -- but it is a bit too late for that. Probably all that can be done at this point is to seek as wide an understanding as possible of the risks that it presents.

Section 5   The Intelligence of the Computer

Almost from the beginning the computer has been referred to as an "electronic brain", and scientists have been intrigued by the question of just how "intelligent" this device might become. No definitive answer to that question has yet been obtained, but some impressive and interesting programs have been written in the course of such investigations.

The following sections offer brief glimpses of this provocative subject. Some references for further reading are cited in Section 5.4.

5.1 What does a Computer Understand?

On the basis of the examples presented so far, and your understanding of the programming concepts from Part I, it would seem like this question is easily answered -- the computer "understands" nothing; it just mechanically executes a sequence of detailed instructions. While this is certainly true, you might consider the implications of the following example.

A program named SAM was written by Lehnert at Yale (see References), using an interactive system such as the one described in Section II.7. The following is an example of its use. Initially, the following text is supplied to SAM as data (shown here as normal English text, not necessarily in the exact format required by SAM):

"John went to New York by bus. On the bus he talked to an old lady. When he left the bus, he thanked the driver. He took the subway to Leone's. On the subway his pocket was picked. He got off the train and entered Leone's. He had some lasagna. When the check came, he discovered he couldn't pay. The management told him he would have to wash dishes. When he left, he caught a bus to New Haven."

After this initial input, the user can conduct a question and answer dialog with SAM using an interactive terminal. The following is the display of the results of an actual dialog.

The user's questions are marked with a "Q"; SAM's answers are marked with an "A".

Q1: WHY DID JOHN GO TO NEW YORK?
A1: BECAUSE JOHN WANTED TO GO TO LEONE'S.

Q2: HOW DID JOHN GET TO LEONE'S?
A2: JOHN TOOK A BUS TO NEW YORK AND THEN HE TOOK THE SUBWAY TO LEONE'S.

Q3: DID ANYTHING UNUSUAL HAPPEN ON THE BUS?
A3: I DON'T REMEMBER ANYTHING.

Q4: DID ANYTHING UNUSUAL HAPPEN ON THE SUBWAY?
A4: A THIEF PICKED JOHN'S POCKET.

Q5: WHAT DID JOHN ORDER?
A5: JOHN ORDERED LASAGNA.

Q6: DID ANYTHING UNUSUAL HAPPEN AT THE RESTAURANT?
A6: JOHN DISCOVERED THAT HE COULDN'T PAY THE CHECK AND SO HE HAD TO WASH DISHES.

Q7: WHY COULDN'T JOHN PAY THE CHECK?
A7: BECAUSE JOHN DID NOT HAVE ANY MONEY.

Q8: WHY DIDN'T JOHN HAVE ANY MONEY?
A8: BECAUSE A THIEF PICKED JOHN'S POCKET.

Q9: HOW DID JOHN GET BACK TO NEW HAVEN?
A9: JOHN WENT FROM LOENE'S BY SUBWAY AND THEN HE WENT TO NEW HAVEN BY BUS.

Q10: HOW WAS JOHN ABLE TO TAKE THE BUS TO NEW HAVEN?
A10: PROBABLY JOHN HAD A TICKET.

This is really a remarkable program. The input story, and the questions are very similar to what is found in elementary exercise books on reading. If you were shown this input, and the corresponding dialog, without being told that a computer was involved, you would certainly conclude that the reader was able to read and <u>understand</u> the story. Moreover, the reader apparently had some background knowledge of his own in the subject area of the story, since his answers involve information that is not explicitly provided in the story. For example, notice that the reader <u>exercises some judgement</u> as to what are unusual events on a cross-country bus, and what is unusual on a New York subway. (You may not agree that pocket-picking is a rare event in New York, but the reader may have lead a rather sheltered life.) The reader also apparently knows something about restaurants. For example, he knows that in order to <u>have</u> some lasagna, as stated in the story, John had to <u>order</u> some lasagna, which is not mentioned in the story. And the reader recognizes that the <u>reason</u> for washing dishes is the lack of

III 5.1 What does a Computer Understand?

money -- which is implied in the story, but not explicitly stated. The reader seems to have some <u>common sense</u>, or some power of <u>deduction</u>, since when asked how John returned to New Haven, he described a subway and bus trip, presumably based on the earlier description of the trip <u>from</u> New Haven, since the story does not detail the return. Finally, the reader is even able to <u>speculate</u> as to how John managed the bus trip without any money. There are surely other possibilities, but the one suggested in the answer to question 10 is not implausible.

But now consider this analysis of the answers in light of the fact that they were <u>produced by a computer</u>. By now you know enough about programming to realize that computers understand nothing, have no common sense, never speculate, and certainly have no experience in buses, subways or restaurants. Computers only execute programs. So you know that what happened in this case is that someone wrote a very clever program whose <u>actions appear to exhibit</u> all those human characteristics. The programmer found a way to encode her own knowledge and understanding of a certain situation into a program. She did this in such a way that the program could manipulate these data so that to an external observer, the computer <u>appears to understand</u> something of the <u>meaning</u> of the input.

Before you become too comfortable with this distinction between <u>understanding</u> and the <u>appearance of understanding</u>, consider what it would mean in a different context. How does a teacher conclude that a student understands some concept -- say, the idea of a "loop" in programming? By means of questions or exercises the teacher looks for the appearance of understanding. If there is sufficient appearance the teacher concludes that the student does in fact understand. But we are not willing to make the same assumption for the computer. The computer may appear to understand, but we know it doesn't really, because a computer can only add, compare, read, write, etc., and understanding surely isn't made up of such actions. But what do we really know about the mechanism of understanding in the human brain? Probably very little. So a conclusion that a program cannot "understand" something is really more of an emotional or theological argument than one of demonstrable fact.

Curiously, when we ask a question about what a computer can do we often learn more about ourselves than about the computer. We ask whether or not a computer can "understand". We discover that although we have a vague intuitive notion of what it means to "understand", we are hard-pressed to make it precise enough to decide whether or not some object possesses the property. We know precisely what a computer does, and we know only vaguely what it means to "understand" -- so we conclude that the two are not compatible.

5.2 <u>Creative Programs</u>

Whether or not a computer can be considered "creative", is largely a matter of agreeing on a precise definition of creativity. For example, it is a reasonable conjecture that none of the "poems" displayed in Section II.6.4 has ever been written before. That is, it is unlikely that ever before in the entire history of the human race has that particular sequence of words been set down on paper. So if creativity simply means producing something never seen before -- then unquestionably the program POET was creative.

You might protest that the creativity was actually exercised by the programmer who produced POET, but this doesn't really seem fair. If the author of those lovely poems in II.6.4 had been human, you would not attribute any creativity they might represent to his <u>teacher</u>.

This suggests looking at the question from another point-of-view. Suppose someone showed you one of those poems (after suitably copying it onto less revealing paper, and using normal upper and lower-case printing) without revealing its origin. While you might not be impressed with its message, you probably would concede some degree of originality, or imagination, or some similar attribute. Then when the origin of the poem is revealed, you might feel a little uncomfortable with your conclusion. Obviously, there is some subtle connotation of human agency in the word "creativity", and we are somewhat reluctant to attribute that property to a machine. This may verge on theology, or at least metaphysics, but objectively, the situation is quite clear: a program is readily capable of producing output which, <u>if it had been produced by a human</u>, would unquestionably be considered creative.

The creativity question often becomes confused with the issue of <u>quality</u>. You might well not be impressed with the poems exhibited, but it would be rash to claim that <u>all</u> poems written by human poets would necessarily be better than these. One humanistic defense against these disturbing arguments rests on the fact that humans <u>selected</u> this output -- we discarded some efforts that were complete gibberish (even worse than those shown), and selected the ones that seemed the most intriguing. But this is not entirely unlike the role played by critics and editors of human-produced poems. Society has rather elaborate machinery for discouraging some would-be poets, and for grading the work of more promising authors. For whatever it is worth, it seems highly likely that with a program little more sophisticated than POET, and enough patience, one could eventually obtain a poem of "publishable quality".

It is not really a satisfactory escape to say that a program "simulates creativity", since this seems to imply that the <u>manner</u> in which it operates somehow mimics or approximates the corresponding human process. Usually only the most rabid of the "artifical intelligence" community ever venture onto that shaky ground. Perhaps the best resolution is to say that the program exhibits "quasi-creativity", or "pseudo-creativity", where the qualification means that if a human did this is would be "true creativity", but we aren't (yet) willing to attribute that property to a machine.

It is really more instructive to look at the program for POET in some detail, than it is to quibble over the intellectual attributes of its output. We wanted to produce text that looked something like a poem. We figured out that poems consisted of stanzas, which consisted of lines, which were built up from phrases. So we constructed a program with nested loops to reflect this structure of a poem. Then we figured out detailed rules for punctuation and presentation of the poem. Finally we obscured the mechanical nature of this process by superimposing some random variability. In effect, we defined a certain type of text and wrote a program that would produce samples of it. If you decline to call this text "poetry", because by definition only humans can write poetry -- then the argument is over. But if you decline to call it poetry because of some specific shortcoming in the output, then in precisely describing that shortcoming you are probably providing all the information needed to change the program to remedy that shortcoming.

For example, POET does not in general produce lines that rhyme, but it would not be difficult to change the manner in which POET chooses line-terminating phrases so that their final syllables are similar. If POET's productions are too repetitive for your tastes -- just expand the vocabulary, and reduce the probability of direct repetition. The point is that you should now understand very clearly what is involved in designing and writing a program to produce somewhat poetic output. You should realize that the only way you can command a computer to "write a poem", is if someone has written a program something like POET, and that the characteristics of the resulting poems are completely specified in the details of that program.

To carry the question a little further, consider the following poetry-writing program:

```
      CHARACTER*100  V(12), LINE
      INTEGER   WD1, WD2, NEXT
      INTEGER   CHOICE
      INTEGER   POEMS, POEMNO
      REAL   SEED, RN
      V(1) = 'AGAIN'
      V(2) = 'AND'
      V(3) = 'DOWN'
      V(4) = 'GO'
      V(5) = 'I'
      V(6) = 'LONELY'
      V(7) = 'MUST'
      V(8) = 'SEA'
      V(9) = 'SEAS'
      V(10) = 'SKY'
```

```
      V(11) = 'THE'
      V(12) = 'TO'
      READ, POEMS, SEED
      RN = RAND(SEED)
C
      DO 100 POEMNO = 1, POEMS, 1
          PRINT, 'POEM NUMBER:', POEMNO
          PRINT, ' '
          LINE = ' '
          NEXT = 1
          DO 30 WD1 = 1, 8, 1
              RN = RAND(RN)
              CHOICE = (RN*12) + 1
              LINE(NEXT:100) = V(CHOICE)
              NEXT = LENGTH(LINE) + 2
 30       CONTINUE
          PRINT, LINE
          LINE = ' '
          NEXT = 1
          DO 60 WD2 = 1, 7, 1
              RN = RAND(RN)
              CHOICE = (RN*12) + 1
              LINE(NEXT:100) = V(CHOICE)
              NEXT = LENGTH(LINE) + 2
 60       CONTINUE
          PRINT, LINE
          PRINT, ' '
          PRINT, ' '
100   CONTINUE
      STOP
      END
```

This program will produce a number of two line poems (the number is specified by the user-supplied value of POEMS). The first line of each poem will have eight words, the second line will have seven words. In both lines the words will be drawn randomly from the following vocabulary:

again,	go	must	sky,
and	I	sea	the
down	lonely	seas	to

This program will probably produce some two-line poems that have never been written before -- but you may not consider it reasonable to call such random generation "creative". However, suppose the program happens to produce the following lines:

   I MUST GO DOWN TO THE SEAS AGAIN,

   TO THE LONELY SEA AND THE SKY,

There are very long odds against choosing a seed that will result in these particular lines, but that is beside the point. If the program does happen to produce this particular pair of lines it will not be original in doing so -- because John

Masefield wrote them previously. But if Masefield had never lived, then would the program be creative? Or suppose the program had been run first, and Masefield wrote later? Then the program would be creative and Masefield would be a plagiarist.

Our point is not to try to convince you one way or the other on the question of whether computers can be creative. It is rather to illustrate how pointless it is to attach much significance to such questions. Whether or not you call it creative, POET is interesting and somewhat provocative. When you understand what the computer can actually do, you can appreciate the intriguing things that ingenious programmers can make the computer appear to do, without getting upset over whether or not this represents some special intellectual activity -- like creating, feeling, understanding, learning, etc.

5.3 Programs that Write Programs

Up to this point all of our examples and discussion have rested on two premises:

1. Computers can only execute programs -- a computer must be given a program, or it can do nothing at all.

2. Programs are written by people.

These premises are clearly very comforting, since they strongly imply that the programmer is in complete control of the situation, and the computer is simply following directions.

The first of these premises is fairly realistic, but eventually one must question the second. Is it necessarily true that only people can write programs? What is implied, of course, is the question of whether perhaps a computer could write its own programs.

Since we understand that computers only execute programs, this means that the real question is:

Can a program be written that will write other programs?

Superficially, the answer is obviously "yes". For example, the following program writes a program:

```
        PRINT, '    PRINT, ''AHOY'''
        PRINT, '    STOP'
        PRINT, '    END'
        STOP
        END
```

To be sure, it doesn't write much of a program, but nevertheless it does write a complete, syntactically-correct FORTRAN program.

So since our question was so easily (and uselessly) answered we obviously didn't ask the right question.

You might reasonably feel that the program above didn't really write a program -- it just printed one that had been supplied to it. So perhaps, a significant question would be:

> Can a program be written that will really <u>create</u> a program -- that is, write some program that was not really supplied by the original programmer.

But having just been through a discussion of computer creativity you should realize that the answer to this question is also obviously "yes".

For example, recall the poetry-writing program of Section II.6.4. It should be clear that we could write a comparable program that would generate text that represented a FORTRAN program. Each execution of this program would produce a valid FORTRAN program. Moreover, by using the RAND function appropriately in the generating program, each output program would be different, and to a certain extent would be a surprise to the author of the generating program. Whether or not any of these random programs would be interesting or useful is another question -- comparable to asking whether any of the poems generated are interesting or pleasing.

So in any reasonable sense of the words, a program <u>can</u> be written that would <u>write</u> other programs; a program can be written that will <u>create</u> other programs; and a program can be written that would at least occasionally generate an <u>interesting</u> program.

So again, our question didn't produce an interesting answer. Perhaps a meaningful version of the question is something like the following:

> Can a program be written that is capable of creating a useful program to perform a specific task?

How would we describe the required task? For example, suppose the task is the following:

> Scan through all the records in a file describing boats for sale. Select records for those boats shorter than thirty-five feet, and from each of these selected records, print the name of the builder, the length of the boat and the reference-file number.

More succinctly, we could describe the task as follows:

```
     FOR ALL BOATS WITH LENGTH < 35,
     PRINT A LIST OF: BUILDER, LENGTH, FILENBR.
```

You will undoubtedly recognize this as a "program" in a

programming language called ASAP (Section III.1.5), but it is nevertheless a problem description roughly similar to what you might give to a human programmer. So, in effect, the ASAP compiler is a program that will create a useful program to perform a specified task. (Any compiler is such a program; we use the ASAP compiler just because its input happens to look a good bit like English.) But this still wasn't what we had in mind, so apparently we still haven't got the question right.

Perhaps what we are really concerned about is whether a program could "choose" the task for which a program is to be written? But precisely what does it mean to "choose a task"? By the time we have precisely defined what we mean, we will probably have come very close to describing an algorithm from which the required program can be written.

While we haven't really answered the question, we have at least illustrated the typical course of such inquiries. It requires extreme care and considerable subtlety to phrase questions in such a way that the answers illuminate the limits of computers.

Probably what we are really worried about is whether computers could ever "get out of control" and "take over". This has been a recurring theme in science fiction for many years. A good example is the mutiny of the HAL-9000 in Arthur Clarke's "2001". Almost any version of the take-over question that is precise enough to be answered intelligently will have to be answered "yes". It is easy to imagine the construction of control-computers that will not permit a "pilot" to override their decisions. In effect, the designer may have more confidence in the computer than the pilot. After all, a speed governor in an automobile is just such a device, and there are now computer-controlled braking systems that act to minimize skidding in spite of any frantic pressure on the brake pedal. HAL was, in effect, just an extreme example of such a system. Whether it forecasts a real hazard is very difficult to say.

5.4 Artificial Intelligence

"Artifical intelligence" is the name given to that branch of computer science concerned with very complex information processing, and in particular with processes that seem to represent or at least simulate some human intellectual task. The title itself is interestingly chauvinistic -- implying that the only real intelligence is human, and whatever a machine might do would by definition be "artificial".

Some of the areas that have been studied are game-playing (chess in particular), pattern-recognition, conceptual learning, and theorem-proving in mathematics.

The area has been controversial from the outset, perhaps inevitably since it seems to threaten certain inherently human prerogatives -- questions such as understanding, creativity, and purposeful action as noted in the preceding sections. But some of the controversy has resulted from exaggerated public optimism as to how rapidly and how effectively computer programs could achieve certain key benchmarks.

There is no question that some remarkable programs have been written -- programs that perform tasks that would constitute intelligent behavior if performed by a human (or some other animal). Invariably these studies have lead to better understanding of the tasks in question. They have also contributed some ideas of programming languages and algorithms that have been useful for less esoteric applications.

Two interesting viewpoints on results and prospects in this area are given by Feigenbaum and Feldman in <u>Computers and Thought</u>, and Dreyfus in <u>What Computers Can't Do</u>. A less scholarly (but more entertaining) collection of material is given by Van Tassel in <u>The Compleat Computer</u>. (See References.)

A general assessment of the future prospects for computing, and for this type of computing in particular, is given by Kahn and Wiener (<u>The Year 2000</u>, page 89):

"If computer capacities were to continue to increase by a factor of ten every two or three years until the end of the century, then all current concepts about computer limitations will have to be reconsidered. ... Even if the rate of change slows down by several factors, there would still be an overall improvement of some five to ten orders of magnitude. Therefore, it is necessary to be skeptical of any sweeping but often meaningless or nonrigorous statements such as 'a computer is limited by the designer -- it cannot create anything he does not put in,' or that 'a computer cannot be truly creative or original'. By the year 2000, computers are likely to match, simulate, or surpass some of man's most 'human-like' intellectual abilities, including perhaps some of his aesthetic and creative capacities, in addition to having some new kinds of capabilities that human beings do not have. These computer capabilities are not certain; however, it is an open question what inherent limitations computers have. If it turns out that they cannot duplicate or exceed certain characteristically human capabilities, that will be one of the most important discoveries of the twentieth century."

Section 6   Popular Wisdom Concerning the Computer

Let us summarize by examining a few of the statements that represent the basis of the current popular wisdom about computers. For such a young device the computer has already accumulated a substantial folklore. It has provided grist for cartoonists and feature writers for many years (see Van Tassel for examples). By now everyone is generally aware of the computer's existence, and vaguely concerned with it as a possible threat to their privacy and livelihood. Everyone uses computers, directly or indirectly, but still relatively few have any substantive knowledge or experience of how they work. So what has emerged is a set of popular conceptions, or rather misconceptions, of what the capabilities and potential powers of this machine are. Let us examine a few such statements critically, in the light of your new understanding of what computers and programming are really like.

6.1 Myth versus Fact

Proposition 1 <u>Computers are not (yet) very reliable, and occasionally make silly (or tragic) mistakes</u>.

We are bombarded with news stories headlined "Computer Goofs Again". These reports about million dollar checks and lost records are somehow comforting -- a fallible machine is not quite so intimidating. However, the fact of the matter is that the modern computer is an incredibly reliable device, performing its programmed sequence of operations with absolute precision. Malfunctions are generally self-detected, and the systems automatically shut-down until repaired, rather than continue and produce suspect results. Mechanical components, such as card readers and printers, are a good deal less reliable than the electronic core of the machine -- but by far the biggest source of trouble in computing is the <u>program</u>.

It is understandable why programmers are happy to have this state of affairs generally misunderstood, but the fact is that these "computer goofs" are almost always attributable to an inadequate program. Either the program had a latent flaw that was finally exposed by some rare combination of circumstances, or the program did not reasonably provide for some peculiar combination of circumstances and data -- which amounts to the same thing. You should understand enough about programming by now to appreciate the extreme difficulty of providing for every conceivable eventuality, and then providing for the inconceivable eventualities. Ordinary human beings are not especially impressive in that respect, and most programs are written by very ordinary human beings.

Reliability is a serious problem in computing -- but it is not the reliability of the machine itself that is at question. There are ways of providing essentially perfect machine dependability (by using suitably redundant systems) and these techniques are used in critical applications -- space vehicle control, air traffic control, medical life-systems monitoring, etc. Most computing systems, like university computing centers for example, are not configured to provide this degree of dependability simply because it is not considered to be worth the cost. So the real essence of the reliability question is the correctness of programs.

Proposition 2 <u>Computers are no better than the data they are provided</u>.

There is obviously some truth to this proposition, but of course the same thing could be said about any other kind of machine -- or for the most part about human beings as well. But taken literally, the statement is just not true. Computers can clearly be <u>at least a little better than their data</u>, as witness the PL/C compiler (and to a lesser extent the WATFIV compiler) which receives as its data programs containing errors, and is often able to repair errors and consequently execute <u>better programs than it receives</u>. In many cases it would be possible for programs to do at least modest repair of errors in the data supplied -- so that if they do not do so, it is just because the programmer never thought of including such provisions in the program.

So, in general, this indictment should really be directed against:

1. Programmers who write programs that do not perform every check possible on the quality of the data received, and even perform repair when that is practical.

2. The human beings who encode and deliver information to the computing system in the first place.

Proposition 3 <u>A computer is no better than the person who programs it</u>.

This is a key tenet to maintaining our posture of human superiority over a machine -- but it doesn't really bear up under close examination. It can be faulted in several different ways.

In the first place, the machine is obviously better than its programmer is some regards -- it is certainly faster, its memory may or may not be larger (the "capacity" of the human memory is not well-understood) but it certainly has more reliable recall, and its arithmetic accuracy is unquestionably superior. It may be argued that these are just quantitative differences in dimensions -- the significant difference lies in the quality, and not the size or speed of the process. But even in this regard it is clear that a computer can surpass the capability of its programmer. There are obvious and convincing examples where a machine can play some game (checkers, or chess, for example) better than the programmer who "taught" it the game.

We can often program a computer to perform some task better than we could do in person, just because the programming process offers a chance to plan the execution exceedingly carefully, and in particular, to <u>work out all the errors</u> by repeated trials -- with confidence that once exorcised, an error will not slip back in.

Proposition 4 <u>Computers have no "common sense" -- they just do what they are told</u>.

Implicit in this proposition is the suggestion that humans performing similar tasks would somehow be more humane -- which is not an entirely supportable hypothesis. By any measure, common sense is an uncommon commodity, and it seems discriminatory to fault the computer for its absence. Moreover, any particular instance cited to illustrate the computer's lack of common sense probably exposes a programmer who just didn't think of this possibility or who didn't think it would occur with sufficient frequency to be worth programming. The assumption that a human could or would do, in routine processing, what a programmer failed to do in preparation for processing, is itself an interesting proposition.

The second part of the statement is equally interesting -- a computer <u>does what it is told</u> to do. This, in fact, is a principal virtue of the computer, and a major failing of many other "processors", including humans. It is always interesting to watch neophyte programmers slowly discover this unique characteristic of the computer -- that it does <u>precisely</u> what it is told. That is, not what you meant, but precisely what you said. Little in human experience prepares us for the awesome responsibility of having an absolutely literal-minded servant.

Proposition 5 <u>Computer capabilities are inherently limited because the machine lacks certain "intellectual" abilities</u>. For example:

       a. it can never really "understand" anything
       b. it cannot learn anything
       c. it cannot deduce a result or procede by induction
       d. it cannot produce anything really original
       e. ... etc.

There is a sort of ritual game involved in testing such propositions. It goes something like the following:

<u>Statement</u>: A computer can certainly never exhibit property X.

<u>Response</u>: Precisely what do you mean by property X?

By the time agreement has been reached on a definition of property X that provides sufficient precision that one could objectively decide whether or not a computer had exhibited the property -- generally the information is at hand to allow the preparation of a program that does, indeed, exhibit property X. Many programs (and many theses) have been written just to exhibit some rudimentary form of some characteristic that was presumably the exclusive property of the human race. It is not necessary that the program simulate the human version of the process -- only that it exhibit the agreed-upon evidence of its presence.

The eventual result of such an inquiry is usually the following:

1. It turns out that property X is not very well understood. It is difficult to define precisely, and difficult to recognize objectively.

2. A program <u>can</u> be written that will exhibit at least some rudimentary form of property X -- at least enough so that a fair-minded observer would have to concede that if a human had done the same thing it would have been judged to represent property X.

3. The original question turns out not to be nearly as profound or as illuminating as it seemed initially. It does very little to help understand the ultimate limits on what a computer could be programmed to do.

6.2 The Computer Age

The modern computer age really began in the late 1940s in laboratories at Harvard, the University of Pennsylvania and Princeton. Commercial production and use of computers began in the early 1950s. So we are at most thirty years into the computer age. Yet in that brief time the computer has become both ubiquitous and indispensable. The growth rate has, by any standard, been spectacular.

Now the question is prediction. Will this growth continue? When will demand approach saturation and growth level off? What else is there that computers can do for society?

To understand the difficulty of even attempting to guess at answers to that question you should realize that many of the things computers are used for today <u>were not envisioned as computer applications</u> a few years ago.

Cornell's experience is probably typical. In 1953 Cornell installed its first "high-speed computer" -- an IBM Card-Programmed-Calculator capable of the magnificent speed of 150 arithmetic operations <u>per minute</u>. It seemed unlikely at the time that there was enough computational work on the entire campus to keep that machine busy. But somehow the work appeared, and by 1956 the C-P-C was overloaded and had to be replaced by a faster machine. This cycle has been repeated every few years ever since. The current central computer (an IBM 370/168) can perform more arithmetic operations in one minute than the C-P-C could manage in a year of around-the-clock operation. Moreover, there are at least 100 other computers on the Cornell campus in addition to the main central facility.

The question is where did all this computing work come from? The answer is that in a sense the computers <u>created their own work</u>. Each successive machine dramatically reduced the cost of performing a given amount of computation -- and thereby increased the class of problems that could be attacked by computation. Most of the things done on the computer today were not even considered computational problems twenty years ago. Think back over the examples given in Part II and realize that few of these would have been considered computing tasks in 1950. So now the question is what areas will be opened up as opportunities for computer use by further reductions in the cost of computing? There is no question that the cost of computing will be further reduced. The devices that represent the computer systems of the early 1980s exist in development laboatories today, and they are significantly smaller, faster and cheaper.

Tiny special-purpose computers called "microprocessors" are now being installed in other machines to perform various control functions. They are cheaper and much more flexible than the electro-mechanical devices (rotating switches, cams, eccentric linkages, etc.) that used to perform these tasks. They are already used in automobiles, sewing machines, automatic washers, microwave ovens and many other appliances, and this transition has just begun.

But the really intriguing question is what will happen when general-purpose programmable computers, comparable to what you have been using to run sample programs, become generally available at very low cost. It is clear that by the early 1980s computers capable of all the tasks illustrated in the programs of this book will be available for a few hundred dollars. (They can be purchased for only a few thousand today.) It is estimated that there are approximately 200,000 such "mini-computers" in use today -- and that that number is increasing at a rate of 60,000 per year. Couple this with the fact that a substantial fraction of today's college students (as well as many high school students) are learning what the capabilities of such machines are, and how they are programmed, and the prospects become awesome. It is hard to guess what new kinds of applications will result -- or more to the point, it is even harder to make any useful statements about what computers will not be used for. It seems very likely that the computer age is just beginning; the growth rate in the next decade may well exceed that of the past.

APPENDIX A   Summary of the Poet's Subset of FORTRAN

The following is a summary of the subset of the FORTRAN language that is used in the body of this book. It simply indicates what elements of the language are included, and shows the general form of each construction. It does not explain what it does or how it should be used. The page number shown at the right for each item indicates the section of the text in which it is introduced, or the principal section in which it is discussed.

With the exception of character string handling, all of the subset constructs are common to virtually all FORTRAN IV implementations. Specific usages have been chosen to directly correspond to WATFIV. WATFIV is a diagnostic FORTRAN compiler developed at the University of Waterloo. Character manipulation (substring specification) is taken from the draft proposal for a new national FORTRAN standard, FORTRAN 77. Appendix E provides methods for translating the Poet's subset constructs to versions of FORTRAN without explicit character facilities.

Job Deck Structure   page 12

```
    Job card(s)              (get local instructions)
        Declarations
        Statements
        STOP
        END
    $ENTRY                   (may require local instructions)
     Data list
    End-of-job card(s)       (get local instructions)
```

Data List

One item per card.

An item is: a decimal number
            a character string (enclosed
                                    in single quotes)

Declarations   page 18

```
    INTEGER          list of names

    REAL             list of names
```

CHARACTER*100 list of names

Names can be simple: name

             or list: name(number of values)

Statements

numeric variable = arithmetic expression   page 68

string variable = string expression   page 75

IF (condition) statement   page 42

READ,   list of names   page 9

PRINT, list of names and/or titles   page 9

DO ### counter = first, last, increment   page 30
    statements of the body of the loop
CONTINUE

GO TO ###   page 47
    statements to be skipped
statement

The "###" is used to indicate a statement number. The number used in DO must correspond with the number on the CONTINUE. Similarly, the number used in the GOTO must appear on the target statement.

Operators in Expressions   page 69

Arithmetic: + - * /

Substring Specification   page 76

string variable(first position:last position)

Relations in Conditions   page 43

.EQ. .NE. .GT. .GE. .LT. .LE.

Built-in Functions   page 73

ABS(real number)   IABS(integer number)
IFIX(real number)   FLOAT(integer number)
SQRT(real number)

Appendix A - Subset Summary

Miscellaneous Rules

1. Names in a program begin with a letter (not a digit) and must consist of six or fewer characters.

2. Numbers are given in the program or in the data list in ordinary decimal form; integer values must not have decimal points. A negative number has a minus sign as a prefix. (Numbers are not enclosed in quotes).

3. Real numbers are displayed in exponential (scientific) notation, with the decimal point preceding the first digit, and the power of ten specified to properly locate the actual decimal point. That is, 3.14159 is given as 0.314159E 01.

4. The two quantities compared by a condition must be of the same type -- either both numbers, or both strings.

5. In comparing strings of different lengths in a condition, the shorter string is automatically extended with blanks on the right to match the length of the longer string.

6. The values of strings are compared according to an extended form of alphabetical ordering called the "collating sequence". Blank is lowest, then punctuation characters, then letters (in alphabetical order), and then the digits.

7. Place all declarations together at the beginning of the program.

8. Any statement (but not a declaration) can be used in the body of a loop. DO, IF, CONTINUE, or declarations cannot be made the subject of an IF statement.

Program Format Rules

1. Statements start in column 7 or further to the right. Statement numbers, if present, appear in starting in column 2. Each statement appears on a separate card, except that both the IF statement and the statement depending upon it appear on the same card.

2. Indent the statements in the body of a loop, with respect to the DO statement:

          DO ### ...
             statements in the body of the loop
      ###   CONTINUE

3. When using IF(condition) GO TO ... to skip a short set of statements, indent the statements to be skipped with

respect to the IF statement:

```
IF(condition) GO TO ###
      statements to be skipped
### statements to be executed regardless of the IF
```

4. When a statement must be continued onto a second line, a $ should be punched in column 6 to indicate the continuation. The body of the continued portion of the statement should be indented further than the initial line.

5. When a statement must be continued onto a second line, divide the statement <u>between</u> elements, not in the middle of an element (a word, a number, etc.).

6. Comments may be inserted in the program by punching a C in column 1. The remainder of the card will be printed, but otherwise ignored.

7. Insert blank comments to separate different parts of the program.

Punctuation Rules

1. Commas are used to separate items in a list, separate the control values of a DO statement, and to separate READ and PRINT statements from their associated lists of items.

2. Colon is used to separate the starting and ending positions of a substring specifier.

3. The period is never used for punctuation -- only as a decimal point.

4. Parentheses are always used in matched pairs.

5. Use parentheses to specify the order in which operations in an expression are to be performed. Operations in the innermost parentheses are performed first.

6. Parentheses must surround the condition in an IF statement:
     IF (condition) statement

7. Character strings must be quoted (single quotes) when they appear in the program or in the data list.

8. To put the quote character itself in a string, you must give the quote twice (so it will not be mistaken for the closing quote). For example, "today's data:" would be given as 'TODAY''S DATA:'.

APPENDIX B   Additional Topics in FORTRAN

B.1 <u>Program Notes</u>

Programs have to be read by people as well as computers. It is useful to include "comments" in a program that are intended <u>solely for human readers</u> and are ignored by the computer. Any card with a "C" in column 1 is a comment card. We have already used blank comments (cards with only a C in column 1) to mark off the logical sections of some of the larger program examples. Comments appear on the source listing, but have no effect on the execution of the program.

One way in which comments can be especially helpful to the reader of a program is by describing the <u>purpose</u> of a section of the program. For example:

```
C      LOAD PHRASES FROM DATA
       READ, NBRPHR
       DO 30 I = 1, NBRPHR, 1
          READ, PHR(I)
30     CONTINUE
C      REPLACE LEADING STAR WITH A BLANK
       DO 50 I = 1, NBRPHR, 1
          IF(PHR(I)(1:1) .EQ. '*') PHR(I)(1:1) = ' '
50     CONTINUE
```

A second use of comments is to describe the <u>role</u> of a particular variable. Recall that in Section II.6.4 we gave a separate list, explaining the role of each variable in the poetry program. By using comments, this information could be included directly in the program. For example:

```
       INTEGER   STZNBR
C                STANZA NUMBER
       INTEGER   NBRSTZ
C                NUMBER OF STANZAS TO BE WRITTEN
```

B.2 Formatted PRINT Statements

It is possible to achieve precise control of the format of printed output by using the formatted version of the PRINT statement. The form is:

          PRINT ###, list of items

The statement number, "###", refers to the FORMAT statement which contains the specifications for the format of the output. The form is:

          ### FORMAT(list of formats)

Each item in the print statement will be printed according to the format item specified in the FORMAT statement. The principal formats are:

> Aw which means print a string in the next w positions on the line. The first character of the string is in the first of the w positions. (It is said to be left-justified). If the string has more than w characters, only the first w will be printed. If the string has fewer than w characters, the remaining positions will be filled with blanks.
>
> Iw which means print a number of type INTEGER in the next w positions on the line. The rightmost digit of the number is in the last of the w positions. (It is said to be right-justified). Remember to make w large enough for the minus sign which will be printed if the value is negative.
>
> Fw.d which means to print a number of type REAL with d digits to the right of the decimal point in the next w positions on the line. The value will be right-justified. Remember to make w large enough for the decimal point and for the minus sign.

One of these formats must be present for each item on the output list. The first item is associated with the first A, I, or F format item, the second with the second, etc.

Another type of format item that is not associated with a data item is:

> wX which means to skip the next w positions on the line.

A literal character string may also be included in the FORMAT statement. The characters of the string literal will occupy the appropriate number of characters at the current position on the line.

Appendix B - Additional FORTRAN

One additional characteristic of formatted output must be considered. <u>The first character of the output line will not be printed</u>. This character, called the "carriage control character", is used to control the vertical spacing of the line. The legal characters are:

    ƀ   which means to print on the next line, i.e. normal single spacing.

    0   which means to skip an extra line before printing, i.e. double spacing.

    -    which means to skip two extra lines before printing, i.e. triple spacing.

    /   which means to skip to the top of the next page.

    +   which means to print over the previous line. Most often used for underlining.

For example, if the value of AVG is 6.12845, the following statements:

```
          PRINT 1, AVG
 1        FORMAT('0', 9X, 'RESULT IS:', F8.2)
```

will cause this line to be printed (where ƀ represents a blank):

    ƀƀƀƀƀƀƀƀRESULT IS:ƀƀƀƀ6.12

Note that the value of AVG has been <u>truncated</u> to fit in the specified space.

B.3 Formatted Input

Sometimes it is convenient not to have to quote string values on a data card. This can be done if you use a formatted version of the READ statement (similar to the formatted PRINT in B.2):

```
          READ ###, variable
 ###      FORMAT(A80)
```

The variable must be a string variable.

Other types of variables may be READ using FORMAT statements. This is particularly useful when a large quantity of data is to be read, and the number of cards becomes cumbersome using the free-format methods. A complete discussion of formatted input is provided in Cress-Dirksen-Graham, Chapter 9.

B.4 Doubly-subscripted Variables

It is often useful to have a *table* or <u>two dimensional array</u> of values for a variable. Such a variable has two subscripts:

The first subscript specifies the <u>row</u> of the table.

The second subscript specifies the <u>column</u> of the table.

The form of the declaration is:

type attribute   name(number of rows, number of columns)

For example, suppose an exam with ten questions is given to twenty students. The scores are recorded in a table with 20 rows and 10 columns. Each row represents the scores of a particular student; each column represents the answers to a particular question. The table could be declared:

```
      INTEGER SCORES(20,10)
```

The following program segment could be used to compute the average score of the Ith student. (That is, the student whose row is the value of variable I).

```
      SUM = 0
      DO 30 J = 1, 10, 1
         SUM = SUM + SCORES(I,J)
30    CONTINUE
      AVG = SUM/10
```

The following would compute the average of all 200 scores:

```
      SUM = 0
      DO 30 I = 1, 20, 1
         DO 20 J = 1, 10, 1
            SUM = SUM + SCORES(I,J)
20       CONTINUE
30    CONTINUE
      AVG = SUM/200
```

Appendix B - Additional FORTRAN

B.5 Additional Built-in Functions

Some of the more commonly used built-in functions are listed below. For completeness, the functions already described in the text are also included here. In the descriptions, "int" stands for an expression of the type INTEGER; "nbr" stands for an expression of type REAL.

ABS(nbr)   gives the absolute value of nbr; that is, the value of nbr as a positive number.

ALOG(nbr)   gives the natural logarithm of nbr.

ALOG10(nbr)   gives the common (base 10) logarithm of nbr.

AMAX1(nbr1, nbr2, nbr3, ...)   gives the greatest of the values of all the arguments.

AMIN1(nbr1, nbr2, nbr3, ...)   gives the least of the values of all the arguments.

ATAN(nbr)   gives the arctangent of nbr in radians.

COS(nbr)   gives the cosine of nbr, assuming nbr is in radians.

EXP(nbr)   gives the result of raising e to the power nbr, where e is the base of the natural logarithm system.

FLOAT(int)   gives the REAL value corresponding to int.

IFIX(nbr)   gives the first integer less than the value of nbr.

INT(nbr)   gives the integer arrived at by simply removing all digits to the right of the decimal point.

MAX0(int1, int2, int3, ...)   gives the greatest of the values of all the arguments.

MIN0(int1, int2, int3, ...)   gives the least of the values of all the arguments.

SIN(nbr)   gives the sine of nbr, assuming nbr is in radians.

SQRT(nbr)   gives the square root of nbr. The value of nbr must be non-negative.

TAN(nbr)   gives the tangent of nbr, assuming nbr is in radians.

B.6 User-Defined Functions

The most important concept in programming that has been omitted from this book has to do with "sub-routines". A sub-routine is a segment of a program that is written in such a way that it can be used in several places in a program without having to be rewritten. The built-in functions we have used are actually examples of sub-routines. For example, there is a short program that takes the square root of a number. This program is given the name SQRT and is written in such a way that whenever you need the square root of a number, you just have to write this name -- SQRT(nbr) -- in order to use this program.

"Square root" is one of many sub-routines considered to be so useful to so many programmers that it is "built-into" the FORTRAN language. For built-in functions, you don't see the programs they represent, but they are nonetheless present. These built-in functions are just a beginning. Each programmer can add to this standard repertoire of sub-routines in order to "personalize" the programming language for his particular type of programs. For example, we have already added LENGTH and RAND to the set of functions that are used by this book.

In FORTRAN, a programmer creates sub-routines by writing SUBROUTINEs or FUNCTIONs. FUNCTIONs are used just like built-in functions. That is, a FUNCTION produces a value and can be used as a term in an expression wherever that value is required. SUBROUTINEs are more flexible and can do things other than just produce a value. SUBROUTINEs are used by means of the CALL statement. For example, you could write a SUBROUTINE to extract each separate word from a given string, and print each word on a separate line (essentially like the program given in Section II.1.1). Say this SUBROUTINE was named WRDPRN. Then whenever you wanted to perform this action in your main program, say with respect to a string named LINE, you would write the statement:

    CALL WRDPRN(LINE)

At some other point, if you wanted to perform the <u>same action</u> on a <u>different string</u> -- say, NEWLIN, you would write:

    CALL WRDPRN(NEWLIN)

This description is only to advise you that something important has been left out -- not to really explain how it works. The mechanism is a bit complicated and since we don't need it for the relatively short programs presented here, we didn't spend the time to explain it. We refer you to Chapter 10 of Cress-Dirksen-Graham.

As one starts to construct programs larger than the examples given in this book, this sub-routine capability becomes essential. It really means that very large programs can be built in small pieces. A large program consists of many

Appendix B - Additional FORTRAN

procedures -- none of which is individually any larger than the examples we have shown. Each of these separate procedures can be studied and understood independently, and then the main procedure can be understood in terms of the actions of the various sub-routines. In this way, very large and complicated programs can be constructed out of pieces that are individually no more complex than those we have shown.

B.7 <u>Logical Connectives</u>

The IF statement in the Poet's subset allows only very simple conditions to be tested. Additional facility is provided by the logical connectives .AND., .OR., and .NOT.

.AND.

It is often necessary for more than one condition to be true before a statement (or a set of statements) is to be executed. Consider the following section taken from the PYS retrieval program in II.5.2:

```
      DO 150 I = 1, FILSIZ, 1
         IF(QRIG .NE. RIG(I)) GO TO 150
            IF(QLLEN .GT. LENGTH(I)) GO TO 150
               IF(QULEN .GE. LENGTH(I)) SELECT(I) = 1
150      CONTINUE
```

These statements set SELECT(I) to 1 only if <u>all</u> three conditions are true:

```
         QRIG  .EQ. RIG(I)
         QLLEN .LE. LENGTH(I)
         QULEN .GE. LENGTH(I)
```

Alternatively, we could use the connective .AND. to form a single (albeit long) IF statement that checks all three of these conditions. The loop would then be:

```
      DO 150 I = 1, FILSIZ, 1
         IF((QRIG .EQ. RIG(I)) .AND.
     $      (QLLEN .LE. LENGTH(I)) .AND.
     $      (QULEN .GE. LENGTH(I))) SELECT(I) = 1
150      CONTINUE
```

.OR.

The ability to test whether <u>any</u> of a group of conditions is true is provided by the .OR. connective. For example, in the Match-Snatch program of Section II.7.2 the statements:

```
IF(WHO .EQ. 'YOU') GO TO 70
IF(WHO .EQ. 'ME') GO TO 70
```

could be replaced by:

```
IF((WHO .EQ. 'YOU').OR.(WHO .EQ. 'ME')) GO TO 70
```

.NOT.

It is often useful to be able to <u>reverse the sense</u> of a condition. Recall this was done in order to make a compound statement conditional. For example, the reversal of:

```
IF(COMAND .EQ. 'RANGE') RA = 'YES'
```

is:

```
    IF(COMAND .NE. 'RANGE') GO TO 30
        RA = 'YES'
        GO TO 10
30  ...
```

However, when the condition has several parts, reversing its sense by replacing the relations can be tricky. The .NOT. connective provides an easier and safer method. For example, suppose the condition to be tested is:

```
((A .GT. 5).AND.(A .LT. 9)).OR.(B .EQ. 1)
```

Now if a compound statement must be skipped if this condition is not true, we could write:

```
IF(((A .LE. 5).OR.(A .GE. 9)).AND.(B .NE. 1))...
```

Or we could write:

```
IF(.NOT.(((A .GT. 5).AND.(A .LT. 9)).OR.(B .EQ. 1)))...
```

The two are equivalent, but the latter is easier to derive and better represents the desired condition.

B.8 WATFIV Extended IF Statements

WATFIV provides an extended form of the IF statement that allows more straightforward construction of conditional compound statements. The form of the IF is:

```
IF(condition) THEN DO
   statements
END IF
```

The statements between the IF and the END IF will be executed if the condition is true.

There is also a more general form:

```
IF(condition) THEN DO
   statement set 1
ELSE DO
   statement set 2
END IF
```

The meaning is:

Execute either statement set 1 <u>or</u> statement set 2 -- statement set 1 if the condition is true; statement set 2 if the condition is false.

An example using IF - THEN - ELSE is given in Appendix B.10

B.9 WATFIV Conditional Loops

WATFIV provides the following alternate form of the DO loop:

```
WHILE(condition) DO
   ...
END WHILE
```

The meaning is:
1. Evaluate the condition; if it is true, execute the statements of the body of the loop; if it is false, skip to the statement following the loop.

2. After each execution of the statements of the body of the loop, return to step 1 - that is, re-evaluate the condition, etc.

Effectively, this means that the execution of the loop is repeated as long as the condition remains true -- which implies that the statements of the body of the loop had better eventually cause the condition to become false or the program will never terminate.

An example using WHILE DO is given in Appendix B.10.

B.10 Example: Queue Simulation

The following program is equivalent to the program given in Section II.6.5, but in this version the program uses some additional features not included in the Poet's subset.

```
C
C   SINGLE CHANNEL QUEUE SIMULATOR
C
      REAL   NXTARV, NXTCMP, TIMLIM
C         NEXT ARRIVAL, COMPLETION, TIME LIMIT
      INTEGER  NBRINQ, NBRINS
C         NUMBER IN QUEUE, NUMBER IN SERVICE
      REAL   CUMST, IDLTIM, LSTEVN
C         CUMULATIVE STATE, IDLE TIME, LAST EVENT
      REAL   MEANST, FRCIDL
C         MEAN STATE, FRACTION IDLE
      REAL   RN, SEED
      REAL   ARVMN, SERVMN
C         ARRIVAL MEAN, SERVICE MEAN
      INTEGER  EVENT
C
      READ, TIMLIM, ARVMN, SERVMN, SEED
      RN = RAND(SEED)
      NXTARV= 0
      NXTCMP = 0
      NBRINQ = 0
      NBRINS = 0
      CUMST = 0
      IDLTIM = 0
      LSTEVN = 0
C
C   RUN UNTIL TIME LIMIT IS REACHED
      WHILE((NXTARV .LE. TIMLIM) .OR. (NXTCMP .LE. TIMLIM)) DO
C       RECORD (STATE * TIME)
          CUMST = CUMST + (NBRINQ + NBRINS) *
     $            (AMIN1(NXTARV, NXTCMP) - LSTEVN)
          LSTEVN = AMIN1(NXTARV, NXTCMP)
C       PROCESS NEXT EVENT
          IF(NXTARV .LE. NXTCMP) THEN DO
C           NEXT CUSTOMER ARRIVES
              NBRINQ = NBRINQ + 1
              RN = RAND(RN)
              NXTARV = NXTARV + (2 * ARVMN * RN)
          ELSE DO
C           SERVICE COMPLETION
              IF(NBRINQ .GT. 0) THEN DO
C               SERVER REMAINS BUSY
                  NBRINQ = NBRINQ - 1
                  NBRINS = 1
```

```
                        RN = RAND(RN)
                        NXTCMP = NXTCMP + (2 * SERVMN * RN)
                   ELSE DO
C                     SERVER GOES IDLE
                        NBINS = 0
                        IDLTIM = IDLTIM + (NXTARV - NXTCMP)
                        NXTCMP = NXTARV
                   END IF
              END IF
         END WHILE
C
C    PRINT CONTROLS AND RESULTS
         PRINT, ' '
         PRINT, ' '
         PRINT, 'SINGLE CHANNEL QUEUE SIMULATOR'
         PRINT, 'RUN LENGTH:', TIMLIM
         PRINT, 'MEAN TIME BETWEEN ARRIVALS:', ARVMN
         PRINT, 'MEAN SERVICE TIME:', SERVMN
         PRINT, 'RANDOM NUMBER SEED:', SEED
         MEANST = CUMST / TIMLIM
         PRINT, ' '
         PRINT, 'MEAN STATE:', MEANST
         FRCIDL = IDLTIM / TIMLIM
         PRINT, 'FRACTION OF TIME IDLE:', FRCIDL
         STOP
         END
```

APPENDIX C   WATFIV Options

The following are options that affect the manner in which a program is executed. They are specified by punching them on the $JOB card that precedes the program.

Only a few of the WATFIV options are given here. Your installation should have a more complete listing along with local $JOB card conventions.

DEC
Causes REAL values to appear in a form that is more readable than the scientific (exponential) form. All of the examples in this book were run using this option.

NOEXT
Do not print diagnostic messages when a WATFIV extension to FORTRAN is used. Since most CHARACTER usages are extensions, NOEXT will help make your listing easier to read.

NOLIST
Omit the normal printing of the source listing. The execution output will still be printed. This might be used after the testing of a program has been completed, since in using a finished program you often do not need a copy of the source listing each time the program is run.

APPENDIX D   Keypunching

The following are basic instructions for operating the IBM Model 029 Keypunch. In general, you will be better off having someone who knows, show you how -- but if you are all alone, these instructions may help a little.

<u>To turn the machine on (or off)</u>
The main power switch is hidden under the table -- by your right knee. Up is on, down is off.

<u>Card Supply</u>
Load a small stack of cards in the "supply hopper" at the upper right corner of the machine. Cards are loaded <u>right-side-up</u> with the <u>printed side facing you</u>.

<u>Card "Release"</u>
The AUTO FEED switch at the top of the keyboard must be in ON position. Press the "Release" key (marked REL at the right of the keyboard) to move a card. Cards released from the hopper move down, then across from right to left, and finally into the "stacker" on the upper left. Important: <u>two cards</u> must be in the opening below the hopper before the machine is ready to punch. If you are starting with the machine empty, press REL twice to move cards down from the hopper.

<u>Punching</u>
When two cards are in the opening below the hopper, you are ready to start punching holes in the front one of these two cards. Each keystroke on the keyboard will punch in one column of the card, and move the card one column to the left ready to punch into the next column. Cards are punched as they move from the rightmost opening into the center opening.

To determine <u>which column will be punched next</u>, read the number directly over the pointer in the window in the upper center of the machine.

Many keys on the keyboard have <u>two characters</u> printed on their face. If the ALPHA key (lower right corner of the keyboard) is held down while the key is pressed, the <u>lower</u> of the two characters will be punched. If the NUMERIC key (lower left corner of the keyboard) is held down, the <u>upper</u> of the two characters will be punched.

When finished punching a card, press REL. That will release the card to the center position, and bring another card down into the right position. The machine is then ready to begin punching the next card. When the second card is finished and is released to the center position, the first card will automatically move up to the stacker.

<u>Printing</u>
The machine will print along the top margin of the card only if the PRINT switch in the top center of the keyboard is in the ON position.

<u>Skipping</u>
The keypunch can be made to provide "tab stops"; the first so you can skip past the statement number and others, every three columns, so you can easily indent the lines of your program.

You need to punch a "drum card". Punch a card as follows:

```
                    1         2         3         4
    columns     1234567890123456789012345678901234567890
    content     1aaaaa1aa1aa1aa1aa1aa1aa1aa1aa1aa1aa1aa1

                    5         6         7         8
    columns     1234567890123456789012345678901234567890
    content     aaaaaaaaaaaaaaaaaaaaaaaaaaaaaaaa-&&&&&&&
```

Have someone help you install this card on the control drum behind the window in the upper center of the machine. (It is easy to demonstrate, but hard to describe.) Activate the drum by pressing the <u>left side</u> of the toggle switch below the window.

Put the AUTO SKIP switch at the upper left of the keyboard in the ON position.

To skip to the next "tab stop" (columns 7, 10, 13, 16, 19, 22, 25, 28, 31, 34, 37, 40) press the SKIP key (right end of keyboard).

With this drum card in use, the keyboard is automatically in "alpha mode" -- the equivalent of holding down the ALPHA key continuously. This means that <u>unless you hold down the NUMERIC key</u>, the machine will always <u>punch the lower character</u> on each key. Use the NUMERIC key to override this -- whenever you want to punch the upper character.

this drum card will also prevent you from accidentally punching anything in column 73 to 80 -- it will automatically release the card when you reach column 73.

APPENDIX E Living Without the Substring Specifier

Many of the programs that appear in this book use the substring specifier to manipulate portions of character strings. Many current FORTRAN compilers do not implement the substring specifier; the purpose of this appendix is to present a set of replacement techniques.

We will use the subroutine ASSIGN (actual code appears at the end of this appendix) to perform substring assignments of the form:

      LINE(FIRST, LAST) = WORD(START, STOP)

This assignment would become:

      CALL ASSIGN(LINE, FIRST, LAST, WORD, START, STOP)

Notice that the six arguments of ASSIGN are in the same order as the six variables of the original assignment. ASSIGN must be given all six arguments. The two string variables (LINE and WORD in the example) must be CHARACTER*100 variables; the other arguments are all INTEGER variables, constants, or expressions.

We are going to use ASSIGN as the basic component of all character string manipulations. The method we will use is to rewrite all string statements that involve substring specifiers as series of statements, each of which either deals with entire character strings or with substring assignments that can be handled by ASSIGN. In the following examples, we assume

      CHARACTER*100 SUBSTR, SBSTRN

has been added to the declarations to create two local, temporary variables.

Assignments dealing with an entire string, such as:

        LINE(LPOSN:RPOSN) = NEWORD
        WORD = LINE(FIRST, LAST)

are equivalent to:

Appendix E - Substring Specification

```
          LINE(LPOSN:RPOSN) = WORD(1:100)
          WORD(1:100) = LINE(FIRST:LAST)
```

which will convert directly to:

```
          CALL ASSIGN(LINE, LPOSN, RPOSN, WORD, 1, 100)
          CALL ASSIGN(WORD, 1, 100, LINE, FIRST, LAST)
```

Constants are handled similarly:

```
          WORD(POS:POS) = '*'
```

can also be written as:

```
          SUBSTR = '*'
          WORD(POS:POS) = SUBSTR(1:1)
```

which converts to:

```
          SUBSTR = '*'
          CALL ASSIGN(WORD, POS, POS, SUBSTR, 1, 1)
```

IF statements can be handled by assigning any substrings to complete strings and comparing these, e.g.:

```
          IF(WORD(POS:POS) .EQ. LINE(CHR:CHR)) ...
```

can be written as:

```
          SUBSTR = WORD(POS:POS)
          SBSTRN = LINE(CHR:CHR)
          IF(SUBSTR .EQ. SBSTRN) ...
```

You should satisfy yourself that you know how to convert

```
          IF(LINE(POS:POS) .LT. 'A') GO TO 10
```

The examples in this book were prepared using these techniques. Each program was first punched just as it appears in the book and then each statement using the substring specifier was converted to a comment and translated into ASSIGN calls immediately following the comment. For example, the poetry composition program of Section II.6.4 becomes:

Appendix E - Substring Specification

```
      INTEGER   STZNBR
      INTEGER   NBRSTZ
      INTEGER   LINNBR
      INTEGER   MAXLIN
      INTEGER   PHRCNT
      INTEGER   PHRNBR
      INTEGER   GROUP
      INTEGER   PHRGRP
      CHARACTER*100  LINE
      INTEGER LSTCHR
      CHARACTER*100  PHR(20)
      INTEGER   PHRLEN(20)
      REAL   RN
      REAL   PIN2
      REAL   PIN5
      REAL   SEED
      REAL   PREP
      REAL   PSKIP
      REAL   PCOMMA
      REAL   PTRMLN
      REAL   TRMST
      CHARACTER*100  SUBSTR
      SUBSTR = ' '
C
      READ, SEED, NBRSTZ, MAXLIN
      IF(NBRSTZ .LE. 30) GO TO 10
         PRINT, 'TOO MANY STANZAS'
         NBRSTZ = 30
C
 10   IF(NBRSTZ .GT. 0) GO TO 20
         PRINT, 'NO STANZAS'
         NBRSTZ = 1
C
 20   IF(MAXLIN .LE. 10) GO TO 30
         PRINT, 'TOO MANY LINES'
         MAXLIN = 10
C
 30   IF(MAXLIN .GE. 1) GO TO 40
         PRINT, 'NOT ENOUGH LINES'
         MAXLIN = 1
C
 40   SEED = ABS(SEED)
      IF(SEED .GT. 1) SEED = 1/SEED
      IF(SEED .LT. 0.1) SEED = SEED+0.1
      READ, PREP, PCOMMA, PTRMLN, PTRMST
      READ, PIN2, PIN5, PSKIP
      DO 100 PHRNBR = 1, 20, 1
         READ, PHR(PHRNBR)
         PHRLEN(PHRNBR) = LENGTH(PHR(PHRNBR))
 100     CONTINUE
      RN = RAND(SEED)
      GROUP = 0
C
C  CHOOSE TITLE
      RN = RAND(RN)
```

318   Appendix E - Substring Specification

```
            PHRNBR = 1 + 10*RN
            PRINT, ' ', PHR(PHRNBR)
            PRINT, '        A POEM'
            PRINT, ' '
C
C    GENERATE THE REQUESTED NUMBER OF STANZAS
            DO 550 STZNBR = 1, NBRSTZ, 1
                DO 450 LINNBR = 1, MAXLIN, 1
                    LINE = ' '
                    LSTCHR = 0
                    IF(LINNBR .EQ. 1) GO TO 150
                        RN = RAND(RN)
                        IF(RN .LT. PIN2) LSTCHR = 2
                        IF(RN .LT. PIN5) LSTCHR = 5
C
C            CHOOSE PHRASES AND ADD TO LINE
  150               DO 350 PHRCNT = 1, 10000, 1
                        IF(PHRCNT .EQ. 1) GO TO 250
                        RN = RAND(RN)
                        IF(RN .GE. PREP) GO TO 250
                            IF(PHRLEN(PHRNBR) + LSTCHR .GT. 97) GO TO 400
                            LSTCHR = LSTCHR - 1
C**                         IF(LINE(LSTCHR:LSTCHR) .LT. 'A') GO TO 200
                              CALL ASSIGN(SUBSTR,1,100, LINE,LSTCHR,LSTCHR)
                              IF(SUBSTR .LT. 'A') GO TO 200
                                LSTCHR = LSTCHR + 1
C**                             LINE(LSTCHR:LSTCHR) = ','
                                SUBSTR = ','
                                CALL ASSIGN(LINE,LSTCHR,LSTCHR, SUBSTR,1,1
C200                        LINE(LSTCHR+2:100) = PHR(PHRNBR)
  200                       CALL ASSIGN(LINE,LSTCHR+2,100, PHR(PHRNBR),1,
                            LSTCHR = LSTCHR + 1 + PHRLEN(PHRNBR)
                            GO TO 400
C
C            RANDOM PHRASE SELECTION
  250                   RN = RAND(RN)
                        GROUP = GROUP + 1 + (2*RN)
                        IF(GROUP .GT. 3) GROUP = GROUP - 4
                        RN = RAND(RN)
                        PHRGRP = 1 + (5*RN)
                        PHRNBR = (5*GROUP) + PHRGRP
                        IF(PHRLEN(PHRNBR) +LSTCHR .GT. 98) GO TO 400
C**                         LINE(LSTCHR+1:100) = PHR(PHRNBR)
                            CALL ASSIGN(LINE,LSTCHR+1,100, PHR(PHRNBR),1,
                            LSTCHR = LSTCHR + PHRLEN(PHRNBR)
C
C            PUNCTUATION PROCESSING
C**                     IF(LINE(LSTCHR:LSTCHR) .LT. 'A') GO TO 400
                            CALL ASSIGN(SUBSTR,1,100, LINE,LSTCHR,LSTCHR)
                            IF(SUBSTR .LT. 'A') GO TO 300
                        RN = RAND(RN)
                        IF(RN .GT. PCOMMA) GO TO 300
                            LSTCHR = LSTCHR + 1
C**                         LINE(LSTCHR:LSTCHR) = ','
                                SUBSTR = ','
```

Appendix E - Substring Specification

```
                        CALL ASSIGN(LINE,LSTCHR,LSTCHR, SUBSTR,1,1
 300                RN = RAND(RN)
                    IF(RN .LT. PTRMLN) GO TO 400
                    LSTCHR = LSTCHR + 1
 350            CONTINUE
 400        PRINT, LINE
C
C           STANZA TERMINATION
C**             IF (LINE(LSTCHR:LSTCHR) .EQ. '.') GO TO 500
                 CALL ASSIGN(SUBSTR,1,1, LINE,LSTCHR,LSTCHR)
                 IF(SUBSTR .EQ. '.') GO TO 550
                RN = RAND(RN)
                IF(RN .LT. PTRMST) GO TO 500
                RN = RAND(RN)
                IF(RN .LT. PSKIP) PRINT, ' '
 450        CONTINUE
 500        PRINT, ' '
 550    CONTINUE
C
        PRINT, '                        ', '-ANON.'
        PRINT, ' '
        PRINT, ' '
        PRINT, SEED, NBRSTZ, MAXLIN, PREP, PCOMMA
        PRINT, PTRMLN, PTRMST, PIN2, PIN5, PSKIP
        STOP
        END
```

Although the LENGTH function given in Section I.6.2.2 could be handled using these techniques, a new version is presented which directly implements the techniques used to prepare the ASSIGN routine. ASSIGN and LENGTH are as follows:

Appendix E – Substring Specification

```
      SUBROUTINE ASSIGN(TARGET,TFIRST,TLAST,SOURCE,SFIRST,SLAST)
C
C     TARGET(TFIRST:TLAST) = SOURCE(SFIRST:SLAST)
C
      CHARACTER*100 TARGET,SOURCE
      CHARACTER*100 TSTR,SSTR
      CHARACTER     T(100),S(100)
      EQUIVALENCE (TSTR,T),(SSTR,S)
      INTEGER TFIRST,TLAST,SFIRST,SLAST
      INTEGER I,TPOS,SPOS
      IF((TFIRST .EQ. 1) .AND. (TLAST .EQ. 100)) TARGET = ' '
      TSTR = TARGET
      SSTR = SOURCE
      TPOS = TFIRST
      SPOS = SFIRST
      DO 20 I = 1,10000,1
         IF (TPOS .GT. TLAST) GO TO 30
         IF (SPOS .LE. SLAST) GO TO 10
            T(TPOS) = ' '
            TPOS = TPOS + 1
            GO TO 20
10       T(TPOS) = S(SPOS)
         TPOS = TPOS + 1
         SPOS = SPOS + 1
20    CONTINUE
30    TARGET = TSTR
      RETURN
      END




      INTEGER FUNCTION LENGTH(STRING)
      CHARACTER*100   STRING, S100
      CHARACTER*1 S(100)
      INTEGER  POS
      EQUIVALENCE (S100,S)
      S100 = STRING
      LENGTH = 100
      DO 10 POS = 1, 100, 1
         IF(S(LENGTH) .NE. ' ') GO TO 30
         LENGTH = LENGTH - 1
10    CONTINUE
20    RETURN
      END
```

REFERENCES

Ahl, D. H., <u>BASIC Computer Games</u>, Creative Computing, P.O. Box 789-M, Morristown, N.J. 07960

American National Standards Institute, <u>Draft Proposed ANS FORTRAN</u>, SIGPLAN Notices, Volume 11, No. 3, 1976 March

Barr, A. J., J. H. Goodnight, J. P. Sall, J. T. Helwig, <u>A User's Guide to SAS 76</u>, SAS Institute, Inc., Raleight, N. C. 27605, 1976

Bennett, Wm. R., Jr., <u>Scientific and Engineering Problem Solving with the Computer</u>, Prentice-Hall, 1976
(Don't be put off by the title. In particular, see Chapter 4 on languages.)

Conway, R. and D. Gries, <u>Introduction to Programming, 3rd Edition</u>, Winthrop, 1978

Conway, R., <u>Primer on Disciplined Programming</u>, Winthrop, 1978

Cousins, N., "The Computer and the Poet", <u>Saturday Review</u>, 1966

Cress, P., P. Dirksen, and J. W. Graham, <u>FORTRAN IV with WATFOR and WATFIV</u>, Prentice-Hall, 1970

Cress, P., P. Dirksen, and S. J. Ward, <u>WATFIV Implementation Guide</u>, Department of Applied Analysis and Computer Science, University of Waterloo, 1969

Dreyfus, H. F., <u>What Computers Can't Do</u>, Harper and Row, 1972

Feigenbaum, E. and J. Feldman, <u>Computers and Thought</u>, McGraw-Hill, 1963

Hughes, J. K., <u>PL/I Programming</u>, Wiley, 1973

Kahn, H. and A. J. Wiener, <u>The Year 2000: A Framework for Speculation on the Next Thirty-Three Years</u>, MacMillan, 1967

Leavitt, R. (editor), <u>Artist and Computer</u>, Creative Computing Press, Morristown, N. J., 1976
(A collection of articles (original, not previously published) by artists who use a computer as their medium. Well-described and beautifully illustrated.)

Lehnert, W., "Question Answering in a Story Understanding System", Research Report 57, Department of Computer Science, Yale University, 1975

Mowshowitz, A., *The Conquest of Will: Information Processing in Human Affairs*, Addison-Wesley, 1976

Mowshowitz, A., *Inside Information: Computers in Fiction*, Addison-Wesley, 1977

Nie, N. H., C. H. Hull, J. G. Jenkins, K. Steinbrenner, D. H. Bent, *SPSS - Statistical Package for the Social Sciences, 2nd Edition*, McGraw-Hill, 1975

Rice, J. K., and J. R. Rice, *Introduction to Computing with FORTRAN*, Holt, Rinehart and Winston, 1973

Sammet, J. E., *Programming Languages: History and Fundamentals*, Prentice-Hall, 1969

Van Tassel, D. L., *The Compleat Computer*, SRA, 1976
"Being a compendium of: Tales of the Amazing and Marvelous, Poetry, Informative News Items, Articles for Edification and Enjoyment, Cartoons, plus Many Other Illustrations, with a special section of Splendiferous Science Fiction Art in full color." (from the book's cover)

Weizenbaum, J., "ELIZA - A Computer Program for the Study of Natural Language Communication Between Man and Machine", *Communications of the Association for Computing Machinery*, Volum 9, Number 1, January 1966

Weizenbaum, J., "Contextual Understanding by Computers", *Communications of the Association for Computing Machinery*, Volum 10, Number 8, August 1967

INDEX

A format item, 300
ABS function, see Built-in functions
Abuses, 271
Addition, 68, 69
ALGOL, 250
Algorithm, 22, 25, 118, 244
ALOG function, 303
ALOG10 function, 303
ALPHA key, 313
Alphabetic ordering, 45
Alphabetic shift, 313
AMAX1 function, 303
AMIN1 function, 303
.AND., 305
APL, 250
Argument, 303
Arithmetic expressions, 68, 69
Arithmetic operators, 71, 296
ASAP language, 252, 255
Arrays, 82, 86, 87, 302
Artificial intelligence, 287
Assembly language, 249
Assignment of value, 67, 79, 296
    from internal values, 67
    from the data list, 12, 17
    to substrings, 78
Assignment statement, 67, 296
ASSIGN function, 315, 319
Auto feed switch, 311
Auto skip switch, 314
Automatic repair of errors, 269
Automation, 278
Automobile analogy, 2, 244
Average, 161, 302

BASIC language, 250
Batch processing, 227
Blank character, 44, 65
Body,
    of a compound statement, 48
    of a loop, 30
Branching, 46
Bridge-playing programs, 7
Brokerage program, 179, 229, 252

Bubble sort, 149
Built-in functions, 72, 79, 296, 303
   ABS, 72, 73, 74, 303
   ALOG, 303
   ALOG10, 303
   AMAX1, 303
   AMIN1, 303
   ATAN, 303
   COS, 303
   EXP, 303
   IABS, 72, 73, 303
   IFIX, 303
   INT, 303
   FLOAT, 197, 303
   LENGTH, 76, 79, 319
   MAX0, 303
   MIN0, 303
   RAND, 194, 303
   SIN, 303
   SQRT, 73, 74, 303
   TAN, 303
Byron, 131

Call statement, 315
Card deck, 10
Card formats, 11
   control cards, 11, 12
   data cards, 11
   drum cards, 314
   program cards, 11
Card reader, 10, 13
Carriage control, 301
Character variables, see Variables
Character listing program, 113
Characters, 12, 45
   collating sequence of, 45
   ordering of, 43
Chess-playing programs, 6, 238, 287
Clark, A., 5, 288
COBOL, 250
Coin-tossing program, 192, 197, 200
Collating sequence, see Characters
Colon, 298
Combinatorial programs, 258
Commas, 298
Comments, 298, 299
Comparison, 42, 53
Competitive programs, 233
Compilers, compilation, 248
Composing lines, 122, 138
Compound statement, 43, 48
Computer, 2
Concordance, 144
Conditional execution, 40, 41, 52, 53, 296, 307
Conditional loops, 307

Index

Conditional statement, 40, 41, 52, 53, 296
Conditions, 42, 75
Confidence limits, 161
Constants, 62
Continuation of a line, 11, 63, 64
CONTINUE, 31, 35, 38, 41
Control cards, 11, 295
   end-of-job cards, 295
   $ENTRY, 12
   job cards, 12, 295
Control values in data, 33
Conversational programs, 239
Cornell University, 252, 276, 293
COS function, see Built-in functions
Cosine function, see Built-in functions
Counter variable, 30, 38
Creation of a variable, 17
Creativity, 282
Crime, 276
Cybernetics, 277

Dana, R. H., Jr., 133
Data list, 32, 295
Data listing programs, 48, 58, 60, 104, 115
Dating, 190
Data bank, 273
Debugging, 89, 96
DEC option, 311
Decimal notation, 19, 311
Decimal point, 19, 20, 21
Declarations, 17, 18, 21, 295
   form, 18, 295
   of character variables, 82, 296
   of arrays, 82, 296
   of integers, 17, 18, 295
   of lists, 82, 295
   of numeric variables, 17, 18, 295
   of string variables, 9, 18, 296
   of tables, 302
   of REAL variables, 17, 25, 295
   of variables, 17, 18
Decomposing lines, 133, 136
Definite repetition, 50, 51
Default, 90
de Stael, 125
Detection of errors, see Errors
Diagnostic statements, 94, 96
Dialog, 239
Dictionary, 171
Dimensions, 82, 86, 87, 302
Display, see PRINT statement
Division, 70, 71
DO loop, see DO statement,
DO statement, 30, 41, 296
Doubly-subscripted variables, 302

Dreyfus, H., 288
Drum card, 314

Editing, 121
ELIZA, 239
ELSE, 307
Embezzlement, 275
END, 9
   of compound statement, 307
   of loop, 307
   of program, 11
End-of-job card, 12
English as a programming language, 252
English translation, 172
$ENTRY, 12
.EQ., 43
Equal, 43
Errors, 90, 96, 265, 289
   data, 266
   during execution, 16, 90
   program, 269
   messages, 16
   repair of, 269
   syntactic, 90
Escape, 51
Expanded printing, 113
Espy, 111
Execution, 13
   errors, 16
   of a program, 13, 15
   output, 13, 16
Exit from a loop, 51, 54
EXP function, see Built-in functions
Exponential notation, 19
Expressions, 68, 79, 86, 296
   arithmetic, 69
   string, 74, 79, 296

F format item, 300
FORMAT statement, 300, 301
Factorials, 115
False, 41, 42
Feigenbaum, E., 288
Feldman, J., 288
Fibonacci sequence, 114
Files, 200
Format,
   in keypunching, 11
   item, 300
   of a program, 11, 25, 297
   of character strings, 12
   of input, 301
   of integers, 19, 26
   of job deck, 12
   of numbers, 19, 20, 26

    of printed output, 14, 15, 18, 20, 26, 61, 65, 129, 300
    statement, 300, 301
FORTRAN, 8, 248
Fraud, 275
French translation, 172
Frequency, 145
Function subprograms, 304
Functions, see Built-in functions

Games, 6, 7, 233, 240, 287
Gardiner, M., 111
.GE., 43
Gilliatt, P., 111
GO TO statement, 46, 47, 53, 54, 296
Greater than, 43
.GT., 43

HAL computer, 5, 288
Handicap rating, 81
Hull speed, 81, 189

IABS function, see Built-in functions
I format item, 300
IF statement,
    standard form, 40, 41, 53, 296
    WATFIV extended form, 307
Implicit declaration, 90
Increment of a loop, 30, 31, 38
Indefinite repetition, 50, 51
Indentation, 11
Industrial revolution, 277
Initial value, 22
Initialization, 22
Input, see READ statement
INTEGER variables, see Variables
Integers, 18, 25, 295
Intelligence, 279
Interactive systems, 227
Interchange of values, 149
Iverson, K., 250

Job card, 11, 12, 295
Job deck, 11, 12, 295
Jump, 46
Justification, 138

Kahn, H., 256, 288
Kennedy, J., 137
Keypunching, 10, 313
Kipling, R., 140

Labeling results, 57, 61
Lehnert, W., 279
LENGTH function, see Built-in functions
Length of a string, 44, 76, 79

Less than, 43
Line formatting, 129, 138
Line skipping, 60
List, see Data list
LIST, see READ or PRINT
List-printing programs, 28, 32, 113
List variable, 81, 87
Loading of a program, 13
LOG function, see Built-in functions ALOG and ALOG10
Logical connectives, 305
Logo program, 258
Loop, 29, 41, 296, 307
Lower-case letters, 64
.LE., 43
.LT., 43

Machine language, 249
Masefield, J., 66, 284
Matching programs, 180
Match-Snatch program, 233
Matrix, 302
MAX function, see Built-in functions
Maximum number program, 103, 104
McCarthy, J., 256
Mean, 161
Melville, H., 126
Memory, 4, 9, 20
MIN function, see Built-in functions
Minsky, M., 264
Multiplication, 70, 71

Names, 21
Natural languages, 22, 171
.NE., 40, 43
Nesting, 34, 46, 52, 71
NIM-playing program, 233
NOEXT option, 311
NOLIST option, 311
.NOT., 306
Not equal, 43
Notation, 19, 20, 311
    decimal, 20
    exponential, 19, 20, 27
    scientific, 19, 20, 27
Notes, see Comments
Numbers, 17, 22
NUMERIC key, 314
Numeric shift, 314
Numeric variables, see Variables
NYYC, 81

Operators, 68, 71, 79, 296
Options, 311
 OR., 306
Order of operations, 71, 79

Ordering of characters, 45
Output, see PRINT statement

Palindromes, 109
Parentheses, 71, 72, 298
PASCAL, 250
Period, 298
PL/C language, 252, 269
PL/I language, 250
Poe, E., 216
Poem-generating programs, 208, 283
Precedence of operations, 71, 79
Precision, 18
PRINT statement, 9, 16, 26, 57, 65, 300
Privacy, 273
Program, 1, 25
   debugging, 89, 96
   errors, 16, 269
   execution, 13, 14, 15
   format, 11, 297
   loading, 13
   reliability, 270
   testing, 89, 96
Program options, see Options
Programming, 1, 243
Programming language, 244
   ALGOL, 250
   APL, 250
   ASAP, 252, 255
   Assembly, 249
   BASIC, 250
   COBOL, 250
   English, 252
   for lists, 245
   for poems, 247
   FORTRAN, 248
   PASCAL, 250
   PL/C, 252, 259
   PL/I, 250
   WATFIV, 11, 12, 228, 248, 269, 311
Prompting, 229
PS-PACK program, 161, 266
Psychiatrist program, 239
Punched cards, 3
Punctuation, 298
PYS-Retrieval program, 179, 228, 252

Queries, 183, 188
Queuing, 221, 308
Quotes, 12, 62, 65, 298

Rand function, see Built-in functions
Random numbers, 194
Random processes, 192
Range, 161

Rating rule, 81
READ statement, 9, 17, 25, 59, 301
REAL, 17, 25, 295
REAL variables, see Variables
REL Key, 314
Relations, 42, 75, 296
Remarks, see Comments
Repair of errors, 269
Repetition, 28, 50, 118
Running a program, 13
Runs in a random process, 201

SAM program, 279
Sammet, J., 250
SAS, 165, 168
Scientific notation, 18
Searching a list, 144
Seed, 194
Selection programs, 179
Sequence, collating, 45
Shaw, G. B., 108, 239
Shift on keypunch, 314, 315
Significant digits, 18
Simon, H., 256
Simple variable, 81
Simulation, 238, 308
SIN function, see Built-in functions
SKIP key, 314
Skip on keypunch, 314
Skipping lines on output, 60
Sorting, 149
Source listing, 13
SPSS, 165
SQRT function, see Built-in functions
Square root, 73
Standard deviation, 161
Statement,
   assignment, 67, 296
   compound, 43, 48
   conditional, 40, 52, 53, 296
   continuation of, 64
   CONTINUE, 31, 35, 38, 41
   diagnostic, 94, 96
   DO, 30, 41, 296
   ELSE, 307
   FORMAT, 300, 301
   GO TO, 46, 53, 296
   IF 40, 53, 296, 307
   input, see READ
   number, 11, 53, 296
   output, see PRINT
   PRINT, 9, 12, 17, 19, 57, 65, 296, 300
   READ, 9, 12, 17, 25, 59, 301
   repetitive, 28
   WHILE DO, 307

Index

WRITE, see PRINT
Statistical system, 160
STOP, 9
Stored program, 4
Stowe, H. B., 135
String, 9
   assignment, 78, 79
   comparison, 42, 53
   constants, 62
   declaration, 9, 12
   expression, 74, 79, 296
   length, 44, 76
   variable, 9, 12
Subroutine, 304
Subscripted variables, 82, 86, 87, 302
Sub-strings, 75, 78, 87, 296, 315
Subtraction, 68
Summing program, 98, 115
Swapping values, 149
Syntactic errors, 91

Tab stops, 316
Tables, 302
TAN function, see Built-in functions
Target statement, 46
Teitelbaum, T., 239
Terminal, 228
Testiil program, 263
Test cases, 93
Testing programs, 89, 96
Text-editing, 121
THEN, 307
Thurber, J., 111
Time-sharing, 228
Titling of output, 57
Translation, 6, 8, 171
True, 41
Truncation, see Built-in function INT
Truthtest program, 261
Turing, A., 254
Turtle race program, 203
Type,
   of value, 17, 21
   statements, 17, 21, 296

Undecidable problems, 261
Understanding by a program, 279
Uninitialized variable, 22
Upper-case letters, 64
User defined functions, 304

Values,
   assignment, 67, 79, 296
   character, 12, 45, 296
   comparison, 42

        control, 33
        initial, 22
        numeric, 17
        types of, 17, 25
        "UUUUUU", 22
Van Loan, 142
Van Tassel, 144, 289
Variable, 25
    assignment of value, 67
    character-valued, 12, 45, 298
    creation of, 17, 21, 295
    declaration of, 17, 21, 295
    initialization of, 22
    INTEGER, 17, 295
    list, 82, 86, 87
    name of, 21
    REAL, 17, 25, 295
    simple, 81
    string, 9, 12, 45, 292
    subscripted, 81, 86, 87, 302
Vector, 82, 86, 87
Vowelless printing program, 107

Waterloo, University of, 11, 249, 295
WATFIV, 11, 12, 229, 248, 269, 295, 311
Weizenbaum, J., 239
WHILE loop, 307
Whiteside, T., 275
Wiener, A. J., 256, 288
Wiener, N., 277
Wirth, N., 251
Word assembly program, 101
Word extraction, 136
Write, see PRINT statement

X format item, 300

Yacht broker program, 179, 229, 252